Praise for *Consider Your Options*

"The best primer we've seen."—*Forbes Magazine*

"Should be required reading for anybody receiving options as compensation."—*Roy Lewis, co-author, The Motley Fool's Investment Tax Guide*

Praise for Our Web Site

"One of our favorite sites."—*Newsweek Magazine*

"One of the top 50 financial web sites."—*Money Magazine*

"A good newsy site, easy to navigate and fun to read. Its explanations are crystal clear."—*The Boston Globe*

Also by the Author

Consider Your Options:
Get the Most from Your Equity Compensation
2004 Edition

Fairmark Guide to the Roth IRA:
Retirement Planning in Plain Language
2004 Edition

Capital Gains, Minimal Taxes

The Essential Guide for Investors and Traders

2004 Edition

Kaye A. Thomas

A Plain Language Guide From
FAIRMARK PRESS INC. LISLE, ILLINOIS

Capital Gains, Minimal Taxes
The Essential Guide for Investors and Traders

This edition of *Capital Gains, Minimal Taxes* reflects relevant legal authorities as of December 20, 2003.

Published by:

Fairmark Press Inc.
P.O. Box 353
Lisle, Illinois 60532

Publisher's Cataloging-in-Publication Data
Thomas, Kaye A.
    Capital gains, minimal taxes : the essential guide for investors and traders / Kaye A. Thomas. — 2004 ed.
    p. cm.
    Includes bibliographical references and index.
    LCCN: 00-192553
    ISBN: 0-9674981-1-2

    1. Investments—Taxation—Law and legislation—United States.
2. Capital gains tax—Law and legislation—United States. 3. Tax planning—United States I. Title.

KF6415.T46 2001   343.7305'24
                                   QBI00-864

Table of Contents

About the Author

Kaye Thomas has over 20 years of experience as a tax lawyer dealing with matters relating to business transactions, finance and compensation. His extensive writings include both technical articles for tax professionals and publications like this book, designed for people with no tax training. His first book, *Consider Your Options: Get the Most from Your Equity Compensation,* received rave reviews and sold over 25,000 copies within nine months.

As part of his never-ending battle for truth, justice, and a less taxing American way, he maintains a free web site called the *Tax Guide for Investors* located at **www.fairmark.com**, providing hundreds of pages of plain language tax guidance. The web site also features a message board where Kaye and other tax professionals respond to questions and comments from readers.

Kaye's law degree is from Harvard Law School, where he was selected to be an editor of the Harvard Law Review and graduated *cum laude* in 1980.

Acknowledgments

I received invaluable editorial and other assistance in preparing the first edition of this book from: Larry Belvin, Rich Carreiro, Colin Cody, Curt Freeman, Alan Kalman, Jennifer Leib and Bob Zerby. Beth Mowry Thomas provided detailed comments on the text but also encouragement and understanding, without which this book could not have been completed.

In addition, I offer a note of thanks to Andrea Kramer, who introduced me to many of the topics discussed in this book during the period I was privileged to work with her.

Sole responsibility for any errors rests in my evil twin.

Chapter 1
The Big Picture

When you open a brokerage or mutual fund account you enter a fascinating world of opportunity. How you explore that world is up to you. Some people believe the best way to accumulate wealth is through long-term investments in a diverse portfolio of established companies. Others relish the excitement (and risk) of jumping into individual stocks of young companies that may become the next Cisco. Still others sit at their computers trading in and out of stocks so quickly that the exercise has turned into a video game.

All these investors and traders have one thing in common. The choices they make affect not only the size of their investment accounts but also the amount of taxes they pay. The result can be bewilderment—and sometimes costly errors—when it comes time to file a tax return. Of equal importance, most investors overlook opportunities to reduce their taxes with timely actions throughout the year.

This book tackles both problems. You'll acquire the knowledge you need to report the correct amount of gain and loss from buying, owning and selling stocks, mutual funds and stock options. You'll also learn ways to reduce your tax bill, often with little or no change in the way you handle your investments.

Having said that, I should perhaps point out what you *won't* learn here. This isn't an all-purpose book on taxation of investments. You won't learn about Roth IRAs or variable annuities or even the rules for reporting interest from government bonds. The goal is to do one thing well: explain how people who buy and sell stocks, mutual funds and stock options can handle their taxes correctly and efficiently.

A few assumptions. This book covers federal tax rules that apply to citizens or residents of the United States. It doesn't cover special rules for nonresident aliens. It also doesn't cover the income tax rules of individual states. The descriptions assume that you don't hold stock as part of a business, except in Part V, which deals with the business of trading.

Here's how the book is organized:

- Part I covers the rules for capital gains and losses the typical investor is most likely to encounter, from the capital loss limitation to the infamous wash sale rule.

- Part II explains how to deal with dividends and investment expenses.

- Part III is for investors who pursue advanced strategies such as short sales and trading in stock options.

- Part IV summarizes rules for gifts, including custodial accounts for minors and charitable gifts.

- Part V tells how to determine if you're a *trader* as defined in the tax law, and how that status affects your taxes.

- Part VI provides help with issues related to filing returns and paying taxes.

- Part VII brings together tax planning ideas that can reduce your taxes.

Part I
Capital Gains and Losses

This is the heart of the book: the main rules about capital gains and losses. These seven chapters cover all the situations you're likely to encounter in the course of ordinary investing. If you get fancy with your trading—selling short or trading in options—you'll have to turn to Part III for the more advanced tax rules.

Part I
Capital Gains and Losses

Chapter 2
Capital Gain Basics

How do people become wealthy? For a lucky few, winning the lottery is the answer. Another small slice of humanity achieves wealth by earning extraordinarily large amounts of income—perhaps as a star athlete or entertainer. Yet most people who build great wealth use a different method that's available to all of us: they own assets that increase in value. Capital gain is the source of most wealth.

This chapter covers the basic tax rules that apply to capital gains and losses. You'll learn the answers to the following questions:

- How do *capital gain* and *capital loss* differ from *ordinary income* and *ordinary deductions*?

- At what point does a capital gain become taxable?

- How do you measure capital gain and loss? What are the meanings of the terms *basis* and *amount realized*?

- How long before a capital gain is *long-term*? How do you measure the *holding period* of an asset?

Capital Gain and Ordinary Income

Capital gain is your profit from selling an asset that has gone up in value. If you buy something for $30 and sell it for $40, you have a capital gain of $10. In this book we're mainly concerned with capital gains from buying and selling stocks and mutual funds, but the same idea applies to gains from almost any kind of asset, from beanie babies to real estate.

All other kinds of income are called *ordinary income*. That's true even for income from unusual sources, like breaking the bank at a Las Vegas casino or winning a beauty pageant. In this context, the word "ordinary" simply means income other than capital gains.

If capital gain is income from selling something that went up in value, you might wonder about merchants who buy inventory at wholesale and sell it at a higher, retail price. The tax law says inventory is not a *capital asset*. That means the profit from selling goods to customers is ordinary income, not capital gain.

Deductions. We also distinguish capital losses from ordinary deductions. Generally you have a *capital loss* when you sell an investment asset that declined in value while you held it. All other deductions, from the most commonplace to the casualty loss you had when an asteroid destroyed your PT Cruiser, are considered *ordinary deductions*.

Note that capital loss generally relates to sale of an *investment* asset such as stock. A loss from selling a *business* asset (for example, equipment used in your profession) is generally an ordinary loss. Also, you aren't allowed to claim a deduction for a loss from selling a *personal use* asset such as your home.

	Ordinary Items	Capital Items
Income	Ordinary income	Capital gain
Loss	Ordinary deduction	Capital loss

When Capital Gains Are Reported

Once in a while, someone who's new to investing asks a question something like this:

> **Q:** I bought stock last May, and by the end of December it was up $3,000. When do I have to report this on my taxes?

That's a legitimate question. When your investments go up in value, your wealth increases. The money is there for the taking: all you have to do is sell the stock. Yet the tax law says you don't have income until you make the sale. You can continue to hold the stock for years while it increases in value many times over without paying a dime of income tax. This is one of the reasons long-term investing in stock is a great way to build wealth.

To be a little more precise, you don't report capital gain or loss until you have a *sale or exchange*. If you exchange one asset for another, you may have to report capital gain even though you didn't receive any cash in the transaction. Not all exchanges are taxable, though. In fact, not all *sales* result in capital gain or loss. In later chapters we'll look at various rules that postpone or eliminate capital gain or loss incurred in a sale or exchange. An example is the wash sale rule (Chapter 6), which says you can't claim a deduction if you sell stock at a loss and buy it back right away.

Conversely, in some special situations you can be treated as if you sold your stock even though you still hold it. For example, you're treated as if you sold stock at the end of the year in which it becomes worthless (Chapter 7). Also, traders who elect to use the mark-to-market method of accounting (Chapter 25) are treated as if they sold all their stock at the end of the year.

> ▪ **Terminology:** When you make a sale or exchange, a tax pro would say you *realized* a gain or loss (in other words, turned it from a "paper" gain or loss to a "real" one). A gain or loss affects your tax if it is *recognized*. A gain or loss that does not affect your tax (as in the case of a wash sale described above) is *realized but not recognized*.

These terms tend to cause confusion, so I avoid them whenever possible. We'll see below, though, that the term used for the precise measure of what you received in a sale is the *amount realized*.

The rule that ties capital gains and losses to sales and exchanges may seem like a big yawn, but it's the key to powerful tax savings. Other forms of income—wages, interest, dividends—arrive according to someone else's schedule. When it comes to capital gains and losses, you're in the driver's seat. Using principles we'll explain in Chapter 30, you can use your control over the timing of sales to take gains and losses when they produce the most favorable tax consequences.

Q&A About Capital Gain Timing

Q: *I sold stock at a profit but used the money right away to buy more stock. Do I have to report a capital gain?*

A: I'm afraid so. With very limited exceptions, you have to report the gain. It doesn't matter that you reinvested the proceeds—even if you bought more stock in the same company.

Q: *I moved money from one mutual fund to a different one in the same family. Do I have to report capital gain?*

A: Yes. When you move your money from one mutual fund to another, you're actually *selling shares* in the fund you're leaving. That means you have to report gain or loss, even if you never see the money because it goes directly to another fund in the same family.

Q: *I didn't want to sell my stock, but was forced into a sale when another corporation bought my company. Do I still have to report the gain?*

A: Most capital gains come from voluntary sales, but the fact that a sale is involuntary doesn't excuse you from reporting gain or loss. A merger in which you receive stock may be partly or completely tax-free (see Chapter 7), but there's no deferral rule for forced sales that result from a taxable merger.

Q: *For tax purposes, when does a sale of stock occur?*

A: As explained in Chapter 4, stock purchases and sales occur on the *trade date*.

Measuring Capital Gains and Losses

The size of your capital gains and losses affects the amount of income tax you have to pay, so it's important to have a precise way of measuring these gains and losses. The basic idea is to determine how much you invested in the relevant asset, and then compare the amount you received when you sold it.

Under the tax law, the term used for your investment in an asset is *adjusted basis*. Roughly speaking this is the amount you paid for the asset, so people sometimes refer to it as *cost basis*. The term *adjusted basis* reminds us that the basis of an asset may change from its original cost. We'll look at adjusted basis in a moment.

The tax law also gives us a term for the amount you receive when you sell an asset. This is called the *amount realized*. It may seem obvious that the amount realized is the cash you receive when you sell an asset, but there are a few potential points of confusion we'll cover below.

With these terms in hand, we're ready to state more precisely how to measure capital gain or loss:

> ▪ The amount of a capital gain or loss is the difference between the amount realized and the adjusted basis of the asset you sold.

Adjusted Basis

The rules for determining adjusted basis are a precise way of measuring the amount you have invested in a capital asset. The normal starting point is the amount you paid to acquire the asset, including any expenses you incurred in making the purchase. When you buy stock, for example, you generally pay a brokerage commission, and that becomes part of your basis in addition to the actual price paid for the stock.

> **Example:** You bought 50 shares of XYZ at $30 per share, paying a $20 brokerage commission. Your basis in the stock is $1,520, or $30.40 per share.

After you've bought an asset, it's possible that something will happen to change its basis. For example, the company may declare a stock split. You started out with 50 shares, but now you have 100. When this happens, your basis splits, too. If you had a basis of $30.40 per share before the split, your new basis is $15.20 per share. The total amount of basis remains the same, but the basis per share has been adjusted.

Suppose you sell stock before there have been any adjustments to basis. It may seem that the term *adjusted basis* can't apply here because there haven't been any adjustments. Yet the tax law uses this term to refer to your basis with relevant adjustments, *if any*. If there haven't been any adjustments, your adjusted basis is the same as your initial basis.

▪ **Basis.** In the rest of this book the word "basis" by itself will mean the same thing as "adjusted basis." If I need to specify your basis in property before any adjustments apply, I'll refer to the *initial basis*.

In Chapter 7 we'll go over many of the situations that may cause adjustments to basis in stock. For now you may want to note that there are some general principles that usually make it easy to guess what the result will be in most situations. One is that your basis goes up if you report income or gain. For example, when you exercise a nonqualified stock option, you report compensation income equal to the bargain element in the option. This income gets included in your basis, together with the amount you actually paid to exercise the option. That way you won't be taxed on the same income again when you sell the stock.

Conversely, in a situation where no gain or income is reported, generally the basis of the stock remains the same. For example, if you receive stock as a gift from your spouse, your initial basis for the stock will be the same as your spouse's adjusted basis at the time of the gift. That's because your spouse didn't report gain or loss at the time of the gift.

Amount Realized

At first glance it may seem obvious how much you received in a sale. There are three points of potential confusion, though: costs of selling, treatment of debt, and property received in an exchange.

Costs of selling. Your amount realized on a sale is reduced by any costs directly related to the sale. The most obvious cost in a typical stock transaction is the commission charged by the broker. If you sell stock for $2,400 and pay a commission of $30 on the sale, the amount realized is $2,370. Most brokers will report the net figure in their tax reports, but they aren't required to do so. The tax form they send you (Form 1099-B) has a checkbox where they indicate whether they reported the gross amount or the net amount. If they reported the gross amount, it's up to you to make sure you get credit for the commission you paid on the sale. See Chapter 26 for details.

There's another cost of selling that's so small you may not notice it: the *SEC fee*. You may see this after a stock sale if you scrutinize your brokerage statement carefully. The fee provides funding for SEC supervision of the securities markets. The current rate is 1/300 of one percent of the total value of the sale. If you sell $30,000 worth of stock, you'll incur a whopping $1.00 fee. It's not exactly a big deal, but it's another cost that reduces your amount realized on a sale.

The main thing to keep in mind about these expenses is this: *you aren't allowed to claim them as a separate deduction.* They're always part of calculating your capital gain or loss.

- **Commission rebates.** Some brokers provide a partial rebate of their brokerage commissions in certain situations. For example, you might receive a credit against your commissions if you have a minimum number of transactions per month. Strictly speaking, this rebate reduces the cost of sale for every sale that occurred during the month. I believe the best way to handle this type of rebate in most cases is to show it as a short-term capital gain.

Treatment of debt. Some people get confused about the amount realized on a sale if they had debt on the property they sold. The rule here is to include the debt as part of the amount realized.

Example: You bought stock for $12,000. Its value rose to $18,000 and you took a margin loan of $5,000 against this stock. Later, you sold the stock for $20,000, receiving $15,000 after paying the $5,000 margin loan. If you compare the $15,000 you received in the sale with the $12,000 you paid to buy the stock, it looks like a $3,000 gain. But your amount realized includes the $5,000 loan that was paid off when you sold the stock. You actually have a gain of $8,000.

Capital Gain Calculation	
Net sale proceeds	$15,000
Debt repaid	5,000
Amount realized	*20,000*
Basis	(12,000)
Capital Gain	**$ 8,000**

It may seem unfair that you have to report $8,000 of gain when you ended up with only $3,000 more than the $12,000 you originally used to buy the stock. Yet you received another $5,000 in the form of a loan. Even if you no longer have that $5,000—perhaps you spent it before you sold the stock—it's part of your profit from the purchase and sale of this stock.

Gain greater than net proceeds. It's worth noting that you can end up with *gain* that's greater than the amount of *money* you receive in a sale. That's one reason to plan carefully when you use debt to acquire investment assets. You may have to come up with money from other sources to pay the tax on your gain.

> **Example:** You bought stock for $12,000. Its value went sky high and you were able to take a margin loan of $15,000 against this stock. Then the value of the stock dropped and you sold it for $20,000, receiving $5,000 after paying the $15,000 margin loan. This time your cash proceeds are only $5,000, but you still have to report gain of $8,000 because you bought the stock for $12,000 and sold it for $20,000.

Capital Gain Calculation	
Net sale proceeds	$5,000
Debt repaid	15,000
Amount realized	20,000
Basis	(12,000)
Capital Gain	**$ 8,000**

There's only one thing worse than having to report gain that's greater than your net sale proceeds, and that's having *the tax itself* be greater than the net sale proceeds. In fact, you can have a gain even with no net sale proceeds at all! In the example above, the stock could have dropped all the way to $15,000 before you sold. That's just enough to pay off the margin debt, leaving you with no sale proceeds. Yet you still have a gain of $3,000, because you bought the stock for $12,000 and sold it for $15,000.

Whether you have a problem in this situation depends on what you did with the money you borrowed when you took out the margin loan. If that money is gone, you need to come up with cash from some other source to pay tax on your gain.

Property received in an exchange. If you receive something other than cash in exchange for stock or another capital asset, the amount realized includes the fair market value of the other property. For example, if you exchange shares of one company for $10,000 in cash plus $6,000 worth of shares of another company, your amount realized is $16,000, just as if you received that much cash. That's true even if you haven't sold the property you received—and even if for some reason you *can't* sell it.

As mentioned earlier, not all exchanges are taxable. You may exchange shares as a result of a tax-free merger, for example. We'll look at the tax rules for this type of transaction in Chapter 7. Even when dealing with those rules, though, you may need to know the amount realized, and that figure includes the value of shares or other property received in the exchange.

Holding Period

You're only partway home when you know the amount of gain or loss on a sale. You also need to know the *holding period* of the asset you sold, to determine whether your gain or loss is short-term or long-term.

Year and a day. To have a long-term capital gain or loss, your holding period has to be at least a year and a day. Exactly one year is not enough. To be more precise, if you sell stock on the anniversary of the date you bought it, your gain or loss will be short-term. The first day you can have a long-term gain is the anniversary of *the day after* the date of purchase.

Some people figure this has to be wrong. If you sell on the anniversary, you've held the stock on 366 days (or 367, if you held the stock on February 29 in a leap year), and that should be enough. That's not the way the rules work, though. When you figure your holding period, you count the date of sale but not the date of purchase. As a technical matter, your holding period begins the day after the date of purchase, and that's why you have to wait until the anniversary of the day after the date of purchase if you want a long-term capital gain.

Quiz: You bought shares on February 28. The following year is a leap year. Which is the first day you can sell for a long-term capital gain or loss?

    (a)   February 27

    (b)   February 28

    (c)   February 29

    (d)   March 1

Many people are inclined to choose (c), because it seems you've held the stock "a year and a day" by February 29. Pat yourself on the back if you selected (d). Your holding period *began* the day after the date of purchase—March 1. You must hold until March 1 of the following year to have a long-term gain or loss.

> ▪ **Flip side.** What if you *bought* in a leap year? If you bought on February 29, your holding period began on March 1, so you have to wait until March 1 of the following year to sell for a long-term gain. But you also have to wait until March 1 of the following year if you bought on February *28* of a leap year. Your holding period began the day after your purchase, on February 29. To sell *more than one year* later, you have to wait until March 1 of the following year.

Special holding periods. Your holding period for an asset doesn't necessarily begin when you acquire it. For example, if you receive stock as a result of a stock split, the holding period of the new shares will be the same as for the old shares. Similarly, if you receive stock as a gift, your holding period is transferred from the person making the gift. If that person held the stock more than a year before you received the gift, you'll have long-term capital gain or loss on a sale even if you sell the same day you receive the gift.

Special holding periods go along with special basis rules, both of which are covered in Chapter 7. There's a general rule that makes it easier to remember when you have a special holding period. Generally, if you have a "tax-free" transaction such as a gift or a stock split, the holding period for the asset continues. Taxable transactions (most commonly sales) start a new holding period.

Chapter 3
Taxation of Capital Gains and Losses

The reason we make such a big deal about capital gains and losses, of course, is that they have some special tax rules. This chapter explains those rules, answering the following questions:

- How do tax rates and tax brackets work when you *don't* have capital gains and losses?

- What difference will you see when you add short-term capital gains and losses to your other income? How do capital loss carryovers work?

- How will long-term capital gains and losses affect your taxes?

- How do capital gains and losses interact when you have both short-term and long-term gains and losses?

Life Without Capital Gains and Losses

As explained in the previous chapter, *ordinary income* includes all forms of income other than capital gain. If you don't have capital gains and losses, your *taxable income* is simply your ordinary income reduced by your ordinary deductions. Taxable income is an important number: it's the one used to calculate your tax. It's almost always less than the amount of money you earn, because nearly everyone gets at least some deductions. There's a *standard deduction* for people who don't claim itemized deductions,* and you can generally claim at least one *personal exemption* (for yourself) unless your parents claim you as a dependent. In the year 2004, the standard deduction for a single person is $4,850 and the deduction for a personal exemption is $3,100. That means a single person who makes $30,000 and "doesn't claim any deductions" probably has $7,950 in "automatic" deductions, and taxable income of $22,050.

Tax rates, tax brackets. Everyone knows tax rates start out low and get higher when your income grows, but things get hazy after that. The confusion usually comes from talk about *tax brackets.* When people say they're "in the 25% bracket," it sounds like all their income is taxed at the 25% rate. That's not how it works.

Income tax rates start at 10%. No matter how large your income is, your first chunk of taxable income is taxed at the 10% rate. If your income is large enough, you'll have another chunk that's taxed at the 15% rate. That process continues through the other rates, up to a maximum of 35%. If you make a gazillion dollars, most of your taxable income will be taxed at the 35% rate, but you'll still have income that's taxed at the lower rates.

There's another way tax brackets sometimes cause confusion. Some people get the idea that the amount they earn at their regular job establishes their tax bracket, even if they have gobs of money from other sources. Sorry, that's not the case. Your tax bracket depends on your overall taxable income, which includes not just wages but also income like interest and dividends from sources other than your regular job.

When we say you're in the 25% tax bracket, we're really saying your taxable income is high enough so that some of it is taxed at the 25% rate, but not high enough for any of it to be taxed at 38%, the next higher rate. Knowing your tax bracket lets you know how much more tax you'll pay if you earn another $100, or how much

---

* There's one situation where the standard deduction is *zero*: when you are married filing separately and your spouse claims itemized deductions.

you'll save if you come up with another $100 deduction. If you're in the 28% bracket, the answer in each case is $28. But consider the following:

Q: *Suppose your taxable income is just $100 below the borderline between the 28% bracket and the 33% bracket. Now you get an additional $200 of income. How much will your tax go up?*

A: The answer is $61. Although you're in the 28% bracket at the time you receive the added income, you have room for only $100 more in that bracket. So $100 will be taxed at the 28% rate and another $100 will be taxed at the 33% rate for a total tax of $61.

Q: *Suppose your taxable income is* exactly *on the line between the 28% bracket and the 33% bracket. If your income goes up by $100, how much more tax will you pay? If instead your deductions go up by $100, how much will you save?*

A: If your income goes up by $100 you'll pay $33 more in tax because there's no more room in the 28% bracket. Yet an additional $100 deduction will save only $28 because it eliminates income that was taxed in the 28% bracket. Of course, if you had *both* an added $100 of income and $100 of deduction, they would cancel each other out for no change in your tax.

These examples illustrate that knowing your tax bracket doesn't necessarily tell you exactly where you stand as to additional income or deductions. That's especially true when you're near the borderline between the 15% bracket and the 25% bracket—a jump of 10 percentage points! Still, it's a good idea to know your tax bracket because it's usually a pretty good indication of how income and deductions will affect your taxes.

Short-Term Capital Gains and Losses

Now we're ready to see what happens when you throw capital gains and losses into the mix. We'll begin with short-term capital gains. Generally, you have a short-term capital gain if you sell stock for a profit after holding it *one year or less*. If you lose money on your sale—the amount realized was less than your basis—you have a capital loss.

Short-term capital gains alone. Suppose you have the good fortune to have no losses. Every time you sold stock, you had a short-term capital gain. The rule here is simple: your short-term gain is taxed at the same rates as ordinary income.

Consider the example above where you are in the 28% bracket but just $100 below the 33% bracket. We saw that adding $200 of ordinary income would increase the tax by $61, because half would be taxed in each bracket. The same would be true if we added $200 of short-term capital gain.

This isn't to say that short-term capital gain is *exactly* the same as ordinary income. We'll see in a few moments that short-term capital gain is *better* than ordinary income when you have capital losses. And there's another important difference that will become important in Part V of this book: capital gain doesn't count as self-employment income, even if you qualify as a trader.

Short-term capital gains and losses. Your luck won't always be that good! If you do enough trading, you're bound to have some losing trades. For now we're still excluding any long-term trades to get a clear picture of what happens with short-term gains and losses.

Start by finding a total for each category. Add up all your short-term gains to get the total amount of gain. Same thing with the losses. Then you subtract the total loss from the total gain.

- If the gain is greater than the loss, you end up with a positive number: a *net short-term capital gain*. That number gets added to your other income. It will be taxed at the same rate as if it were ordinary income.

- If the gain is exactly the same size as the loss, you end up with zero. The tax law isn't always sensible and fair, but in this case it is: you broke even in your stock trading, so the activity has no effect on the amount of income tax you pay.

- You may have losses that exceed your gains: a *net short-term capital loss*. In this unfortunate situation you may take some comfort in knowing that the Treasury will share your pain—but only up to a limit.

Capital loss limitation and carryover. A net capital loss is a deduction that reduces your other income, up to a maximum of $3,000. If your capital loss is $3,000 or less, you get to claim the entire loss. If the loss is more than $3,000, you claim $3,000 and "carry" the rest to the next year.

> **Example:** Suppose your ordinary income and deductions leave you with taxable income of $40,000. In addition you have short-term capital gains that add up to $8,000 and short-term capital losses that add up to $10,000. Your net capital loss is $2,000. That's less than $3,000, so you can deduct the full amount, reducing your taxable income to $38,000.

Notice that you're getting the full benefit from $10,000 of capital losses. Some people get in a panic thinking they'll only get $3,000 of capital losses regardless of their gains. The $3,000 limitation doesn't come into play until after you net out the losses against the gains.

How carryovers work. A carryover sounds like something fancy and technical. Actually it's a pretty simple concept. Whatever capital loss you don't use this year because of the $3,000 capital loss limitation is treated like a brand-new loss in the same category (short-term or long-term) at the beginning of the following year.

Example: Your capital gains add up to $2,000 and your capital losses add up to $10,000, leaving you with a net capital loss of $8,000. You get to deduct only $3,000 of the capital loss this year. The remaining $5,000 is carried over to the following year. That means you're treated as if you had a new capital loss at the beginning of the following year.

Capital Loss Carryover	
Total short-term capital gain	$2,000
Total short-term capital loss	(10,000)
Net short-term capital loss	(8,000)
Used in current year	3,000
Carryover to next year	$ (5,000)

The $5,000 capital loss carryover works just like any other capital loss in the carryover year. If you have other capital gains and losses, it goes into the mix just like a "real" loss. If you don't have any other capital gains or losses, you can deduct $3,000 of this loss, and carry the remaining $2,000 to the *next* year. There's no time limit on this, because each year it's treated as a new loss. You can't take it with you, though, or even leave it behind: any unused capital loss carryover remaining at your death is worthless.

> ▪ **Forward, not back.** Some kinds of losses (called *net operating losses,* or *NOLs*) carry back to previous years. Not capital losses! Unless you're a corporation, your capital losses carry forward only, never back.

I heard a sad story about someone who fell into a trap with these rules. She had a great winning streak in 1999 when the stock market was strong, piling up $400,000 in gains. When the air went out of some of the tech stocks early the next year she lost the whole bundle. She didn't even save enough to pay taxes on gains from the prior year! There's really nothing you can do in this situation. You can't carry the loss back to the previous year. In the current year the deduction is limited to $3,000. And unless you get another hot streak going, at $3,000 per year it's going to take more than 100 years to use up a $397,000 capital loss carryover.*

Ordinary income less than $3,000. You might run into a situation where you don't get the full benefit of a capital loss deduction because your taxable income without this loss is less than $3,000, perhaps because you're a student or you spent the entire year trading stock. In this situation, you may burn up less than $3,000 of your capital loss, giving you a larger carryover to use in future years. If you qualify for a personal exemption, though, you may find that much or all of the $3,000 allowance counts against your capital loss carryover even though your benefit from the capital loss is much smaller. If you're in this situation, use the capital loss carryover worksheet in the instructions for Schedule D (Form 1040) to determine the amount you're allowed to carry over.

Long-Term Capital Gains and Losses

We've seen how ordinary income and deductions work without any capital gains or losses, and also what happens when you throw short-term capital gains and losses into the mix. Now let's eliminate the short-term gains and focus on what happens when you have long-term gains and losses: gains and losses from stocks and other assets held more than a year.

---

* In Chapter 25 we'll see that individuals who qualify as traders can make the *mark-to-market election*, which converts trading gains and losses into ordinary income and loss. Traders who make this election can use trading losses against ordinary income, and carry losses *back* as well as forward.

> ▪ **"Pass-through" gains.** Depending on your invest-
> ments, you may have a long-term capital gain that
> gets "passed through" from another source—for
> example, a capital gain dividend from a mutual
> fund. These are treated the same as long-term
> capital gains you have from selling stock or other
> assets.

Long-term capital gains alone. We'll start the same
way we did for short-term gains and losses, looking at the
situation where you have gains but no losses. The tax rate
for long-term capital gain is lower than the rate for
ordinary income. For long-term capital gain that falls into
the first two tax brackets (10% and 15%), the rate is 5%. A
15% rate applies to all other long-term capital gain.*

To determine whether the gain "falls into" the two
lowest brackets, you need to know what your taxable
income is *without* the long-term capital gain. Then you
figure out what rate would apply if you added more
income to your total. If your taxable income is large
enough to put you in the 25% bracket or higher without
any long-term capital gain, *none* of your gain will fall in
the first two brackets.

Example: For single individuals in 2004, the 15%
tax bracket ends when taxable income reaches
$29,050. Suppose your taxable income that year is
$27,050—in other words, $2,000 less than the
limit. If your long-term capital gain is $2,000 or
less, the entire gain will be taxed at 5%. If your
long-term capital gain is greater than $2,000, then
the 5% rate applies to the first $2,000 and the 15%
rate applies to the rest.

Example: Suppose your taxable income, before
taking any long-term capital gain into account, is

---

* These rates are in effect for long-term capital gains realized after
May 5, 2003. Long-term capital gains realized before that date are
taxed at 10% or 20%. Higher rates apply to some long-term capital
gains, as explained in Chapter 8.

$50,000. In this case, the 15% rate will apply to all your long-term capital gain.

The tax consequences of long-term capital gain are always tacked onto the end of your ordinary income, even if the gain came from a stock sale on January 1, before you earned any ordinary income. The rate that applies to the gain depends on how much ordinary income and short-term capital gain you had throughout the entire year. If that's enough to push the gain out of the 15% bracket (where it would be taxed at 5%), the 15% rate will apply to the gain.

By the same token, long-term capital gain never pushes ordinary income into a higher bracket. Some people worry that they'll lose some of the benefit of the lower rates from long-term capital gain if it causes their ordinary income to be taxed at a higher rate. That doesn't happen: the tax rates apply first to ordinary income as if you didn't have any long-term capital gain, and then the special 5% or 15% rate applies to the capital gain.

Indirect effects. Long-term capital gain can affect the rate you pay on ordinary income *indirectly*. That's because the gain is included in your *adjusted gross income*. That figure is used to determine whether various tax benefits should be reduced. A long-term capital gain, like any other additional income you might have, could reduce your itemized deductions or the deduction for personal exemptions, for example. Likewise, long-term capital gain can reduce the amount you're allowed to contribute to a Roth IRA, or reduce your deduction for a regular IRA contribution.

> - The special treatment of long-term capital gain is an important fact of life for people who buy and sell stocks. Knowledgeable investors seek to take advantage of this tax break whenever possible. An opportunity to receive long-term capital gain in place of ordinary income or short-term capital gain is a chance to preserve wealth by reducing your rate of tax on that income.

Long-term capital gains and losses. We've seen what happens if the only thing you have on your tax return, other than ordinary income such as wages, is long-term capital gain. If we throw long-term capital losses into the mix, we'll see a situation similar to the one we had when you had short-term capital gains and losses. You have to add up all your long-term gains, and also add up all your long-term losses. Then you subtract the total loss from the total gain.

If the result is a positive number, you have a net long-term capital gain. This is the amount that will be taxed at the special rates described above. If the gain and loss are exactly equal, they cancel each other out and have no effect on your taxes.

If the loss is greater than the gain, you have a net long-term capital loss. Just as in the case of a net short-term capital loss, you can claim up to $3,000 of the loss as a deduction. That means a net long-term loss of $3,000 or less has exactly the same effect as if the loss were short-term. If the loss is greater than $3,000, though, the category of the loss makes a difference, because the loss carryover will be long-term, not short-term. That could make a difference in your calculations for the following year.

Short-Term and Long-Term Gains and Losses

Now we're ready to put it all together. Let's see what happens in a year when you have both short-term and long-term capital gains and losses.

The first step is to find a total for each of the four types of results: short-term gains, short-term losses, long-term gains and long-term losses. Then you subtract the losses in each category from the gains in the same category. In other words, subtract the short-term losses from the short-term gains, and subtract the long-term losses from the long-term gains. You end up with two numbers: one that represents a short-term gain or loss, and another that represents a long-term gain or loss. There are three possibilities: they are both positive (net gains), both negative (net losses), or one positive and the other negative.

Both positive. If you have a net short-term gain and a net long-term gain, the short-term gain is taxed at the rates that apply to ordinary income, just as it would be if you didn't have any long-term capital gain or loss. The long-term capital gain is taxed at 5% to the extent it falls in the tax brackets below 25%, with any additional amount taxed at 15%.

> **Example:** Before you take capital gains and losses into account, your taxable income is $2,000 below the upper boundary of the 15% bracket. You have a short-term capital gain of $2,000 and a short-term capital loss of $500, giving you a net short-term capital gain of $1,500. In addition, you have a long-term capital gain of $3,800 and a long-term capital loss of $1,300, giving you a net long-term capital gain of $2,500.
>
> The short-term capital gain counts first. You're in the 15% tax bracket with $2,000 to spare, so the entire short-term gain of $1,500 is taxed at the 15% rate. After that, you're only $500 away from going into the next tax bracket. That means $500 of your long-term gain will be taxed at 5% and the rest will be taxed at 15%.

Notice that you would come out better if you could apply the long-term loss against the short-term gain. That would give you a smaller short-term gain and a larger long-term gain, so that more of your gain would be taxed at the lower rates that apply to net long-term capital gain. Unfortunately, the tax rules don't permit you to do this. You always have to net long-term losses against long-term gains before you can apply them against any other kind of income.

> • **Remember:** When it comes to capital gain, long-term is better than short-term. When it comes to capital loss, the opposite is true. Short-term loss is better because it reduces short-term gain.

Both negative. In a bad year you may have a net loss for both short-term and long-term transactions. When this happens, the $3,000 loss limitation applies to the total of *all* your capital losses. In other words, the largest amount of net capital loss you can claim in any year is $3,000, even if you have losses in both the short-term and long-term categories.

You're required to claim the short-term loss first. This rule doesn't matter if the total loss is less than $3,000. If the loss is greater than $3,000, this rule determines how much of your carryover is short-term and how much is long-term.

> **Example:** You have a net short-term loss of $2,500 and also a net long-term loss of $2,500. Your total capital loss is $5,000, but you can claim only $3,000 in a single year. You're required to use the short-term loss first, so the $3,000 you deduct this year will take up the entire short-term capital loss plus $500 of the long-term capital loss. That leaves you with a $2,000 long-term capital loss carryover.

You aren't allowed to use the long-term loss first, or use them both proportionately. The tax law requires you to use the short-term loss first.

Net loss and net gain. You may end up with a net loss in one category and a net gain in the other. When this happens, you apply the loss against the gain. The resulting number will belong to the category of the larger number.

- *Short-term loss greater than long-term gain.* The resulting number is treated as a net short-term loss, just like a short-term loss that arises purely from short-term transactions.

- *Long-term gain greater than short-term loss.* This situation gives you a net long-term gain, which will be taxed at the favorable long-term rates.

- *Long-term loss greater than short-term gain.* In this case you have a net long-term loss. You'll deduct up to $3,000 and carry any excess to the next year.

- *Short-term gain greater than long-term loss.* The result here is a net short-term gain, which will be taxed at the same rate as ordinary income.

That may seem like a complicated mess to try to remember, but in reality there's just one simple rule that applies: whichever item is larger determines the category for the net figure. It may not be pretty, but at least it's logical.

Example: Suppose you net out all your short-term capital gains and losses and end up with a net loss of $2,000. At the same time, when you net your long-term gains and losses you come up with a gain of $8,000. Under these rules, you'll net the short-term loss against the long-term gain, leaving you with long-term capital gain of $6,000.

> ▪ **Tax terminology.** You might think, quite reasonably, that you have a *net capital gain* whenever your total capital gain in all categories is greater than your total capital loss. Technically, though, the term *net capital gain* refers only to a net *long-term* capital gain that remains after subtracting any net short-term capital loss. If you have a net *short-term* capital gain, that gain isn't part of your *net capital gain*. It seems illogical, but that's the way the terms are defined in the tax law.

Why bother with this arcane factoid? The IRS sometimes uses this terminology in its instructions and publications. They may say that a particular rule applies only if you have a *net capital gain*. If you apply the rule to a net short-term capital gain you'll be wrong. I've seen tax pros make this mistake, because it seems so logical to say a net short-term capital gain is a net capital gain.

In a Nutshell

Now we're ready to summarize the principal tax rules for the treatment of capital gains and losses. The best way to do this is to set forth the sequence of steps you go through to determine the correct treatment.

1. Begin by sorting all transactions into four categories: short-term gain, short-term loss, long-term gain and long-term loss. Find the total for each category.

2. Subtract the short-term loss from the short-term gain to arrive at a *net* short-term gain or loss. Do the same with the long-term gain and loss.

3. If you have a gain in one category and a loss in the other, subtract the loss from the gain. The resulting net figure is considered to be in the same category as the larger of the two numbers. For example, if you had a long-term loss and a smaller short-term gain, the resulting number would be a long-term loss.

4a. If you have an overall loss, use up to $3,000 of the loss as a deduction against your taxable income, applying short-term loss before long-term loss. Any loss that isn't used will carry over to the next year as if it were a new capital loss deduction.

4b. If you have an overall gain, the short-term gain (if any) will be taxed at the same rate as additional ordinary income. The long-term gain (if any) will be taxed at the rate of 5% to the extent it falls in the two lowest tax brackets, with any additional amount taxed at the rate of 15%.

Chapter 30 lays out tax planning techniques that take maximum advantage of these rules.

Chapter 4
Special Rules for Stock

So far we've been dealing with rules that apply to sales of all kinds of assets. In this chapter we'll look at some rules for capital gains and losses that apply specifically to shares of stock.

Date of a Purchase or Sale

The holding period for stock is determined the same way as for any other asset. You have to hold the stock at least a year and a day to have a long-term capital gain or loss. Yet there's some ambiguity as to when you buy or sell stock, because in a normal stock transaction two different dates are significant. One is called the trade date, and the other is called the settlement date.

The *trade date* is the date you entered into the transaction. That's often, but not always, the day you tell your broker to buy or sell. If you give instructions on Monday but the transaction doesn't take place until Tuesday (perhaps because you transmitted the instructions after the market closed, or you placed a limit order that couldn't be filled Monday), then your trade date is Tuesday. When in doubt, check the trade confirmation you get from the broker to learn your trade date.

The *settlement date* occurs a few days after the trade date. This is the day the shares and the cash will actually change hands. If you're the buyer, you need to have money in your account by the settlement date.

For tax purposes, the date that controls your holding period is the *trade date*. The settlement date is irrelevant in determining how long you held your stock. That's true for both purchases and sales. If you want to have a long-term gain, you have to make sure the trade date of your sale is on or after the first anniversary of the day after the trade date of the purchase. To get a short-term loss, you need to have the trade date of your sale before the first anniversary of the day after the trade date of the purchase.

> ■ **Year of sale.** The trade date also determines *what year* you sold your stock. People sometimes ask what is the last day to sell stock for a gain or loss in the current year. The answer is December 31 (assuming the stock market is open that day). The fact that the transaction won't settle until January of the next year doesn't delay reporting of the sale. There's an exception for short sales, though. See Chapter 12.

Identifying Shares

If you find yourself holding different batches of shares in the same company, you may want to choose which shares you sell first. In other words, you may want to *identify* the shares you're selling. Choosing wisely can reduce your tax bill.

> **Example:** You hold some shares of XYZ stock you bought years ago, when the stock price was much lower than it is today. You also hold some shares of XYZ you bought recently when the price was higher than the current price. Now you want to sell some of this stock, but not all of it. If you sell the older shares, you'll report a gain, increasing your tax for the year of the sale. If you sell the newer shares, you'll report a loss, and reduce your income tax for that year.

If you don't identify the shares you're selling, you'll be treated as if you sold the oldest shares first. Tax pros call this the *FIFO* rule, which stands for "first-in, first-out." Sometimes the FIFO rule produces the best tax result, but often it doesn't, and that's when you need to identify the shares you're selling.

The rules for identifying shares aren't difficult, but are often misunderstood. It isn't just investors who mess up: many brokers get confused by these rules. Make sure *you* understand them, so your broker's ignorance won't cost you tax dollars.

Background. It's useful to understand the *theory* of the rule for identifying shares. The tax law permits you to decide what shares you want to sell. You have to make that choice *at the time of the sale,* though. You can't go back later, after you see how things turn out for the year, and say you really meant to sell different shares. The rules for identifying shares are designed to do two things:

- Provide a rule for what happens if you *didn't* make any choice at the time of the sale, and

- Provide a way for you to make a choice at that time—and to prove that you made it.

If You Don't Choose

If you don't specify which shares you're selling, the law treats you as if you sold the *earliest* shares you bought. This is called the *first-in, first out* method, or *FIFO*.

Example: You bought 50 shares of XYZ at $40 in 1998 and another 50 at $60 in 1999. In 2004 you sell 50 shares at $80 without specifying which shares you're selling. The tax law says you sold the shares you bought in 1998.

Notice that you would report a smaller gain, and pay less tax, if you specified that you were selling the shares you bought in 1999. Sometimes it pays to choose which shares you're selling.

No averaging. Some people wonder if they can use the *average* basis for the shares they hold. There are averaging rules for mutual fund shares, but for regular stocks you can't use average basis.

Switching permitted. Suppose you sold some shares earlier and didn't identify the shares you were selling. Does this mean you're locked into using the first-in, first-out method? Not at all. The rule for identifying stock applies to each individual sale. You can identify shares for a current sale even if you failed to identify shares from the same stock in the past. (Note, however, that if you elect averaging for mutual fund shares you're locked into that method for all shares of the same mutual fund. See Chapter 5.)

If You Hold Certificates

Shares of stock are represented by *certificates*. It used to be commonplace (and is still not unusual) for shareholders to hold certificates for their shares. Most investors nowadays leave the certificates with the broker.

If you hold certificates for your shares, the way you choose which shares you're selling is to deliver the certificate that represents those shares. It isn't necessary to *identify* the shares in this situation. It's your responsibility to determine which certificate represents the shares you want to sell and deliver that certificate. It won't help to tell the broker (or the IRS) you meant to sell some other shares if you deliver the wrong certificate.

It's possible you'll end up holding a single certificate that represents shares bought at different times or different prices. In that case, assuming you're using a broker to sell the shares, you need to identify the shares you're selling (as explained below) when you deliver the certificate to the broker. If you sell some of the stock represented by a certificate *without* using a broker or other agent, you simply have to maintain a written record of which shares you sold.

Identifying Shares Held by Your Broker

Now we come to the meat of the question. You left the certificates with your broker and you want to sell some but not all of the shares. To identify the shares you're selling you need to do two things:

- *At the time of the sale,* specify to the broker the shares you're selling, *and*

- *Within a reasonable time thereafter,* receive a written confirmation of that specification from your broker.

Clearing the Air

Before we go any further let's clear up the biggest point of confusion. The traditional way to specify the shares you're selling is in the form of an instruction to your broker:

Sell 50 shares XYZ from the lot purchased on March 12, 1996.

This makes it sound like the broker has to do something special—possibly locate those specific shares, or at least make a record of some kind indicating what shares you sold. Some brokers say, "We don't offer that service." But in reality the only thing the broker has to do, besides executing the sale transaction in the normal way, is send you a written confirmation that you specified shares from the lot purchased on March 12, 1996.

Only part of the message shown above is really an instruction. "Sell 50 shares XYZ" is an instruction. The rest of the message is there for the sole purpose of establishing proof acceptable to the IRS that you made a choice at the time of the sale. *Your broker doesn't have to do anything about the second part of the message—except provide written confirmation that they received it.*

If I seem to be shouting here, it's because I've seen brokers time and again misunderstand this rule. They'll tell you it's okay to do your own identification on your tax return, or that their computers aren't set up to handle this, or some other nonsense. Tell them that's all very nice but you need written confirmation of your identification.

Specifying the Shares

When you specify the shares to be sold, you need to identify the shares in a way that makes it clear which shares you sold. Any of the following might do the trick:

- The shares I bought on March 12, 1996.

- The shares I bought for 40-3/8.

- The shares I bought most recently.

In theory, it shouldn't matter if the instruction is meaningless to the broker. For example, you may have had a different broker when you bought the shares, so the present broker has no idea what shares you bought on March 12, 1996. The thing that *does* matter is that your choice is objective and unambiguous, so you can prove to the IRS which shares you sold.

If you do your trading online, you may find that there's no apparent way to give instructions as to which shares you're selling. If you're in this situation, it should be acceptable if you send an email at the same time as your order, saying something like this:

My sale order # 123456 pertains to shares purchased on March 12, 1996. Please acknowledge in writing that you received this message at the time of the sale.

I don't guarantee that they'll respond in writing, but in my view this procedure will work if you can get them to do so. The regulations say you have to specify the shares at the time of the sale, but they don't require you to specify them as part of the process of giving the sale order.

> ▪ Be careful not to send an email that can be misinterpreted as an *additional* sale order.

Instruction need not be in writing. Although you need confirmation from the broker in writing, your *instruction* does *not* have to be in writing. It can be given by email, or orally over the telephone.

Broker's Confirmation

The second requirement is that you receive written confirmation of the identification from the broker within a reasonable time after the transaction. Remember, they're merely confirming *your message*. They don't have to confirm that they actually sold those specific shares. *All you need is written confirmation that you identified the stock at the time of the sale.*

> **Example:** Your broker sends you a message stating "We acknowledge that you identified the 500 shares of XYZ sold on May 18, 2000 as shares purchased on March 12, 1996."

That's it! If you can extract that in writing from your broker within a reasonable time after the sale, you've met the requirement. Traditional brokers who know how to handle identification may acknowledge the identification on the trade confirmation slip, but this isn't a requirement. You just need something in writing that confirms your identification.

> **Email?** An email should be good enough confirmation but there's no guidance on this question. The regulations require a *written document* from your broker, and it's possible the IRS will say email doesn't pass muster. You're safer if you can get your broker to send confirmation of your instructions by regular mail.

> **Note:** One taxpayer won a case where all of the communications were oral, and there was no written confirmation from his broker. I think the result of that case is questionable, so I'm reluctant to rely on it.

Blanket Instructions

Some advisors suggest that you can give your broker a blanket instruction, such as "always sell the shares with the highest basis." If you have written confirmation of such an instruction from your broker it should stand up in court. Bear in mind, though, that there may be times when you want to use a different approach. For example, it may be better to sell the shares with a lower basis because they produce long-term capital gain instead of short-term gain. You may get better results if you make a specific identification each time you sell some but not all of your shares.

Separate Accounts

The regulations don't mention the possibility of holding your shares in separate accounts. It's reasonably clear, though, that if you do so, the separate accounts serve as at least a partial identification of the shares you're selling. If you sell the shares in Account A, you don't have to specify that you aren't selling the shares in Account B, because that's already clear.

Stapling Trade Confirmations

You may hear that you can identify shares by matching up trade confirmations for purchases and sales and stapling them together. That's an urban legend. Nothing in the law supports that procedure. It provides no evidence that you made your choice at the time of the sale, so it's unlikely the IRS will accept this procedure.

Chapter 5
Special Rules for Mutual Funds

When it comes to capital gains and losses, mutual funds present some special problems—and special opportunities. Even basic issues such as when you have to report gain or loss can be confusing, and determining the *amount* of a gain or loss can be a painfully difficult task. Fortunately, the tax law provides some special rules that can make your task easier, and in some cases lower your tax bill.

> - We discuss mutual fund dividends in Chapter 9. For now you should be aware that not all dividends from mutual funds qualify for the 15% tax rate.

Types of Mutual Funds

There are thousands of mutual funds to choose from, and various ways of classifying them. I won't try to give a full picture of what's available, but a few remarks on various types of mutual funds are appropriate.

Open-end mutual funds. This is the type of mutual fund most people are familiar with. The name comes from the fact that these funds grow in an open-ended way by selling shares directly to investors. At the close of each day, the fund determines the total market value of its assets. This number is used to arrive at the *net asset value* of shares in the fund. The net asset value, or *NAV*, is the price you'll see for fund shares in the financial section of your newspaper. Most open-end mutual funds will automatically reinvest your dividends unless you request otherwise.

Closed-end mutual funds. This type of mutual fund has been around for a long time, but has not been nearly as popular as open-end mutual funds. When you want to buy shares in a closed-end mutual fund, you make a purchase in the stock market, just as you would if you were buying regular shares of stock. The price of the mutual fund shares isn't necessarily the same as the value of the assets held by the fund. It can be higher, but more often it's somewhat lower.

Later in this chapter, we'll discuss *averaging* rules that can be used to determine gain or loss from selling mutual fund shares. Although the rules appear to be appropriate mainly for open-end funds, they apply equally to closed-end funds.

Exchange-traded index funds. This is a relatively recent innovation that has quickly become very popular. Like open-end index funds, these funds are designed to mimic the performance of a particular stock index. For example, SPDRs ("Spiders") mimic the S&P 500 index, and QQQs ("Qubes") mimic the NASDAQ 100 index. Yet they look more like closed-end funds, because you buy and sell shares on the stock exchanges. These funds are specially designed to have a market value that closely reflects the value of the underlying stocks, even though in theory they can have a different value, just like traditional closed-end funds.

Here again, the averaging rules described later are available. Although they trade like stocks, these funds are "regulated investment companies" under the tax law, and subject to all the rules that apply to mutual funds.

Money market funds. Some mutual funds are set up to make very short-term investments that are unlikely to change significantly in value. While it's theoretically possible you could have a loss in one of these *money market funds*, that's almost unheard of. You also won't have a gain in one of these funds, because they declare dividends *daily* to keep the price of shares at exactly $1.00. Your profit comes in the form of dividends, not share appreciation.*

Exempt bond funds. Some mutual funds are set up to invest in tax-exempt bonds. Investors sometimes assume that they won't have to worry about taxes on this investment because the bonds are tax-free. Although you won't pay tax on the dividends from exempt interest, you can have taxable gain (or deductible loss) when you sell shares in these funds, or a taxable dividend if the fund has gains from selling bonds. Note also that there's a special rule for losses from these funds, explained at the end of this chapter.

Buying and Selling Mutual Fund Shares

When you invest in a mutual fund, you're buying shares. Many people don't realize this when they invest in an open-end fund, because the investment is usually in terms of a specific dollar amount. You don't say, "I'll purchase 80 shares of mutual fund XYZ." Instead, you send $500 to the mutual fund company. It feels more or less like you're depositing money into a bank account. Yet what you're actually doing is buying $500 worth of shares, usually determined to three decimal places. For example, if you read your mutual fund statement carefully, you might find that your $500 bought 19.273 shares. The number of shares you receive is based on the net asset value of shares as of the end of the day the mutual fund received your money.

More importantly, any time you pull money out of a mutual fund, you're *selling* shares. That's true even if you merely move money from one fund to another in the same family of mutual funds. Perhaps you never saw the money, but for tax purposes you're treated the same as if you sold shares in the first fund—with a gain or loss—and

---

* Money market funds generate most of their income in the form of *interest*, but when they pay this income to their investors, that payment is a *dividend*. Money market bank accounts pay interest.

used the money from that sale to buy shares in the second one.*

I stress this point because it often comes as a surprise to people who are new to mutual fund investing. Perhaps they've grown accustomed to moving money from one fund to another within their 401k account or IRA. There's no gain or loss to report in retirement accounts, so it never hits home that they're buying and selling shares when they make these fund switches. They take the same approach with their non-retirement investments and learn the truth when Form 1099-B arrives at tax time, telling them the amount of the sale that was reported to the IRS.

Basis and Holding Period

To determine how much gain or loss you have on a sale of mutual fund shares, you need to know your *basis* in those shares. Chapter 4 explains the general rule for determining the basis of shares of stock, and that rule applies to mutual fund shares as well: your basis is equal to the amount paid for the shares, including any costs directly related to the purchase. If you paid a brokerage commission or similar charge when you made your investment, that amount is included in your basis. Some mutual funds impose a charge on the initial purchase, called a "load." This would be included in your basis, too.

> **Example:** You invested $20,000 in a mutual fund that charges a 5% front-end load. Only $19,000 was actually used to buy shares, because $1,000 was used to pay the sales charge. Yet your basis for these shares is $20,000, because basis includes expenses incurred in purchasing the shares.

Dividends. Most mutual funds are set up to reinvest your dividends in additional shares of the same fund. The tax law treats you as if you received the dividend in cash,

---

* For a special rule that can limit losses when moving from one fund to another in the same family, see "Load Rollover Rule" later in this chapter.

and then used the cash to buy additional shares. That means you have to report the dividend as income. It also means you have additional shares with basis equal to the amount of the dividend.

> **Example:** You invested $20,000 in a mutual fund, acquiring 828.844 shares at $24.13 per share. Later, when the net asset value of the fund was $24.93, the fund paid a dividend of $1.04 per share. Your dividend is $862.00, and you receive an additional 34.577 shares at $24.93 per share. You now have a total of 863.421 shares, but they don't all have the same basis. Some have a basis of $24.13 per share, and some have a basis of $24.93 per share.

It's also worth noting that your shares don't all have the same holding period. Your holding period for some shares goes back to the date of your original investment, while the other shares have a holding period that begins on the date the mutual fund paid the dividend. This is important when you have to determine whether your gain or loss is short-term or long-term.

> **Example:** You sell your mutual fund shares more than a year after the date of the original investment but less than a year after the date of the dividend. Your gain or loss on the original shares is long-term, but your gain or loss on the shares you acquired from dividend reinvestment is short-term.

Later in this chapter we'll look at methods designed to make it easier to determine the basis of the shares you sell. Yet no matter what method you use, you have to know the holding period of your shares. This information tells you whether some or all of your gain is short-term, and is used for other purposes as well:

- The wash sale rule may apply if you sell some shares at a loss within 30 days before or after a dividend, because the dividend reinvestment is a purchase. Chapter 6 explains the wash sale rule.

- The special rule for sales of mutual fund shares at a loss within six months of purchase (explained later in this chapter) can apply to shares you bought automatically as a result of dividend reinvestment.

Basis of Particular Shares

Determining the basis of particular shares in a mutual fund can be a tedious process. This is particularly true if you've made a large number of purchases over a period of years. Some people make monthly investments in one or more mutual funds. This can be an excellent way to build wealth, but be prepared for some difficult record keeping.

Consider the following example. You've invested $100 per month over a period of four months with the following results:

Date	Amount	Price	Shares
3/1/04	$100.00	25.43	3.932
4/1/04	$100.00	25.80	3.876
5/1/04	$100.00	25.65	3.899
6/1/04	$100.00	26.03	3.842

The price per share of the mutual fund varies from time to time. As a result, the number of shares you receive for each $100 is different.

If you sell all the shares at one time, it's easy enough to see that your basis is $400. But suppose you withdraw only a portion of your account. You take $250, resulting in a sale of 8.477 shares. How do you determine the basis of those shares?

As it turns out, there are four different possibilities. Two of them involve the use of *averaging* methods described later in this chapter. Once you start to use one of those methods for a particular mutual fund, you're locked into that method for all future sales of shares in the same fund. If you haven't previously elected to use one of the averaging methods, all four of these alternatives are available to you:

- First-in, first-out (FIFO)

- Identification

- Single-category averaging

- Double-category averaging

First-In, First-Out

The default method—the one that applies if you don't take action to choose another one—is the first-in, first-out method, or FIFO. The rule here is the same as described in Chapter 4 for regular shares of stock. The only difference is that it's often a great deal more difficult to apply this method in the case of mutual funds because of multiple purchases and fractional shares.

We asked earlier what the result would be if you sold 8.477 of the shares represented in the table. Applying the FIFO method, we would treat the first shares purchased as the first shares sold. Spending a few moments with a calculator, you can determine that you sold all the shares bought on 3/1/00, all the shares bought on 4/1/00, and 0.669 of the shares bought on 5/1/00. You're left with 3.230 of the shares bought on 5/1/00 and all the shares bought on 6/1/00. The basis for the shares you sold is as follows:

Date	Shares	Per Share	Basis
3/1/00	3.932	25.43	$100.00
4/1/00	3.876	25.80	$100.00
5/1/00	0.669	25.65	$17.16
Total	8.477		$217.16

You'll report a sale of 8.477 shares for $250.00, with a basis of $217.16, resulting in gain of $32.84.

This certainly isn't rocket science, but you can see where you could run into a major headache if you continued to buy shares on a monthly basis over a period of years, and in addition had dividend reinvestments to deal with. That's where the averaging methods come in handy. We'll turn to them after a few words about identification.

Identifying Shares

Chapter 4 explains the rules for identifying shares of stock. It's unusual to see investors use those rules for mutual fund shares, yet the same rules apply here. If you can get the mutual fund company to cooperate, you may be able to use identification to reduce your tax bill.

In the example above, you might specify that you're selling the newest shares, rather than the oldest ones. The newer shares have a higher basis than the older ones, and that means you report a smaller gain (or a larger loss) when you sell them. The tax regulations say you have to tell the broker or mutual fund which shares you're selling at the time you give the order to sell. In addition, you have to receive written confirmation of the identification within a reasonable period of time after the sale. It isn't always easy to receive this cooperation from a broker or mutual fund, but if you can meet the requirements, identification can reduce your taxes. See Chapter 4 for more on identification.

Single-Category Averaging

Now we come to a choice that isn't available when selling regular stocks. People sometimes ask whether they can use their average basis to determine gain or loss on a stock sale. The answer is yes—but only when selling shares of a mutual fund.

This method is often quite a bit easier than tracing the basis of particular shares through your records. Some mutual funds make it easier still, by providing you with the information you can put on your tax return. In many cases, the result provided by this method is better than the result you would get using the FIFO method described above. In fact, sometimes you get a better result with averaging than you get when you identify shares.

Eligibility. Nearly everyone who invests in mutual funds is eligible to use the single-category averaging method. There are three situations to watch out for, though:

- You can't use this method if you physically possess certificates representing your shares. Many mutual funds record your investment by a book entry system, and in other cases the broker usually retains possession. In either of these cases you're eligible.

- You can't use this method if you previously elected to use the double-category method (described below) for the same mutual fund.

- If you received some of your mutual fund shares by gift, there's a special requirement described below.

You can use different methods for different mutual funds, including different funds within the same family of funds. And you can use the single-category method even if you sold shares in previous years without using an averaging method. But once you start using an averaging method, you're stuck with it for that fund. You can use other methods for other funds, but you have to continue using the same averaging method for this one.

There's one other eligibility rule. The IRS can deny you the use of this method if it appears you're using it to convert short-term gain to long-term gain, or long-term loss to short-term loss. You shouldn't need to worry about this rule unless you're planning something fancy. If you come up with a clever scheme to benefit from this type of conversion by using the single-category method, you should be aware that the IRS can deny the benefits under this rule.

Averaging information provided by the fund. Many mutual funds do the single-category averaging calculations for you. They send a schedule that tells you the basis per share, the number of shares sold, and the total basis of the shares you sold. This information is not reported to the IRS. In fact, the mutual fund is not required to provide this information at all. It's simply a service that some funds provide.

Just because they send this information doesn't mean you have to use it. You may find that you're better off if you use the first-in, first-out method to determine your gain or loss. If you used averaging for this fund in prior years, you have to stick with that averaging method, but otherwise you're free to use the method of your choice.

Bear in mind that the mutual fund company doesn't know what method you used in prior years. If you used a method other than single-category averaging for any previous sale, their basis calculation won't be correct. That's because the method you use for one sale affects the basis of the remaining shares. If you've used the FIFO method or specific identification in the past and then switch to averaging, you'll have to do your own averaging calculation.

■ **Statement required.** Even if you're using figures provided by the mutual fund company, you have to tell the IRS you've elected to use averaging the first time you use this method for that particular fund. See *Electing an Averaging Method*, later in this chapter.

How single-category averaging works. The single-category method requires you to add the basis of all shares you hold in the mutual fund and divide the total by the number of shares you hold. That average is used as the basis of the shares you sold.

Example: You contributed $100.00 per month to your mutual fund account for a period of 27 months. During that period, $147.00 of dividends were reinvested. Your total basis is $2,847.00. According to your mutual fund statement, at this point you own 112.342 shares, so your average basis is $25.34 per share. Then you take $500.00 from the fund. Your statement says you sold 18.277 shares. To determine your basis in those shares, multiply the average basis by the number of shares. That gives you a basis of $463.14 ($25.34 times 18.277). You'll report a gain of $36.86 ($500.00 minus $463.14).

Before the sale, the total basis of your shares was $2,847.00. Now you've sold shares with a basis of $463.14, so your remaining shares have a basis of $2,383.86. The next time you sell shares, you'll start from this number and increase it for any amounts added to the account, including reinvested dividends.

This may not seem like the easiest calculation in the world, but in a lot of cases it's a far sight easier than determining exactly what shares you sold when you withdrew $500 and figuring the basis of those particular shares. The main thing you have to do when you use this method is keep a running tally of your basis for the mutual fund: your contributions, plus reinvested dividends, minus the basis of shares you sold. Divide that total by the number of shares you held at the time of the sale (a number you can get from your mutual fund statement) to get the average basis.

Single-Category Averaging Calculation	
1 Previous basis	$ 0.00
2 Additions	2,700.00
3 Reinvested dividends	147.00
4 Basis adjustments	0.00
5 Total basis	2,847.00
6 Number of shares owned	112.342
7 Average basis per share	25.34
8 Number of shares sold	18.277
9 Basis of shares sold	463.14
10 Total basis before sale	2,847.00
11 Basis of shares sold	(463.14)
12 Basis remaining after sale	$2,383.86

In this calculation, the "previous basis" is zero because this is the first time using averaging. The next time you sell shares, your "previous basis" will be $2,383.86, the ending number from the calculation above. Lines 2 and 3 will show only the additions and dividends that occurred after the sale reflected in this calculation. Line 4 allows for basis adjustments that may result from return of capital distributions (a negative number) or capital gain allocations (a positive number) described in Chapter 9.

> ▪ Remember, the key to this calculation is a running tally of your basis, adjusted to reflect added investments, reinvested dividends and sales, as indicated above. If you know the total basis of your shares, the averaging calculation is easy.

Holding period. You aren't done yet! In addition to basis, you also have to know your *holding period* for the shares you sold. In other words, you need to know if the shares you sold were all long-term, all short-term, or some of each. You can average your basis, but you can't average your holding period!

When you use the single-category method, you're required to treat the shares you sold as the *earliest* shares you bought. All shares have the same basis, so this rule doesn't affect the amount of gain or loss, but it does affect the *category* of gain or loss. If you have long-term shares, they are treated as the first ones sold, even if you would prefer to sell the short-term shares.

> **Example:** You're selling mutual fund shares at a loss using the single-category method. Because you have a loss, you would prefer to sell your short-term shares. That way you would have a short-term loss, which reduces short-term gain. You aren't allowed to make this choice, though. You have to treat this as a sale of the oldest shares.

In most cases the easiest way to determine whether you sold any shares with a short-term holding period is to look at the shares you *didn't* sell. If the number of shares remaining in your mutual fund account after the sale is greater than the number of shares you acquired (including dividend reinvestments) during the 12 months preceding the sale, then all of your gain or loss on the sale is long-term. If not, you'll have to determine how many of the shares you sold were short-term.

> **How you can benefit.** The most obvious benefit of the single-category averaging method is that it eliminates a big headache if you make partial sales from a mutual fund account in which you have a large number of purchases. Yet the single-category method can also reduce the amount of tax you pay on your sale.

Consider the situation where the value of your mutual fund has gone up quite a bit in the last 18 months or so. Throughout that period you were adding to your investment, but now you want to take some money out. If you use the first-in, first-out method, you'll be selling shares you held more than a year (good) but those shares have the lowest basis, meaning you'll report a large gain (bad). If you identify the shares you're selling as ones you bought more recently, you'll have a smaller gain (good) but your gain will be short-term (bad).

The single-category averaging method provides a solution. You can sell the long-term shares, but report a smaller gain than you would under the FIFO method. That's because the more costly shares you bought recently give you an average basis that's higher than the per-share basis of the older shares. You get the lower rate that applies to long-term capital gain, but your gain is smaller than it would be if you didn't elect to use this averaging method.

More on averaging. Additional rules for averaging appear below under the headings *Averaging When You Have Gift Shares* and *Electing an Averaging Method*.

Double-Category Averaging

There's another method of averaging for mutual fund shares, called the *double-category averaging method*. In the single-category method, you determine your average basis for *all* shares. In the double-category method, you find two different averages: one for your long-term shares, and one for your short-term shares.

As you might expect, the double-category method is somewhat more complicated than the single-category method. When you consider this election, you have to weigh not only the potential tax savings, but also the added complexity you'll have to deal with. That's especially true if your mutual fund company does the single-category calculations for you.

Advantages of the double-category averaging method. The double-category method gives you greater flexibility, because it allows you to specify at the time of a sale whether you're selling short-term shares or long-term shares. You may be able to use this flexibility to reduce your tax from a particular sale. Even without this option, the double-category method can produce better results, depending on how the cost of your newer shares compares with the cost of your older ones. We'll see these advantages in action shortly.

How double-category averaging works. The double-category method requires you to find separate averages for your long-term shares and your short-term shares. Generally you'll do this by finding the total basis of all shares, then determining how many short-term shares you hold and the basis of those shares.

Example: Let's use the same example as in the discussion of the single-category method. You contributed $100.00 per month to your mutual fund account for a period of 27 months. During that period, $147.00 of dividends were reinvested. Your total basis is $2,847.00. According to your mutual fund statement, at this point you own 112.342 shares.

Looking at purchases that occurred during the past 12 months, you find that you paid in $1,200 ($100 per month), and there was a dividend of $105 during that period. That means the total basis of your short-term shares is $1,305. You add up the number of shares bought in all those purchases and find that the total is 57.506 shares. Dividing $1,305 by 57.506, you find that the basis per share for the short-term shares is $22.69.

Next, you need the basis of your long-term shares. That's your total basis ($2,847) minus the basis of the short-term shares ($1,305), or $1,542. Similarly, the number of long-term shares is the total number of shares (112.342) minus the number of short-term shares (57.506), or 54.836. Dividing, you get an average basis for the long-term shares of $28.12.

When you took $500.00 from the fund, your statement said you sold 18.277 shares. That's fewer than the number of long-term shares you hold, so the entire sale came from the long-term category (assuming you didn't identify your shares sold as coming from the short-term category, as explained below). To determine your basis in those shares, multiply the average basis by the number of shares. That gives you a basis of $513.95 ($28.12 times 18.277). You'll report a loss of $13.95 ($500.00 minus $513.95). (See table on next page.)

Notice that you now get to report a loss, whereas you had to report a gain on the same sale if you used the single-category method. That's a little unusual, but it happens here because the older shares were more costly: the value of this mutual fund declined after you bought some of your older shares.

This is a case where the double-category method produces a better result than the single category method. If you don't mind doing the extra calculations, you'll reduce your taxes on the sale. The tax reduction is small in this example, but you may run into a situation where the benefit is more meaningful. Note, however, that once you elect to use the double-category method, you must continue to use it for that fund. You'll have to do these additional calculations, not only for the present sale, but also for all future sales, even though you may not get any tax savings from using this method in the future.

Double-Category Averaging Calculation	
1 Previous basis	$ 0.00
2 Additions	2,700.00
3 Reinvested dividends	147.00
4 Basis adjustments	0.00
5 Total basis	2,847.00
6 Number of shares owned	112.342
7 Basis of short term shares	1,305.00
8 Short-term shares owned	57.506
9 Basis per short-term share	22.69
10 Basis of long-term shares	1,542.00
11 Long-term shares owned	54.836
12 Basis per long-term share	28.12
13 Number of shares sold	18.277
14 Basis of shares sold	513.95
15 Total basis before sale	2,847.00
16 Basis of shares sold	(513.95)
17 Basis remaining after sale	$2,333.05

Identifying short-term shares. When you use the double-category method, you're allowed to determine at the time of a sale whether you're selling long-term shares or short-term shares. Normally you would want to do this if a sale of the short-term shares will produce a loss. If we reversed the facts in the example above, so that the newer shares have a higher basis than the older shares, you might want to sell the newer shares instead of the older ones.

To sell the newer shares, you have to use the same procedure described in Chapter 4 for identifying shares. You have to tell the broker or mutual fund, at the time of the sale, that you're selling short-term shares, and you have to receive written confirmation of this instruction "within a reasonable time thereafter." I suspect that this procedure is used so rarely that most brokers and mutual funds will find it confusing. If you're persistent, though, you may be able to get a letter or other document confirming that at the time of the sale you specified a sale of the short-term shares. It may help to explain that it doesn't matter which shares they *actually* sell. The only thing they need to do is confirm that you made the identification at the time of the sale.

Notice that in this situation it doesn't matter *which* short-term shares you're selling. The basis will be an average of *all* the short-term shares. You merely have to identify the *category* of short-term shares.

More on how double-category averaging works. You may have a situation where you sell some but not all of your short-term shares. This will affect the way you determine the basis of shares in the two categories the next time you make a sale. Here's why.

As time passes, shares move from the short-term category to the long-term category. When that happens, the number of shares in each category changes. The total basis of shares in each category changes, too.

Let's suppose you had 10 shares with a basis of $25.00. For the first year after you bought these shares, the $250.00 of basis represented by these shares was reflected in the short-term category. On the anniversary of the day after you bought the shares, they move to the long-term category, and their basis moves to that category, too.

But now let's suppose that before these shares moved to the long-term category, you sold some short-term shares, using an *average* basis of $25.40 per share. When that happened, the basis of *all* your short-term shares—both the ones you sold and the ones you continue to hold—is adjusted to $25.40 per share. On the anniversary of the day after you bought the shares for $250.00, you'll move $254.00 (*not* $250) to the long-term category.

This rule applies only to short-term shares you held at the time you made a sale of *other* short-term shares to which the double-category averaging method applies. It doesn't apply if you merely sold long-term shares. And it doesn't apply to shares you buy later, unless you make another sale of shares from the short-term category

More on averaging. Additional rules for averaging appear below under the headings *Averaging When You Have Gift Shares* and *Electing an Averaging Method.*

Averaging When You Have Gift Shares

There's a special rule that applies to certain shares received by gift if you elect to use one of the averaging methods. The rule applies only if the shares have a basis greater than their value at the time of the gift. In other words, the rule applies if the person who gave you the shares could have sold them at a loss. The purpose of this special rule is to prevent you from getting the benefit of this loss when you use an averaging method.

If you have gift shares and you want to use an averaging method, you have to do one of the following:

- You can include in your election a statement that you'll use the *date-of-gift* value as the basis of the shares for all purposes. That means you won't get the benefit of the higher basis the shares had in the hands of the person who made the gift. You might do this if the date-of-gift value is only a little bit lower than the donor's basis. Bear in mind, though, this choice will apply to any gift shares you receive in the future, too.

- Your other alternative is to hold the gift shares in a separate account that's excluded from your averaging calculations. This choice involves some added paperwork, but preserves the possibility that you'll benefit from the higher basis if the value of the shares rises. For more about gifts and basis, see Chapter 7.

Electing an Averaging Method

To elect an averaging method, you should attach a statement to your return for the first year you want the election to apply. Remember that the election applies only to a particular mutual fund, so you need to make another election every time you start to use averaging with a new mutual fund.

Your election should state which averaging method has been used to determine gain or loss and specify the fund to which it applies. The election might look like this:

Jane Q. Public
SSN 123-45-6789
Attachment to 2001 Form 1040

The single category averaging method has been used to determine gain or loss for shares of the XYZ Mutual Fund.

If you want the election to apply to gift shares described earlier, you would include an additional statement:

The basis of gift shares that have an adjusted basis in the hands of the donor greater than the fair market value of such shares at the time of the gift shall be the fair market value of such shares at the time they were acquired by gift and such basis shall be used in computing average basis.

> • Be sure to maintain good records of all calculations relating to the use of an averaging method.

I suspect that many thousands of mutual fund investors have used an averaging method without attaching the statement described above. I'm not aware of any case where the IRS denied the benefits of averaging for this reason. I recommend attaching the statement when required, but don't lose any sleep if you failed to do this in the past.

Losses Within Six Months

Here's a rule even your tax pro may not know. If you have a loss from selling mutual fund shares you've held less than six months, you have to treat some or all of that loss as a long-term loss if you received a capital gain dividend (or had to report undistributed capital gain) on those shares. What's more, if you received an exempt interest dividend on those shares, part or all of your loss will be nondeductible.

Background. When a mutual fund pays a dividend, the value of the fund goes down by the amount of the dividend. For example, if your mutual fund shares are valued at $29.75 immediately before a dividend of $1.50 per share, the value will be $28.25 per share immediately after the dividend. No problem there—that's just the way stocks work in general. But that means a special rule is needed for certain capital losses on mutual fund shares.

Suppose you bought the mutual fund shares just before the dividend and sold them shortly afterward. In that situation you might be able to claim a short-term capital loss that was really a reflection of the dividend you received. If the dividend was a capital gain dividend or an exempt interest dividend,* the combination of the dividend and the short-term loss would give you an unfair tax advantage. There's a special rule designed to eliminate that advantage, and it applies even if you didn't intentionally seek to obtain a tax benefit.

Capital gain dividends. Consider what would happen if you bought shares in a mutual fund at $29.75 per share just before the fund paid a *capital gain* dividend of $1.50. You'll treat that dividend as long-term capital gain even if you held the mutual fund shares only a day before the dividend. Then you *sell* the mutual fund at $28.25—the value right after the dividend. Under the normal rules, you would get a short-term capital loss. That could provide you with a significant tax advantage if you also have short-term capital gains.

Example: Overall for a particular year you had $15,000 of long-term capital gain and $5,000 of short-term capital gain. Your short-term capital

---

* Chapter 14 explains the various types of mutual fund dividends.

gain would be taxed at your marginal rate of 33%, while the long-term gain is taxed at 15%. Being a crafty investor, but unaware of the special rule we're discussing, you find a mutual fund that's about to pay a capital gain dividend. You buy enough shares so you'll receive a $5,000 capital gain dividend. Right after receiving the dividend, you sell the shares for a $5,000 capital loss.

Now your totals for the year are $20,000 of long-term capital gain and $0 of short-term capital gain. The $15,000 long-term gain you had before is increased by the $5,000 capital gain dividend from the mutual fund, and the $5,000 short-term gain you had before is eliminated by the $5,000 loss on sale of the mutual fund shares. Your total amount of gain is still $20,000, but now it's all long-term, meaning a lower rate of tax—if this special rule didn't apply!

The rule applies only if you sell your mutual fund shares at a loss *six months or less after you bought them.* (It's OK to sell less than six months after the *dividend,* if you held the shares more than six months.) Note that this doesn't match up with the amount of time you need to hold the shares to have a long-term capital gain or loss upon selling the shares. The idea is that if you've held the shares six months, that's long enough so that your loss (if you have one) probably relates to genuine changes in the value of the mutual fund rather than the effect of a single dividend.

When the rule applies, you have to treat some or all of your short-term loss as a long-term loss. The amount that's treated as a long-term loss is limited to the amount of the capital gain distribution or allocation you received. So if your loss is greater than the amount of that distribution or allocation, the remaining portion of the loss is treated as a short-term capital loss.

> - The same rule applies if, instead of a capital gain dividend, you had to report undistributed capital gain. Chapter 9 explains capital gain distributions and allocations.

It appears that the six-month rule does not apply to qualifying dividends, even though they are taxed at the same rate as long-term capital gains. However, you don't get the benefit of the lower tax rate unless you hold your mutual fund shares at least 61 days. See Chapter 9.

Exempt interest dividends. The same principle applies if you receive an exempt interest dividend and then sell shares at a loss. But in this case, your short-term loss becomes nondeductible.

> **Example:** You buy shares in a municipal bond fund just before it pays an exempt interest dividend of $1,200. Then you sell the shares at a loss of $1,300. If you held the shares six months or less, you're permitted to deduct only $100. The remaining $1,200 represents the exempt interest dividend you received.

This rule does *not* apply to nontaxable return of capital distributions. Those distributions reduce your basis in the mutual fund shares, so your loss calculation automatically takes this item into account.

Load Rollover Rule

There's one other rule that can change the tax consequences when you sell mutual fund shares. It applies if you pay a sales load when you buy shares, but then get to pay a reduced sales load, or none at all, when you switch your investment to a different fund. This rule says that if you have a loss when you move from one fund to the other, you can't deduct the portion of your loss that represents a reduction in sales load relating to a purchase in the preceding 90 days.

Example: You want to invest $20,000 in the XYZ Growth Fund, which charges a 5% front-end sales load. That means $1,000 of your investment will be used to pay the sales charge, leaving you with a $19,000 investment. You're allowed to switch your money between funds maintained by XYZ without paying an additional load.

If the load rollover rule didn't apply, you might be tempted to try the following maneuver. Instead of buying the fund you're really interested in, you would buy the XYZ Balanced Fund, paying the $1,000 load. Then you would immediately switch the $19,000 investment to the XYZ Growth Fund (where you wanted to be all along), claiming a $1,000 capital loss on sale of your shares in the Balanced Fund.

The load rollover rule prevents you from getting a tax advantage if you use this technique. It applies if you paid a sales load during the preceding 90 days and received a reduction in the sales fee on your new purchase. Any loss you have, up to the amount of the reduction in the sales fee for the new fund, is disallowed. The disallowed loss is added to your basis in the shares of the new fund, so your tax benefit isn't lost entirely, just delayed until you sell the shares you bought with the reduced sales load.

Chapter 6
The Wash Sale Rule

When the value of your stock goes down you get that sinking feeling—you've lost money. But the tax law doesn't allow that loss until you sell the stock. In a way that's good, because it means you can control the timing of your deduction, taking it when the benefit is the greatest.

The problem is, you may have a conflict. You want to deduct the loss, but you also want to keep the stock because you think it's going to bounce back. It's tempting to think you can sell the stock and claim the loss, then buy it back right away. And that's where the wash sale rule comes in. If you buy replacement stock shortly after the sale—or shortly before the sale—you can't deduct your loss. At least, you can't deduct it until you sell the replacement stock.

This chapter provides a complete explanation of wash sales under the following headings:

- The basic rule

- Consequences of a wash sale

- Substantially identical securities

- Replacement stock

- Matching Rules

- IRAs and other related "persons"

- Wash sales and traders

- Planning for wash sales

- Reporting wash sales

The Basic Rule

People in business sometimes say a combination of two things that offset each other, eliminating any advantage, is a *wash*. *"The profit from increased sales was just enough to cover the cost of the advertising, so it turned out to be a wash."* This may not be a common use of the word—I checked two good-sized dictionaries without finding a definition corresponding to this meaning—but this use gives us the name of a tax rule that has been with us for many years: the *wash sale rule*.

In general you have a wash sale if you sell stock at a loss, and buy substantially identical stock within 30 days before or after the sale. The two transactions leave you in the same position as before you started: it was a wash.

> **Example:** On March 31 you sell 100 shares of XYZ at a loss. On April 10 you buy 100 shares of XYZ. The sale on March 31 is a wash sale. You can't deduct the loss on this sale.

Wash sale period. The *wash sale period* for any sale at a loss consists of 61 days: the day of the sale, the 30 days before the sale and the 30 days after the sale. (These are calendar days, not trading days. Count carefully!) If you want to claim your loss as a deduction, you need to avoid purchasing the same stock during the wash sale period. For a sale on March 31, the wash sale period includes all of March and April.

Losses only. The wash sale rule only applies to *losses*. You can't wipe out a *gain* from a sale by buying the same stock back within 30 days.

> **Example:** On June 10 you sell 100 shares of XYZ for a $2,000 profit. On June 15 you buy 100 shares of XYZ, replacing the shares you sold. The wash sale rule doesn't apply because you had a gain, not a loss. You have to report the gain.

Consequences of a Wash Sale

The wash sale rule actually has *three* consequences:

- You aren't allowed to claim a deduction for the loss on your sale.

- Your disallowed loss is added to the basis of the replacement stock.

- Your holding period for the replacement stock includes the holding period of the stock you sold.

The first one is clear enough, but the other two may require some explanation.

Basis adjustment. The basis adjustment is important: it preserves the benefit of the disallowed loss. You'll receive that benefit on a future sale of the replacement stock.

> **Example:** Some time ago you bought 80 shares of XYZ at $50. The stock has declined to $30, and you sell it to take the loss deduction. But then you see some good news on XYZ and you buy it back for $32, less than 31 days after the sale.
>
> You can't deduct your loss of $20 per share. But you add $20 per share to the basis of your replacement shares. Those shares have a basis of $52 per share: the $32 you paid, plus the $20 wash sale adjustment. In other words, you're treated as if you bought the replacement shares for $52. If you end up selling them for $55, you'll only report $3 per share of gain. If you sell them for $32 (the same price you paid to buy them), you'll report a loss of $20 per share—unless you buy replacement stock again, creating a second wash sale.

Because of this basis adjustment, a wash sale usually isn't a disaster. In most cases, it simply means you'll get the same tax benefit at a later time. If you receive the benefit later in the same year, the wash sale may have no effect at all on your taxes. There are times, though, when the wash sale rule can have truly painful consequences:

- If you don't sell the replacement stock in the same year as the wash sale, your loss will be postponed, possibly to a year when the deduction is of less value.

- If you die before selling the replacement stock, neither you nor your heirs will benefit from the basis adjustment.

- You can also lose the benefit of the deduction permanently if you sell stock and arrange to have a related person—or your IRA—buy replacement stock. We'll discuss this point later in this chapter.

Holding period. When the wash sale rule applies, your holding period for the replacement stock includes the period you held the stock you sold. This rule prevents you from converting a long-term loss into a short-term loss.

> **Example:** You've held shares of XYZ for years and it's been a dog. You sell it at a loss but then buy it back within the wash sale period. When you sell the replacement stock, your gain or loss will be long-term—no matter how soon you sell it.

In some situations you get more tax savings from a short-term loss than a long-term loss, so this rule generally works against you. If the price of the stock recovers and you sell for a gain, you may benefit from this rule.

Gaps and overlaps. You can have a wash sale because of a purchase that's up to 30 days before or after your sale. That raises an interesting question, because the law says your holding period for the replacement shares "includes" the holding period of the shares that were sold. That raises the question of how to handle gaps and overlaps. For example, suppose you bought the original stock on May 5. Somewhere along the way you had a wash sale, and there was a gap of several days before you bought the replacement shares. If you sold the replacement stock on May 6 of the following year, is your gain or loss long-term, even though several days elapsed between the sale of the original stock and purchase of the new shares? Or do you subtract the days you didn't own the stock?

Curiously, there's no guidance on this question. I'm inclined to believe you should treat the entire period from the original date of acquisition to the final date of sale as your holding period—in other words, ignore the fact that there were a few days you didn't own the stock. My reason: the theory of the wash sale rule is that the interruption in ownership wasn't great enough to prevent you from being considered a continuous owner of this stock. Likewise, I believe you should ignore any overlap period, if you bought the replacement shares before selling the original shares at a loss.

Reasonable minds can differ, though. The law is simply ambiguous on this point. If you want to be certain you have a short-term loss—or your stock has recovered and you want to be certain of a long-term gain—you need to make the least favorable assumption concerning this rule and plan your sale accordingly.

Substantially Identical Securities

You don't have a wash sale unless you buy *substantially identical securities* within the 61-day wash sale period. As a general rule, stock of one company isn't substantially identical to stock of a different one, even if they're both in the same industry. For example, Dell isn't substantially identical to HP. If you have a loss on one of these companies, you can buy the other one without having a wash sale.

This rule presents one of the most effective ways of dealing with the wash sale rule. If you want to report a loss but you're afraid the market will get away from you while you wait out the wash sale period, you can sell your losing shares and buy another stock that's likely to move in the same direction as the one you're holding. Of course, things don't always work that way: one company can have good news while another in the same industry has bad news. What you're doing is *reducing* the chance of missing an upswing in your stock's value, not *eliminating* that possibility.

Related stocks. Sometimes people want to play games with the wash sale rule. You may own stock in a company that's about to be acquired by Bigco. Just before the merger you sell your stock and buy shares of Bigco— shares you would have received in the merger if you hadn't sold your original shares. If you're thinking this isn't a wash sale because you bought shares in a different company, you're wrong. The rule about stock in different companies not being substantially identical isn't hard and fast. If two different stocks are linked together in such a way that any change in the value of one will be reflected in the value of the other, they're likely to be treated as substantially identical securities for purposes of the wash sale rule.

Mutual funds. There's some debate, but no direct authority, on the question of whether two mutual funds keying off the same index are substantially identical for purposes of the wash sale rule. Can you sell one S&P 500 index fund at a loss and buy a different S&P 500 fund the same day without having a wash sale?

Because there is no direct authority dealing with this question, reasonable minds may disagree. It's always possible to identify differences between funds managed by different companies, such as expense ratios and "tax load." Some people conclude on this basis that funds maintained by two different companies should never be considered the same for purposes of the wash sale rule.

My feeling is that those differences aren't enough to prevent the two funds from being *substantially* identical, which is all the wash sale rule requires. The point of the wash sale rule is to determine whether you've changed your position relative to the market. If you can lay the price graph for your new investment on top of the price graph for the old one and never see a significant disparity (as would be the case for two high quality S&P 500 funds), the investments should be considered substantially identical for purposes of the wash sale rule.

If I were sitting with a loss in an index fund and wanted to get around the wash sale rule, I would invest for 31 days in a fund that doesn't precisely track the same index, but emphasizes stocks of the type that are in that index. A fund that has similar stocks but doesn't track the same index shouldn't be considered substantially identical to the index fund. Yet a diversified holding of stocks that are mainly in the same index should have a relatively small likelihood of diverging significantly from the index within 31 days. That's not to say there's zero likelihood of that happening. The managed fund may have some heavy bets go sour during that time. Bear in mind, though, that the reverse is equally likely: the managed fund may outperform the index for this period.

The bottom line is that risk and the wash sale rule are tied together. If you have a strategy that completely eliminates market risk, you bear the *tax risk* that the IRS will say you have a wash sale. The idea is that you can't report a loss for tax purposes without changing your investment position.

Replacement Stock

There are situations where your purchases and sales may fit within the literal language of the wash sale rule, but where the rule shouldn't apply because the stock you bought didn't replace the stock you sold. Unfortunately, you won't find exceptions to cover these situations in the Internal Revenue Code or the tax regulations. Some of the possibilities are covered by common sense, and there's an IRS ruling that covers another one. Still others leave some doubt as to the correct interpretation.

The easiest way to understand what I call the *replacement stock* issue is through a series of examples.

Selling all. On June 1 you buy 200 shares of XYZ for $10,000. On June 12 you sell all 200 shares for $8,000 (a loss of $2,000).

Most people wouldn't even think about applying the wash sale rule here. You know instinctively it shouldn't apply, even though there's a sale at a loss, and a purchase within 30 days before the sale. Your instincts are correct: the wash sale rule doesn't apply because the stock you bought isn't *replacement stock* for the stock you sold. That's because you sold the same stock you bought.

> **Selling half.** On June 1 you buy 200 shares of XYZ for $10,000. On June 12 you sell 100 shares for $4,000 (a loss of $1,000). You continue to hold the other 100 shares.

The answer here is a little less obvious. After the sale, you hold shares identical to the shares you sold, and you bought those shares less than 31 days before the sale. But you probably still feel that the wash sale rule shouldn't apply here. Fortunately, the IRS agrees, at least in situations where you bought the 200 shares in a single lot. They issued a ruling saying this sequence doesn't produce a wash sale.

The result shouldn't change if you gave a single order to buy 200 shares and your broker happened to execute it by buying two lots of 100 shares each. It's clear in this situation that the shares you have left after the sale weren't bought to replace the shares you sold. Yet the IRS ruling telling us you're okay if you buy the shares in a single lot doesn't tell us what happens if a single buy order is split into two lots, so the result here is a little less certain.

> **Separate purchases.** You buy 100 shares of XYZ in the morning, and decide to buy another 100 shares in the afternoon of the same day. Within 30 days you sell the morning shares at a loss.

This is a situation where the wash sale rule probably *does* apply. The shares you bought in the afternoon are likely to be considered replacement shares for the ones you bought in the morning and later sold.

> **Old shares.** You've held 100 shares of XYZ for more than 30 days. You buy an additional 100 shares for $5,000. Less than 31 days later, you sell these

shares (the new ones) for $4,000 (a $1,000 loss). You continue to hold the old shares.

There are no rulings that mention this situation. Yet I believe the implicit requirement for replacement stock should prevent the wash sale rule from applying here. After your sale, you don't hold any shares that were purchased in the preceding 30 days.

Note that you have to use *identification* to sell the newer shares. Unless you follow this procedure (explained in Chapter 4), the tax law assumes you sold the older shares. If you have a loss on a sale of the older shares, the wash sale rule applies because you bought replacement shares within 30 days before the sale.

> **Not so old shares.** This example is the same as the previous one, except the "old" shares aren't as old. You bought the old shares on June 1, the new shares on June 10, and sold the new shares at a loss on June 20.

Once again, you had to use specific identification to sell the new shares. The question is, do you have a wash sale here because you bought the old shares less than 31 days before you sold the new ones?

As a matter of logic, it's clear that the answer should be no. The old shares can't possibly be replacement shares for the newer ones. You bought them before you bought the shares you sold, so it seems they should be ignored in applying the wash sale rule.

Unfortunately, in a ruling dealing with an unrelated issue, the IRS gave an example like the one above, and said the wash sale rule applied. The ruling was designed to cover an entirely different point, and it's probably just an unfortunate coincidence that the example came out the way it did. The person who drafted the ruling may not have thought about the fact that the shares in the example weren't replacement shares. Perhaps if the IRS were to focus on this issue, they would agree with my interpretation. I can't promise that result, though.

> • My feeling is that the wash sale rule should never apply if the replacement shares were bought at the same time as, or earlier than, the shares that were sold. There isn't any opportunity for abusive tax planning in this situation. The issue is in doubt, though, because the IRS has issued a ruling containing an example that seems erroneous.

Matching Rules

There are times when you know the wash sale rule applies, but it isn't obvious exactly *how* it applies because of multiple purchases and sales of the same stock. The tax law provides *matching rules* for telling which shares are affected by a wash sale.

The general rule is to resolve ambiguities by analyzing transactions in chronological order. If there are multiple sales that can match a particular purchase, you match the earliest sale first. Similarly, if there are multiple purchases that can match a particular sale, you match the earliest purchase first. *You're required to follow these rules even if a different way of matching would produce a better tax result.*

Example: You sold 100 shares of XYZ at a loss on March 12. On March 14 you bought 60 shares, and on March 20 you bought another 90 shares. You bought a total of 150 shares during the wash sale period, but only 100 are *replacement* shares under the wash sale rule. You need to know *which* shares are replacement shares because that affects the basis and holding period of those shares. *The replacement shares are the ones acquired earliest:* the 60 shares you bought on March 14 and 40 of the 90 shares you bought on March 20. The other 50 shares you bought on March 20 are not affected by the wash sale rule.

Example: You sold 100 shares of XYZ at a loss on March 12, and another 100 shares, also at a loss, on March 14. On March 20 you bought 150 shares. In this case, *all* of your new shares are replacement shares, but now you need to determine which loss is disallowed. *The wash sale rule applies to the earliest sale first,* so all the loss from the March 12 sale is disallowed. In addition, the wash sale rule disallows the loss from 50 of the 100 shares sold on March 14.

There's one other rule that acts as a tiebreaker. You may have a situation where you can't tell which shares were sold first. In that case, the wash sale rule applies first to the shares you *acquired* first.

Example: On January 5 you bought 100 shares of XYZ at $55, and on January 10 you bought another 100 shares of XYZ at $65. On March 12 you sold 200 shares of XYZ at $40. Then you bought 100 shares of XYZ on March 18, creating a wash sale as to 100 shares of the 200 shares you sold.

First you look at which shares were sold first. You may not be able to tell which were sold first because you sold all 200 shares at the same time. If that's the case, you apply the wash sale rule to the shares you *bought* first: the shares you bought on January 5. Your loss on the shares you bought on January 10 is allowed.

IRAs and Other Related "Persons"

One of the most frequently asked questions about the wash sale rule goes like this:

> *Suppose I sell my stock at a loss and buy the same stock in my IRA. Does the wash sale rule apply?*

The answer is subject to debate. Some tax advisors believe you can claim the loss in this situation. My feeling is that the IRS would probably disallow the loss if they found out about the replacement purchase.

> • **Related persons.** In the strange language of the tax law, the word "person" includes entities as well as human beings. Corporations, partnerships and trusts are all *persons*. Your IRA is a *person*, and it's considered *related* to you because you own it.

The section of the tax law that lays out the wash sale rule doesn't include any rules for related persons. The same is true of the tax regulations. Looking at the Internal Revenue Code and the regulations, you might get the impression that it would be okay to buy replacement stock in your IRA, or to have your spouse or another relative buy replacement stock.

There are cases, though, where the IRS has taken a taxpayer to court for transactions that look like wash sales, where the buyer was an individual or entity related to the taxpayer. None of these cases involve IRAs—all of them came up before there was such a thing as an IRA—so there's no direct authority on the question posed above. Yet it seems to me that if the IRS can disallow the loss in those earlier cases, it can do so when an IRA is involved.

I suspect the reason we haven't seen any cases involving IRAs is that these transactions are difficult to find. It would be unusual for the IRS to audit a taxpayer so thoroughly as to check the trading records of his or her IRA. If the IRS became aware of the situation, though, the results could be pretty painful. Remember, in a normal wash sale your basis for the replacement stock includes the disallowed loss. That makes it possible for you to recover the tax benefit from that loss when you sell the replacement stock. If the replacement stock is in your IRA, though, you'll never recover the tax benefit that was disallowed on your sale. Additional basis for stock in your IRA provides no benefit because IRAs don't report gain or loss on a sale of stock.

Wash Sales and Traders

At one time the wash sale rule didn't apply to *traders* (other than corporations), but Congress changed the law.* If you're a trader under the rules described in Part V of this book, you have to deal with the wash sale rule until and unless you make the mark-to-market election (Chapter 25). That's unfortunate, because by the very nature of what they do, traders normally have a large number of wash sales.

Working through all the basis adjustments for scores of wash sales is a major headache. You need to analyze every trade on which you have a loss to determine if it's a wash sale. If it is, you have to make a basis adjustment to the replacement stock. What's more, the basis adjustment can turn a cash profit into a tax loss, so even profitable trades can result in losses that are subject to the wash sale rule.

> **Example:** You lost $300 on a sale of XYZ and bought the same stock again the next day. That's a wash sale, so you have to eliminate the loss and add $300 to the basis of the replacement stock. Then you sell the replacement stock for a profit of $100 (relative to the purchase price). Because of the extra $300 of basis, this is a loss of $200 for tax purposes. If you have another purchase of the same stock, the wash sale rule can apply again.

Headache relief. Can you avoid all these calculations without making the mark-to-market election? Officially the answer is no. Yet there's one situation where you can prove that the wash sale rule doesn't affect your taxes, even if it applies to many of your trades. If you fit that situation, I believe the IRS will accept your return without a full-blown wash sale analysis.

---

* Tax professionals may note that the regulations still say the wash sale rule doesn't apply to individual traders. That's simply because the Treasury hasn't updated the regulation to reflect this change in the law. *Don't rely on this regulation!*

To eliminate the tax consequences of your wash sales, you need to do two things:

- Prior to the end of the year, eliminate all positions you hold in the particular stock that gave rise to the wash sales, including long, short and option positions.

- Abstain from buying or selling that stock (or options on that stock) until the start of the new year or at least 31 days after your last sale, *whichever is later.*

Example: You close all your positions in XYZ on December 15, 2000. You avoid any transactions in this stock until January 15, 2000.

In this situation, it's clear that you recovered the disallowed loss from any wash sales you made during the year because you sold the replacement stock. Your final sale can't be a wash sale because you stayed out of the stock for 31 days. The wash sale rule doesn't affect the amount of tax you owe, so arguably there's no point in working through the analysis of each individual sale.

Let's be clear: this approach is based on logical analysis of the consequences of the wash sale rule. The IRS has never said you get out of reporting all your wash sales if you take this approach. Yet it's difficult to imagine that the IRS would complain in this situation. By clearing out your wash sales, you made the job of determining your correct tax easier for yourself *and* for the IRS. Once they know you reported and paid the correct amount of tax, they have no interest in forcing you to go through a lot of unnecessary paperwork.

Planning for Wash Sales

Before you spend too much brainpower figuring out how you can plan for wash sales, ask yourself *why* you need to do this planning. In many cases the reason boils down to the fact that you're kicking yourself for buying the stock in the first place, and you'll kick yourself even more if it recovers after you sell it. Try to convince yourself that you should kick yourself just as much if some *other* stock goes up when you don't own it. Sell the loser, and buy something else.

If you're one of those people who can't move on after a loss, you may want to know what you can safely do to plan around the wash sale rule. No technique is completely safe. Here are some ideas to consider:

- Most obviously, you can sell the stock and wait 31 days before buying it again. (Check your calendar carefully!) The risk here is that the price of the stock may rise before you can repurchase it.

- If you're truly convinced the stock is at rock bottom, you might consider buying the replacement stock 31 days *before* the sale. If the stock happens to go up during that period, your gain is doubled. If it stays even you can sell the older stock and claim your loss deduction. But if you're wrong about the stock, a further decline in value could be painful.

- If your stock has a strong tendency to move in tandem with some other stock, you may be able to reduce your risk of missing a big gain by purchasing stock in a different company as "replacement" stock. This is not a wash sale because the stock you're buying is not "substantially identical" to the stock you're selling. Thirty-one days later you can switch back to your original stock if that's your wish. But there's no way to be certain that any two stocks will move in the same direction, or in the same magnitude.

There's no risk-free way to get around the wash sale rule. But then again, continuing to hold a stock that has lost value isn't risk-free, either. In the end it's up to you to evaluate all the risks, and balance them against the benefit you'll receive if you can claim a deduction for your loss.

Reporting Wash Sales

When you report a wash sale, you need to follow special procedures set forth in the instructions for Schedule D. First, you report the loss exactly as you would on any other sale, showing the amount of the loss in column (f). Then, on the line immediately below the line where you reported the loss, write the words "Wash Sale" in column (a) (where you normally describe the item you sold) and in column (f) write the amount of the loss as a positive number. The positive number on this line will cancel out the negative number on the line above where you reported the loss.

When you sell the replacement stock, remember to add the disallowed loss to your cost basis. Also, use the date you bought the original stock as your acquisition date. The IRS asks you to attach an explanation of why you're using a basis other than the actual cost, as described in Chapter 26.

> ▪ Further complexities of the wash sale rule apply to people who engage in short selling, and people who trade stock options. Those specialized applications of the wash sale rule are explained in Chapters 12 and 13.

Chapter 7
Special Transactions

There are a variety of special transactions that can affect the way you figure your gain or loss on shares of stock. Some of them apply to all kinds of property, and others relate only to stock. This chapter covers the situations you're most likely to encounter:

- Stock received as a gift

- Stock acquired from your spouse

- Stock received from a decedent

- Stock dividends and splits

- Mergers and spin-offs

- Dividend reinvestment plans (DRIPs)

- Stock acquired by exercising employee options

- Stock that becomes worthless

- Cash in lieu of fractional shares

Stock Received as a Gift

If you're lucky enough to receive stock as a gift, you need to know the special rules for determining gain or loss on sale of that stock. These rules don't apply to stock you receive from your spouse or from a decedent. We'll get to those rules a little later.

Good news. To begin with, you'll be happy to learn that the value of the gift isn't *income.* The gift may seem as good as a paycheck (or better!) but you don't have to report it or pay income tax. You don't have to pay gift tax, either. If there's a gift tax, the *donor* pays it, not the person who received the gift.

Stock has gone down. The rules for gifts depend on whether the stock is *appreciated* or *depreciated*—in other words, did it go up or down while the donor held it. We'll start with the rule for depreciated stock: stock that has gone down. In other words, we're talking about a situation where the donor's basis (usually the amount paid to acquire the stock) is greater than the current value.

> **Example:** Your uncle bought 100 shares of XYZ when it was at $72. His basis for the 100 shares, including a $50 commission, was $7,250. He gave the stock to you when it was at $60 and had a fair market value of $6,000. If he sold it instead, he would have had a loss of $1,250.

In this case you have *dual basis* for the stock. You use one number for basis if you have a *gain* when you sell the stock, and a different one if you have a *loss*. This may seem confusing, but the rule isn't hard to apply:

- If you sell the stock for more than the donor's basis ($7,250 in the example) you'll use that basis to measure your gain. For example, if you sell for $7,600, you report a gain of $350 ($7,600 minus $7,250).

- If you sell the stock for less than the value at the time of the gift ($6,000 in the example), you use that value to measure your loss. For example, if you sell for $5,250, you report a loss of $750 ($6,000 minus $5,250).

- Another possibility is that you sell the stock for a price somewhere between the value on the date of the gift and the donor's basis. For instance, you might sell for $6,375 in the example. In this case your gain or loss is zero.

The idea behind this rule is to prevent your uncle from transferring a tax loss to you when he makes the gift. At the time of the gift he could have sold the stock for a loss of $1,250. Instead, he gave the stock to you. You get the full benefit of his basis when you sell the stock for a gain, but you aren't permitted to claim a loss unless the stock declines in value after you receive it.

> ■ **Tax planning.** In this situation, it's sometimes better for the donor to sell the stock and claim a loss, then make a gift of the sale proceeds. Otherwise, it's possible that no one will get the benefit of the donor's basis in the stock.

Example: You bought XYZ for $30,000 but it now has a value of $12,000. You want to make a gift to your daughter. If you give the stock and your daughter subsequently sells it for $12,000, no one will get a deduction for the $18,000 loss in value. If you sell the stock for $12,000 and give the cash to your daughter, you can claim the $18,000 loss (subject to the capital loss limitation). If the idea is for your daughter to own XYZ stock, she can use the $12,000 to buy this stock—preferably at least 31 days after your sale, to avoid any risk that the IRS will apply the wash sale rule as explained in Chapter 6. The tax savings from being able to claim the loss may be greater than the costs of this sale and purchase.

Stock has gone up. Now let's look at what happens when the value of the stock has gone up. In other words, the value of the stock is greater than the donor's basis. In that case, your basis for the stock is the same as the donor's basis—with a possible increase if the donor paid gift tax on this gift.

Example: Your grandmother gives you 100 shares of XYZ she bought many years ago. The current value of the stock is $8,500, but her basis is only $1,200.

Unless the gift tax adjustment described below applies, your basis for the stock is the same as your grandmother's: $1,200. If you sell it for $8,000, you must report a gain of $6,800—even though the stock went down while you were holding it.

Gift tax adjustment. Gift tax doesn't apply to most gifts because of the *$10,000 annual exclusion* and the *unified credit*, both of which are explained in Chapter 17. If the gift tax applies in spite of these exclusions, you may be able to increase your basis in the stock you receive. The increase applies only if the stock had a value greater than the donor's basis at the time of the gift. (In tax lingo, this means the stock was *appreciated.*) In this case, your basis includes the portion of the gift tax that relates to the stock's *appreciation.* Here's how you figure the basis increase:

- **Step 1.** Determine the amount of appreciation for the gift. This is the fair market value of the property minus the donor's basis. For example, suppose your mother gave you stock with a value of $50,000, and she had a basis of $20,000. The appreciation is $30,000.

- **Step 2.** Determine the *appreciation ratio.* This is the amount of appreciation (determined in step 1) divided by the amount of the gift. In our example, the appreciation ratio is 60% ($30,000 divided by $50,000).

- **Step 3.** Determine the amount of the gift tax paid on the gift. Let's say your mother paid $9,000 gift tax on this gift.

- **Step 4.** Multiply the gift tax by the appreciation ratio. In our example, you would get $5,400 (60% times $9,000).

In this example, you end up with a basis of $25,400, which includes your mother's basis of $20,000, plus $5,400 gift tax adjustment.

Holding period. As always, it isn't enough to know how much gain or loss you have when you sell something. You also need to know whether the gain or loss is long-term or short-term. In other words, you need to know your holding period.

The rule for stock or other property received by gift is unique. If you end up using the donor's basis to figure your gain or loss on the stock, you take the donor's holding period. In other words, if the donor acquired the stock on June 5, 2003, you're treated as if *you* acquired it on that date.

On the other hand, the rules described above may require you to use the fair market value of the stock on the date of the gift to determine your basis. If your basis is determined under this rule, your holding period begins on the date of the gift, and you'll have a short-term gain or loss if you sell less than a year and a day after receiving the gift.

> ▪ **Tax planning.** When you make a gift of stock, you can transfer the *gain* in that stock to the recipient of the gift. That can mean a smaller tax bill on sale of that stock if the donee is in a lower tax bracket than you are. Just make sure it's a legitimate gift: the IRS is likely to object if you give stock to your child just before a sale, and your child gives you the cash afterwards.
>
> The flip side doesn't work. You can't transfer a loss to someone else by making a gift. If you're thinking of giving away stock that's gone down while you held it, you should consider selling the stock and making a gift of the proceeds.

Stock Acquired from Your Spouse

The usual rules for determining basis don't apply when you acquire stock from your spouse. This is true if you receive stock in any of the following ways:

- You receive a gift from your spouse.

- You buy stock from your spouse.

- You receive stock as part of a settlement or decree in a divorce or separation.

In any of these situations, the rule is very simple, and it is hard and fast: your basis is the same as the basis your spouse had immediately before you acquired the stock. Your spouse's holding period also transfers to you.

> ▪ **Note:** This rule doesn't apply if your spouse dies and you inherit stock from his or her estate. The rules for that situation are described below.

Although this rule is quite simple, it's worth taking a moment to think about what it means.

Gifts. As explained above, there's a tricky little rule that means you can have dual basis for stock you received as a gift. This rule doesn't apply to gifts between spouses. You simply take the same basis and holding period your spouse had.

Purchases. Here's the really strange part of this rule. (So strange, in fact, that even some tax professionals have a hard time believing it.) If you buy stock from your spouse, you get the same basis your spouse had—no matter what you pay for the stock.

> **Example:** Your spouse bought 200 shares of XYZ at $80 per share (a total of $16,000). Later, when XYZ is at $125, you buy the stock from your spouse for $25,000. Your basis is only $16,000. If you sell it the next day for $25,000, you'll have to report a "gain" of $9,000.

This may seem unfair, but there's another side to the coin. Your spouse didn't have to report any gain when you bought the stock. There's no reporting of gain or loss on sales of stock (or anything else) between spouses, and that's why the basis doesn't change.

Divorce and separation. The same rule applies to divorce and separation. Let's suppose you and your spouse are splitting up, and part of what you're splitting includes 100 shares each of two different stocks. One has been Wall Street's darling, rising from $20 to $60; the other has been a dog, falling from $90 to $55. At a tender moment during the divorce proceedings, your spouse says you can take either stock, and your spouse will keep the other one. You can't believe what a dope your spouse is as you grab for Darling, Inc.

But when you sell your Darling stock for $60, you have only $20 of basis and have to report a gain of $40. By the time you're finished with federal and state taxes, you get to keep roughly $50 per share. Meanwhile your dopey spouse is selling Dog Corp. for $55 and paying no taxes at all. In fact, your spouse reports a loss that results in lower taxes. The end result is that your spouse pockets something like $63 per share—$13 per share more than you got out of your Darling stock. All's fair in love and war.

Stock Received from a Decedent

The rules described here apply when stock was held by an individual and passed to another individual at the death of the first one. Different rules may apply in different situations, such as when stock was held in a trust or a family limited partnership. You may need to consult a tax professional to learn the basis of stock you receive in special circumstances.

Background. Cash or other property you inherit from a decedent isn't considered income. You don't have to report it on your income tax return. Of course, if you later receive income from that property (such as dividends on stock) you have to report that income.

Basis and holding period. The basis and holding period rules for property received from a decedent don't follow the pattern for other rules. Normally, the basis of an asset changes only in a *taxable transaction*: an event that requires someone to report income, gain or loss. Also, your holding period for an asset is usually either the actual amount of time you held the asset or a holding period transferred from another asset or another person. There's a certain logic to all these rules, but that logic doesn't apply when it comes to estate property.

Your basis in stock you inherit is the fair market value of the stock on the valuation date. In most cases (see exception below) the valuation date is the date of death. In tax lingo we say the stock's basis is *stepped up* (or stepped down) to the date-of-death value. The basis is adjusted even though no one reported gain or loss at the time the owner died. Furthermore, the holding period for the stock is automatically long-term. That's true even if the decedent bought the stock less than a year before death.

> **Example:** Your grandfather bought 800 shares of XYZ many years ago for a total of $1,600. You inherited the stock when he died. On his date of death, the value of the stock was $32,000. Your basis in the stock is $32,000. If you sell it for $28,000, you have a loss of $4,000; if you sell it for $40,000 you have a gain of $8,000. Your gain or loss is long-term, even if you sell the stock right away after receiving it.

This tax rule provides a significant benefit on these facts. No one had to pay income tax on all that increase in value that occurred while your grandfather owned the stock. Yet you get the same basis as if you bought the stock for $32,000.

This rule can work the other way, though. Suppose your grandfather bought the stock for $32,000, but it was worth only $1,600 when he died. Now the basis will be stepped *down*. No one will receive an income tax deduction for the loss of value while your grandfather owned this stock.

Exception for alternate valuation date. There's a special rule under the estate tax that allows the executor (the person in charge of the estate) to elect a different valuation date in certain cases. If the estate qualifies for this election, and the executor makes the election, the valuation date is six months after the date of death. The principal reason for making this election is to reduce the amount of estate tax that must be paid. Yet the election also has an effect on income tax, because it means you will now use the later date to determine your basis in the stock.

> **Example:** In the example above, the stock had a value of $32,000 on the date of death. Six months later, the stock had a value of $27,000. If the estate qualifies for the alternate valuation date, and the executor makes the election, you'll take the stock with a basis of $27,000.

In this example, you end up with a lower basis, which means you may have to pay more income tax when you sell the stock. Overall, though, the beneficiaries of the estate received a benefit because the alternate valuation date is used in circumstances where it reduces estate tax.

Stock Dividends and Splits

Companies sometimes increase the number of shares outstanding (and at the same time reduce the value of each share) by issuing stock dividends or stock splits. These events are usually nontaxable, but change the number of shares you own and the basis of those shares.*

A stock dividend is generally declared in terms of a percentage. For example, in a 5% stock dividend, you'll receive one additional share for every 20 shares you already own. A stock split is usually declared as a fraction. In a 2-for-1 split, you receive one additional share for every share you own (so that you end up owning two shares for every one you owned before the split). Stock splits can occur at odd fractions. For example, if you stock splits 3-for-2, you receive one additional share for every

---

* In the unusual case where you receive a *taxable* stock dividend, the company should notify you of this fact and explain how to report it.

two you owned before the split (and end up owning three for every two you had before). A 3-for-2 stock split is the same as a 50% stock dividend.

> ■ If your stock pays a cash dividend and the dividend is reinvested, you end up with more stock as a result of the dividend reinvestment, but this is *not* a stock dividend. You have a stock dividend only if the dividend itself is paid in stock.

Determining your basis. When you receive additional shares as a result of a nontaxable stock dividend or split, your total basis in your stock remains the same. The basis is divided among the shares you already owned and the new shares in proportion to the value of the shares. In the usual case, where the new shares are exactly the same as the old ones, the value per share is the same, and basis is allocated equally to each share.

Example: You own 400 shares of XYZ with a basis of $33 per share (total basis of $13,200). XYZ declares a 10% stock dividend. You receive 40 additional shares and now own a total of 440 shares. Your total basis is unchanged, so your basis per share is now $13,200 divided by 440, or $30.

Example: You own 150 shares of XYZ with a basis of $24 per share, and another 100 shares of XYZ with a basis of $28 per share. The stock splits 2-for-1. After the split, you own 300 shares with a basis of $12 per share, and 200 shares with a basis of $14 per share. This is true even if you receive a single certificate representing your 250 new shares.

Holding period. You're treated as if you held the new shares as long as you held the old shares. For example, if you bought 400 XYZ on June 10, 2000 and received 40 new shares in a nontaxable stock dividend on November 10, 2004, any gain or loss on a sale of the 40 new shares will be long-term even if you sell these shares immediately after you acquire them.

Mergers and Spin-Offs

Sometimes one company merges with another, going out of existence and leaving its shareholders with stock in the acquiring company. Other times a company that owns another company (a *subsidiary*) will distribute or *spin off* stock in the subsidiary to its shareholders, who find that they own stock in two companies where they formerly held just one.

Companies engaged in these transactions should provide their shareholders with detailed information about the tax consequences. If you mislaid this information, guidance should be available from the investor relations department of the company. Nowadays, the information is usually available on the company's web site, too.

I urge you to obtain information from the company because it will be more detailed than the guidance offered here. Because of the complexity of these rules, what follows is merely a broad outline of the main points.

Cash merger. In some mergers, the owners of the acquired company receive cash. The owners are treated as if they sold their stock for an amount equal to the cash proceeds. If you have a gain, the fact that the "sale" was involuntary doesn't excuse you from reporting it.

Stock merger. You may receive stock instead of cash in the merger. When this happens, the merger is nearly always tax-free. You don't report gain or loss on the exchange of your old shares for shares of the new company. The new shares have the same basis and holding period as the old shares.

Example: In October 1996 you bought 100 shares of XYZ at $36 (total of $3,600). In January 2004, Bigco acquired XYZ in a tax-free merger and you received 60 shares of Bigco. Your basis for the Bigco shares is $3,600 ($60 per share), and you're treated as if you bought the Bigco shares in October 1996.

Merger for stock and cash. This type of merger can be taxable or tax-free. If it's taxable, you're treated as if you sold your shares for an amount equal to the sum of (a) the amount of cash you received, plus (b) the value of the shares you received. The new shares have a basis equal to their value when you received them, and your holding period for those shares begins when you receive them.

If the merger is tax-free, it may be really only *partly* tax-free because part of your consideration was cash. If you have gain on the exchange, you report that gain, but only up to the amount of cash you received. If you received cash in excess of any gain, you'll reduce your basis in the stock by the amount of excess cash.

Example: Some time ago, you bought 100 shares of XYZ at $36 (total of $3,600). Now XYZ merges into Bigco, and you receive 40 shares of Bigco plus $800 in cash. There are three possibilities:

Gain is larger than cash. Suppose the Bigco shares are worth a total of $4,000. You also received $800 in cash, for total consideration of $4,800. Your gain is $1,200 ($4,800 minus original cost of $3,600). You report gain of $800 because that's the amount of cash you received. Your stock has a basis of $3,600.

Cash is larger than gain. Suppose the Bigco shares are worth only $3,000. Now your total consideration is $3,800, giving you a gain of $200. You report $200 of gain. You received another $600 in cash, and that reduces your basis in the new shares from $3,600 to $3,000.

No gain. Suppose the Bigco shares are worth only $2,000. Your total consideration was $2,800, which is less than you paid for the XYZ shares. You can't report a loss on the transaction, but you get to receive the $800 cash without reporting any gain or income. You have to reduce your basis in the new shares by this $800, from $3,600 to $2,800.

In each case, your holding period for the new Bigco shares includes the time you held the old XYZ shares.

Spin-offs. If you receive stock in a tax-free spin-off, you don't report gain or loss (or dividend). Your basis from the shares you held before the spin-off is allocated among all your shares in proportion to their fair market value at the time of the spin-off. The new shares have the same holding period as the original shares.

> **Example:** You bought 100 shares of Bigco at $72 (total of $7,200). Bigco decides to spin off XYZ, distributing one share of XYZ for every two shares of Bigco. After the spin-off, you hold 100 shares of Bigco and 50 shares of XYZ.
>
> Some people think they should allocate two-thirds of the basis to the Bigco shares, because two-thirds of the shares are Bigco shares. *Don't make that mistake!* The basis allocation is based on relative *value,* not the number of shares. The company should inform you of the proper allocation ratio. The amount of basis allocated to the XYZ shares may be greater than or less than one-third of the total.

If you receive shares in a *taxable* spin-off, you should rely on information from the company to determine the tax consequences.

Dividend Reinvestment Plans

Many publicly traded companies maintain *dividend reinvestment plans* (sometimes called *DRIPs*). If you hold stock in XYZ and participate in a DRIP maintained by that company, cash dividends on your stock are automatically reinvested in XYZ stock. The tax consequences are *not* the same as receiving a stock dividend (a dividend paid in the form of stock).

Different companies design their DRIPs with different features. As a result, the tax consequences of DRIPs may differ. Here are some of the ways plans may vary:

- Some DRIPs charge a periodic service charge, which may be deducted from the dividends paid on your stock. For example, you may be required to pay a service charge of $30 per year to participate in the DRIP.

- Some DRIPs acquire stock directly from the company, while others may use your dividends to buy stock on the open market. If the plan buys stock on the open market, it will incur brokerage commission costs, and the date of purchase will not necessarily be the same as the date of the dividend.

- Some companies that maintain DRIPs will pay brokerage commission costs on purchases made through the plan. In other cases, the commission is paid out of the dividend and reduces the number of shares you receive.

- Some DRIPs permit participants to buy additional shares by sending a cash payment to the trustee of the plan. These are called *optional purchases.*

- Some DRIPs provide a discount on purchases of dividend reinvestment shares, or on optional purchases, or both.

When you're considering whether to participate in a DRIP, you should receive a prospectus that describes the features of the plan. The prospectus will point out advantages of participation, which may include avoiding brokerage commissions or buying stock at a discount. It will also point out possible disadvantages of participation. For example, if you decide to sell the stock you hold in the plan, you may not be able to do so as quickly as if you held the shares in a regular brokerage account.

The prospectus will also include a section describing the tax consequences of participation. If possible, you should rely on that discussion, and on information supplied by the company, to determine how to report. If the tax information in the prospectus isn't available, or isn't clear, the following explanation may be helpful.

You're the owner. The tax law treats you as the owner of shares you hold in a DRIP. The prospectus may refer to a *trustee* that holds your shares and administers the plan, but for tax purposes your stock is *not* held in trust. The administrator of the DRIP is merely acting as your agent, the same way your stockbroker does if you maintain a brokerage account. You don't have to report income when you take your shares out of a DRIP because you owned those shares even before you took them out. If you take cash out of a DRIP, you'll report capital gain or loss on the sale of shares to provide the cash.

Service charges. If your DRIP imposes a service charge, this charge is *not* included in the basis of shares you buy through the plan. Instead, it's an investment expense, which you may claim as a deduction subject to the limitations that apply to investment expense deductions (see Chapter 11).

Amount of dividend. When you participate in a dividend reinvestment plan, the amount of your dividend may not be the same as if you held your shares outside a plan:

- If the plan incurs brokerage commissions to reinvest dividends and the company pays the commissions rather than deducting them from the dividend, your share of the commission is treated as an additional dividend. When this happens, the additional dividend is usually very small.

- If the company provides a discount on dividend reinvestment purchases, the amount of the discount is treated as an additional dividend. The same is generally (but not always) true for a discount on optional purchases.

In general, you can rely on your annual Form 1099 to tell you the amount you must report as a dividend.

Basis in your shares. Your basis in shares you purchase through a DRIP includes:

1. The amount (if any) you paid for the shares, plus

2. The amount taxed to you as a dividend, minus

3. The amount (if any) deducted from your dividend as a service charge.

This basic rule can spin out in different ways:

- Suppose the stock you already own in a DRIP pays a dividend of $300. The DRIP buys shares directly from the company at a 5% discount, so your account is credited with $315 worth of stock. The IRS treats the additional $15 worth of shares as a further dividend, so you're taxed on a dividend of $315, and that's your basis in the shares.

- Suppose the DRIP buys shares in the open market instead of buying them from the company. The company doesn't provide a discount, but it does cover the brokerage commission. The IRS treats your share of the brokerage commission as an additional dividend. If your share of the commission is $8, you're taxed on a total dividend of $308, and that's your basis for the shares.

- Suppose you send in $1,000 to make an optional purchase through the DRIP. The DRIP buys shares directly from the company at a 5% discount. Your account is credited with $1,050 worth of stock. Generally, the IRS will treat the discount as a dividend. When this is so, you report a dividend of $50 (in addition to any other dividend you received) and take a basis of $1,050 in your stock.

Holding period for your shares. For shares that are received in lieu of cash dividends, you're treated as if you bought the stock on the date of the dividend. If you make an optional purchase through a DRIP, you're treated as if you bought the stock on the date the plan makes the purchase (*not* the day you send in your money).

Keeping records. Figuring out your basis and holding period on any particular dividend reinvestment is usually not too hard. If you reinvest dividends over a number of years, though, it may be difficult to reconstruct the basis of your shares unless you keep records as you go along. You'll have many different blocks of shares, each with a different basis and holding period. Determining gain or loss on a sale, especially if you don't sell all your shares at one time, can be a real headache.

It's a good idea to set up and maintain a good system of records for your stocks even if you don't participate in a DRIP. If you *do* use a DRIP, keeping good records is truly a necessity.

> ▪ If you sell some but not all of your DRIP shares, and have a loss on the sale, be alert to the possibility of a wash sale if you had a purchase from dividend reinvestment within 30 days before or after your sale.

Employee Stock Options

Employee stock options come in different varieties with different tax consequences. The subject is too large to cover here; in fact, I've written an entire book on the subject.* Here are some of the main points having to do with reporting gain or loss on a sale:

- If you exercise a nonqualified stock option, you'll report compensation income either at the time of

---

* *Consider Your Options: Get the Most from Your Equity Compensation*, 2004 edition, Fairmark Press Inc. See ordering information in the back of this book.

exercise or when the stock vests. This income increases your basis in the shares, so you don't get taxed twice on the same income. For example, if you pay $800 to exercise an option and report $400 of compensation income, you're treated as if you bought the stock for $1,200.

- You don't report compensation income at the time you exercise an incentive stock option, but you may have to pay alternative minimum tax (AMT). When you sell the shares, you'll have a higher basis (and a smaller gain) under the AMT than under the regular tax.

- If you sell shares from an incentive stock option too soon, you'll have a *disqualifying disposition.** In that case you have to report compensation income equal to the *spread* at the time you exercised the option (the difference between the value of the stock and the amount you paid under the option) or the amount of gain you have on the sale, whichever is *smaller.* If your gain is larger than the amount of the spread, any excess is capital gain (which may be long-term or short-term, depending on how long you held the stock before selling).

- You may have to report compensation income on a sale of shares from an employee stock purchase plan. If you do, the income increases your basis in the shares, so you don't pay double tax on that income.

Worthless Shares

Companies sometimes fail, leaving shareholders with worthless stock. The general rule is that if your stock becomes worthless, you claim a capital loss as if you sold

---

* To avoid a disqualifying disposition, you have to hold the shares until a year after you exercised the option, or two years after the option was granted, whichever is *later.*

the stock on the last day of the year in which the stock became worthless.

Example: You bought XYZ stock in November, 2000. In June of the following year, disaster struck the company and the stock became worthless. Although you held the stock less than a year when it became worthless, you'll have a long-term capital loss because you're treated as having a loss on the last day of the year, and that's more than a year after you bought the stock.

The chief difficulty with this rule is determining which year a stock became worthless. Some companies crash and burn fairly rapidly leaving little doubt as to the year they became worthless, but others die a lingering death. It isn't necessarily enough that trading in the stock has terminated, making it difficult or impossible to sell your shares. Even if the company is in bankruptcy, the stock may not be worthless because some companies emerge from bankruptcy and continue operations. If the stock has any present *or future* value, it isn't worthless. You can't claim your loss in a year before the year the stock becomes worthless.

To make matters worse, you also aren't allowed to claim a loss in a year *after* the stock became worthless. That means you're entitled to the deduction in a particular year only if you can show (1) some identifiable event or events caused the stock to become worthless in the year you claimed the loss, *and* (2) the stock had at least some value at the end of the preceding year. If you postpone your deduction to a later year because you're uncertain whether the stock truly is worthless, the IRS may disallow your deduction on the basis that you should have claimed it in an earlier year. To soften this rule a bit, the law permits you to go back and amend the return in the year the stock actually became worthless, as many as seven years after you filed the return for that year.

Dealing with uncertainty. What should you do if you think your stock is worthless, but you aren't sure? One approach is to try to arrange a sale of the stock. Some brokers will accommodate their customers by purchasing shares that may be worthless for a nominal amount. Then you can claim a loss on the sale, without worrying about whether the stock is worthless. If the stock actually became worthless in an earlier year, though, the IRS may challenge the deduction and say you should have claimed it in the earlier year.*

If you can't arrange a sale, or you don't want to do so, the safest approach is to claim your deduction in the earliest year the stock may have become worthless. It's possible the IRS will challenge the deduction, but there shouldn't be a penalty if you believed in good faith that the stock may have been worthless that year. In fact, the judicial opinion in one case dealing with worthless securities suggested exactly this approach in situations where it's unclear when stock has become worthless.

Cash in Lieu of Fractional Shares

In some of the transactions described above you may receive cash representing the value of a fractional share. Generally this cash should be reported as proceeds from the sale of that fractional share. You allocate basis to that fractional share just as you would if it were a full share.

> **Example:** You paid $8,000 for 100 shares of XYZ. Later, Bigco acquired XYZ in a tax-free merger. Under the formula used in the merger, you're entitled to receive 92.5 shares of Bigco stock. You receive 92 shares plus $75.00 representing the value of the fractional share.
>
> To find your basis per share, divide your total basis of $8,000 by 92.5 (*not* by 92!). Your basis per share is $86.49. Your basis for the fractional share is $43.24, so you'll report a gain of $31.76 ($75.00 received in cash minus basis of $43.24).

* If you have the idea of selling the shares to a relative, or to a business you own, remember that you can't claim a deduction on a sale at a loss to a related person.

Chapter 8
Special Categories of Gains and Losses

So far we've talked about "plain vanilla" capital gains and losses. This chapter discusses special categories of gains and losses that receive different treatment under the tax law:

- Five-year gain or loss

- Unrecaptured section 1250 gain

- Collectibles gain or loss

- Qualified small business stock

- Specialized small business investment companies

The rules for unrecaptured section 1250 gain, and for collectibles gain or loss, usually don't apply to stock. We cover them briefly because it's possible these gains and losses will interact with your gains or losses from buying and selling stock.

Special Rates for Five-Year Gain

The tax law that lowered capital gain rates in 1997 also gave us special, reduced rates for property held more than five years—but delayed the effective date until 2001. Even at that point the benefit applied only to five-year gains that fell in the lowest tax brackets. Then the 2003 tax law effectively eliminated the five-year rates for *all* capital gains after May 5, 2003. Assuming we don't go back to a system where five-year gain received preferential treatment, the special rules for property held more than five years are significant only for gains falling in the 10% or

15% tax brackets—and only if the sales occurred from January 1, 2001 to May 5, 2003. If you had gains meeting this description, the tax rate is 8% instead of the 10% rate that otherwise would have applied. Beginning May 6, 2003 the rate is 5% for long-term capital gains falling in these tax brackets, and there's no added benefit for holding stock more than five years.

Unrecaptured Section 1250 Gain

I can't blame you if your eyes glaze over at the thought of something called *unrecaptured section 1250 gain.* It's possible some of this gain will show up on a year-end statement you receive from a real estate investment trust (REIT), or possibly from a mutual fund that holds stock in one or more REITs. You can also run into this category of gain if you personally sell real property after claiming depreciation deductions, or you're a member of a partnership that does so.

Briefly, this item represents past depreciation deductions that were converted into long-term capital gain. Normally, depreciation deductions reduce ordinary income, which is taxed at higher rates than long-term capital gain. In effect, when you sell property for which you previously claimed depreciation, you're converting ordinary income into long-term capital gain. To reduce the benefit of this conversion, the tax law imposes a maximum rate of 25%, rather than 20%, on capital gain from this source.*

> **Example:** You bought rental property for $80,000. Over the years you held it, you claimed $20,000 of depreciation deductions, reducing your basis to $60,000. Then you sold it for $90,000, securing a $30,000 gain. A portion of this gain ($20,000) is unrecaptured section 1250 gain, taxable at a maximum rate of 25%. The remaining $10,000 is taxed

---

* If the gain falls into a tax bracket lower than 25%, you pay the rate for that bracket instead of the higher 25% rate.

as "regular" long-term capital gain, at a maximum rate of 20%.

Collectibles Gain or Loss

You probably won't run into this item in connection with your stock investing. If you have gains from investing in certain items classified as *collectibles*, though, you'll have to pay tax at a maximum rate of 28%.* Collectibles include works of art, rugs, antiques, metals, gems, stamps, coins and alcoholic beverages. (Contrary to popular opinion, collectibles to not include many other items people collect, at least until the Treasury designates them as such. For example, it appears that baseball cards are not collectibles as defined in the tax law, although I suppose the IRS could argue that they are works of art.) If you hold any of these items more than a year and sell for a gain, your tax will be higher than on a normal long-term capital gain.

> ▪ If you're considering a charitable donation of property, appreciated collectibles held more than a year make a good choice. You get to claim the full value of the property and avoid the 28% tax.

Qualified Small Business Stock

The first two items above are taxed under rules that are less favorable than for regular capital gains. Now we come to a special category that's taxed under *more* favorable terms. To take advantage, though, you have to acquire *qualified small business stock.*

To give a complete explanation of these rules would require an entire chapter—more space than we can afford for a benefit most people can't claim. What follows is an overview that will enable you to get an idea what these benefits are, and find out whether they might apply to

---

* Here again, the maximum rate only applies when gain falls into a higher tax bracket.

you. If it looks as if you might qualify, you'll have to follow up with a tax professional who can look into the details.

Qualified small business stock. Stock you buy in the stock market isn't *qualified small business stock.* To qualify for these tax benefits, you generally have to buy stock directly from the company. This may happen because you're one of the company's founders, or because you've provided venture capital to the company. Another possibility: you worked for the company and exercised an option to buy stock.

The company has to meet various requirements. It must be a "C corporation" (in other words, a corporation that hasn't made the "S corporation" election). It has to be in an active business (not just an investment company)—but various types of active businesses aren't allowed. Among the businesses that don't qualify are professional services, performing arts, financial services, farming, lodging and restaurants. Furthermore, the company may not have more than $50 million in assets at the time you buy the stock (or during certain other specified periods).

Benefits. Two different benefits are potentially available to people who hold qualified small business stock, although the second one has mostly disappeared. The first one allows you to "roll over" gain from qualified small business stock you held more than six months. That means you don't pay tax when you sell the stock, provided that you invest the money in *new* qualified small business stock within the 60-day period beginning on the date of the sale. Your basis for the new stock is reduced by the amount of gain postponed from the sale of the old stock. That means you'll still pay tax on that gain if you sell the new stock. You may be able to avoid that tax altogether, though, if you hold the stock until death or donate it to a charity.

The other benefit is smaller—in fact, it has almost vanished. If you hold your shares *more than five years,* you can exclude half of your gain when you sell the stock, subject to certain limits. But here's the kicker: the part you don't exclude is taxed at 28%. Effectively this rule gives you a 14% rate, which was nice back in the days when you would otherwise pay 20% but a big yawn when the alternative is to pay 15%. And speaking of alternatives, watch out for the alternative minimum tax (AMT) if you claim this benefit.

If this tiny tax break still seems attractive, bear in mind that there are two limits on the amount of gain you can exclude. One limit is pretty generous: $10 million per company in which you invest. The other one is more likely to be a problem for people who get in very early on a very successful business: you can't exclude more than ten times the amount of your basis in shares of that company you sold during that year. For example, if your $5,000 investment turned into $500,000 before you sold it, your exclusion on the sale will be limited to $50,000, ten times the amount you invested.

Specialized Small Business Investment Companies

People sometimes ask me if there's any way they can avoid reporting gain from a sale of stock if they reinvest the proceeds in more stock. Unless you're selling qualified small business stock as described above, the answer is generally *no*. There's an exception if you're willing and able to invest your sale proceeds in a *specialized small business investment company* (SSBIC).

The easy part is that you have to be selling publicly traded securities—in other words, the kind of stock you can buy or sell through a stockbroker. You have 60 days to reinvest the proceeds. The hard part is finding a suitable investment in an SSBIC.

These companies are intended to encourage investment in businesses of entrepreneurs who have been denied the opportunity to own and operate a business because of social or economic disadvantage. If these businesses prosper, the SSBIC may share in that success. Yet these investments involve a great deal of risk. What's more, many SSBICs insist on a minimum investment that's beyond the reach of most investors.

At this writing, the number of SSBICs is small—perhaps 20 or so—and none of them trade publicly. If you're well connected financially and able to absorb the risk involved in such an investment, you might consider rolling your gains to one of these companies. This is not an opportunity for the typical investor, however.

Part II
Other Investment
Income and Expense

Capital gains and losses don't tell the whole story when it comes to taxation and investing. You'll encounter other types of income (such as dividends) and expenses (such as investment interest). These three chapters cover the issues you're most likely to encounter.

Part II Other Investment Income and Expense

Chapter 9
Dividends from Stocks and Mutual Funds

We seem to be coming out of a period of several decades in which dividends dwindled in importance as companies changed their emphasis from cash payouts to stock buybacks. Capital gains became the primary goal for most investors in stocks and mutual funds, partly because of favorable tax treatment and partly because that was where they found the bulk of their investment profits. The last few years have changed the outlook for dividends. Spurred by investor demand and more recently by the new tax rates for qualified dividends, many companies are increasing their dividend payouts, or announcing new dividends when they did not pay any in the past.

We'll begin by looking at the rules for dividends from companies. These are somewhat more complicated than in the past because of the new tax rates for dividends. Later, we'll turn to dividends from mutual fund companies—which are even more complicated.

Dividends from Companies

In the first edition of this book we were able to say dividend income was "simple city." Now we have lower tax rates for qualified dividends, but these come with some added complexity.

Rates. The rates for qualified dividends are the same as for long-term capital gain. In fact, the tax calculation for qualified dividends is combined with the capital gains tax calculation on Schedule D. If the dividend income falls in the lowest tax brackets, you pay 5%. If your other income fills up those brackets before you count your qualifying dividends, you'll pay 15%.

Q: *Does that mean I can use dividends to soak up capital losses?*

A: No. Even though qualified dividends are now taxed at the same rates as long-term capital gains, these dividends are treated as ordinary income for other purposes, including the $3,000 capital loss limitation.

Sixty-one day holding period. There's a special holding period for qualified dividends. Generally you have to hold the stock at least 61 days, not counting the date of purchase but counting the date of sale. You don't have to hold the stock 61 days *before* the dividend, and you don't have to hold it 61 days *after* the dividend—but you have to hold it at least 61 days during the 121-day period beginning 60 days before the ex-dividend date.*

The main idea here is that you can't buy stock just before a dividend, take the 15% rate on that dividend, and then sell the stock, possibly taking a short-term capital loss that will reduce income that would be taxed at a higher rate.

Example: You buy 1,000 shares of XYZ at $40 just before the ex-dividend date and capture a $2 per share dividend. Right after that you sell the stock at $38. You have a $2,000 dividend and a $2,000 short-term capital loss, but overall no economic profit or loss. In this situation your dividend is ordinary income that does not qualify for the 15% rate.

This rule can produce unfavorable tax results even if you aren't trying to do anything fancy.

---

* As originally written, the law refers to a 120-day period, and this causes a problem for people who buy shares one day before the ex-dividend date. As this book went to press, Congress was working on a technical correction to fix the problem.

Example: In the previous example, suppose you already have more than $3,000 of net capital loss for the year. The additional short-term capital loss will not do you any good except as a carryover to a later year. Yet you still have to report the dividend as ordinary income.

Example: Going back to the previous example again, suppose you have an overall capital gain for the year, but all your gain is long-term. Now you'll be able to use the capital loss from selling the XYZ shares, but the loss will count against income that would have been taxed at the 15% rate for long-term capital gains. Meanwhile, your dividend income doesn't qualify for that rate because you didn't hold the stock long enough.

These problems existed before the change in the law, but they are likely to crop up more often now that companies are paying more dividends and many investors are seeking out dividend-paying stocks. The moral of the story: be wary of dividends if you do short-term trading.

Preferred stock. You have to meet a longer holding period requirement—91 days instead of 61 days—if you hold preferred stock that pays a dividend attributable to a period of more than 366 days. Otherwise the normal 61-day period applies to preferred stocks.

Mutual fund dividends. Mutual fund dividends can include income from various sources: long-term capital gains, short-term capital gains, interest and dividends. The part of a mutual fund dividend that comes from qualified dividend income *received by* the mutual fund gets treated as qualified dividend income on *your* return—just as you get the benefit when the mutual fund distributes long-term capital gains. Other portions of the mutual fund dividend have to be treated as ordinary income, taxed at the regular tax rates. For example, if part of the mutual fund distribution represents interest income or short-term capital gains received by the mutual fund, you'll report that part of the mutual fund distribution as a nonqualified dividend.

> ▪ The tax information you get from the mutual fund in January will tell you how much of the dividend qualifies for the lower rates.

REITs. The idea behind the lower dividend rate is to make up for the fact that corporate income is taxed twice: the corporation pays tax on this income, and then the shareholder pays tax on the same income when it is paid out as a dividend. Real estate investment trusts (REITs) that follow certain rules don't pay tax on their income, so the lower rates don't apply to most REIT income. REIT dividends that come from income that was subject to corporate income tax will qualify for the lower rates, but this is normally a small fraction of REIT income, if any.

> ▪ The tax information you get from the REIT in January will tell you how much of the dividend qualifies for the lower rates.

Dividends from foreign companies. Foreign companies can pay qualified dividends if their stock trades on an exchange in the United States. This includes stock that trades through ADRs.* It's also possible to receive qualified dividends from a foreign company that does not trade on a U.S. exchange, so check the tax information you receive from the company.

Investment interest deduction. As explained in Chapter 10, qualified dividends don't count as investment income for purposes of applying the limitation on investment interest expense deduction unless you choose to give up the benefit of the lower tax rates.

Don't get fancy. Advanced trading techniques or special transactions can disqualify you from claiming the

---

* ADRs are basically a substitute for actual shares of stock, used to overcome certain difficulties in trading stock of a foreign company.

lower rate on dividends. There's a rule that says you don't have a qualified dividend if you're obligated to make a payment to someone else with respect to the dividend. That rule would apply if you sell stock *short against the box* as explained in Chapter 12. And there's another rule that says you aren't treated as the owner of the stock, for purposes of the 61-day holding period, during any period when you've used stock options or similar arrangements to protect yourself against loss from a decline in the value of the stock.

> **Example:** You hold 1,000 shares of XYZ and decide to sell short 1,000 shares of this stock while continuing to hold these shares. XYZ pays a dividend of $1.25 per share while the short position is open.

In this situation, you have to pay $1,250 to the person from whom you borrowed the shares to make a short sale. You also receive $1,250 as a dividend on the shares you continue to hold. This is not a qualified dividend, however, because you were obligated to make a payment related to this dividend.

More on Dividends

People sometimes get tripped up if they have cash dividends reinvested. It's important to keep a record of dividend reinvestments, because they count as additional purchases of stock. These purchases create *basis* in your shares, and that means you'll report a smaller gain (or larger loss) when you sell the shares. You may be disappointed if you assume the company will be able to reconstruct these records for you at the time you sell, particularly if you hold the stock for many years. Losing these records may mean paying additional tax.

In theory, a regular company can pay a tax-free return of capital dividend, although this rarely happens. A company can pay this type of dividend only after it has paid out all its "earnings and profits," not just for the current year, but over its entire life as a corporation. If you receive a notice telling you part of your dividend is a tax-free return of capital, read about this type of dividend in the discussion of mutual fund dividends below.

Mutual Fund Dividends

Mutual fund dividends can be much more complicated. In fact, mutual funds can pay four different types of dividends, and in addition make two different types of *allocations* that affect your tax return. Some of these items are further broken down into subcategories. That may seem like a lot to learn, but chances are that any one mutual fund you invest in will generate only two or three of these items.

We'll start by looking at the reports you'll receive from your broker or mutual fund company. Then we'll identify each type of dividend and explain how to handle it.

Note: Your mutual fund dividends are taxable even if you choose to reinvest them. Generally, when you choose to reinvest your dividends you're treated the same as if you received the dividend in cash and then used it to buy additional shares.

Reports you'll receive. From time to time during the year you may receive statements concerning activity in your mutual fund account. Those statements will provide information concerning dividends, but these are not your official tax reports. The tax reports normally arrive in January or early February, and consist of one or more of the following items:

- Form 1099-DIV, Dividends and Distributions

- Form 2439, Notice to Shareholder of Undistributed Long-Term Capital Gains

- A tax report from the mutual fund company or your broker

Form 1099-DIV. This form reports up to three types of dividends, plus your share of the fund's foreign tax payments, if any. Mutual fund companies are permitted to use the official IRS form, or to provide you with a *substitute* Form 1099-DIV that gives the same information. The substitute form doesn't have to be on a separate sheet of paper. It can be printed on the same page as other information. This form tells you:

- The total *ordinary dividends* you received for the year, in box 1 of the form.

- The total *capital gain distributions* you received for the year, in box 2a of the form. Subcategories of capital gain distributions are broken out in boxes 2b, 2c and 2d.

- The total *nontaxable distributions* you received for the year, in box 3 of the form.

- Your share of the fund's *foreign tax paid* for the year in box 6 of the form.

Form 2439. This form reports information about undistributed long-term capital gains that are *allocated* to you, even though they were not paid out to you. If you didn't get one of these forms, don't worry. Most mutual funds don't make this type of allocation, so most mutual fund investors don't receive this form. If you *do* get one, read the discussion of mutual fund capital gain allocations below.

Mutual fund tax report. The mutual fund may send you a report providing additional tax information. If the fund paid any exempt-interest dividends, this report is where you'll find that information. The report may provide other tax information, too:

- How much of your exempt-interest dividend is potentially subject to alternative minimum tax (AMT).

- How much of your exempt-interest dividend is from various states. (This information doesn't affect your federal income tax return, but may affect your state income tax return.)

- How much of the ordinary dividend represents interest on federal obligations that's exempt from state income tax.

There's no special format for this report, but it's usually easy enough to identify. Just make sure you don't throw out anything you receive from your mutual fund or broker in January or February!

January dividends. There's a special rule you should be aware of if you receive dividends in January. Mutual funds are permitted to treat certain January dividends as if they were paid in the previous year. It may seem like a mistake when the mutual fund reports this income as if you received it in December of the previous year. It's not a mistake though, just a special feature of the way the tax law treats mutual funds.

Ordinary Dividends

Most mutual funds pay at least some ordinary dividends. Even if the mutual fund is designed to generate other types of income, such as tax-exempt interest, it may have a small amount of income it must pay out as an ordinary dividend.

Almost any type of income other than long-term capital gain or tax-exempt interest will be treated as an ordinary dividend when paid out by a mutual fund. In particular:

- *Taxable interest* that's received by a mutual fund will be treated as an ordinary dividend when the mutual fund pays this income to its shareholders. That's why you'll get a dividend report, not an interest report, if you invest in a money market mutual fund. If the taxable interest includes interest on federal obligations, you may be able to exclude that portion on your state income tax return.

- *Short-term capital gain* that's received by a mutual fund is also treated as an ordinary dividend when paid to the shareholders.

That last statement may seem surprising if you're familiar with the way capital gains work. Short-term capital gains often end up being taxed at the same rate as ordinary income, but they're not *treated* the same as ordinary income. In particular, if you have a large capital loss— long-term or short-term—you may be better off if you have short-term capital gain than if you have ordinary income. That's because you can deduct only $3,000 of the loss against ordinary income.

Nevertheless, you aren't allowed to treat any part of your mutual fund dividend as short-term capital gain. That's true even if the mutual fund includes information in its report telling you how much of the dividend came from short-term gains. You have to treat that amount as part of your ordinary dividend.

Capital Gain Distributions

If a mutual fund has long-term capital gains, it can designate part of its dividend as a capital gain distribution. The shareholders report this part of the dividend as if it were their own long-term capital gain. These amounts are called *capital gain distributions* or *capital gain dividends*. As noted above, this treatment does *not* apply to short-term capital gains.

A capital gain distribution is taxed as long-term capital gain. That's true even for shareholders who have held the mutual fund shares less than a year. Generally this means favorable rates apply: you're likely to pay less tax on this type of dividend than on an ordinary dividend. Be alert to special categories of capital gain that may appear in boxes 2b, 2c or 2d of Form 1099-DIV. If you see amounts reported in these boxes, follow the instructions on the form carefully.

> • **Important:** Many people who receive capital gain distributions don't realize they need to do a special tax computation to get the benefit of lower tax rates for long-term capital gains. There's a long calculation on page 2 of Schedule D, and a shorter one in the tax return instructions for people in simpler situations. The calculation may seem like a pain in the neck, but be sure to do this because this is where you get your savings from the lower capital gains tax rates.

Note: If you receive a capital gain distribution and subsequently incur a short-term capital loss on mutual fund shares held six months or less, read about the special rule for losses within six months in Chapter 5.

Capital Gain Allocations

Mutual funds that have long-term capital gains have a choice. They can pay the capital gains out to their shareholders: a capital gain dividend. If they don't want to do that, they can retain the capital gain, pay a tax, and make a *capital gain allocation.*

It's easy to tell which one you received. Capital gain dividends are reported in box 2a of Form 1099-DIV, as described earlier. If the mutual fund decides instead to make a capital gain allocation, this item won't appear on Form 1099-DIV. Instead, you'll receive a special form: Form 2439, *Notice to Shareholder of Undistributed Long-Term Capital Gains.*

Where is it? This form may arrive at a different time than other tax forms. Mutual funds and other companies are supposed to provide Form 1099-DIV by the end of January. They have 60 days after the end of their tax year (which isn't necessarily December 31) to provide Form 2439. If your shares are held by a nominee, this form may arrive even later.

What to do. When you receive Form 2439, you need to do four things:

- Report the capital gain on your income tax return for the year.

- Claim a credit for the tax paid by the mutual fund.

- Attach copy B of Form 2439 to your completed tax return.

- Adjust the basis of your shares in the mutual fund.

Reporting the capital gain. You'll report the capital gain from this form in the same way as a capital gain dividend, discussed earlier. Be sure to do the tax rate calculation for capital gains, or you lose the benefit of the lower rates. The rule for losses on shares held less than six months applies to capital gain allocations as well as capital gain distributions.

Claiming the credit. Now for the good part. You get to claim credit for the tax paid by the mutual fund. That tax is paid at the rate of 35%, and that's higher than the amount of tax you pay because of the capital gain allocation. As a result, receiving Form 2439 usually means paying *less* tax with your return, not more. If this additional credit means you have an overpayment, you can use it to claim a refund.

Add the amount from box 2 in every Form 2439 you receive and report the total on the line near the end of Form 1040 that refers to Form 2439. When you complete Form 1040, you'll get credit for this figure just as if it were an additional amount of tax you paid to the IRS.

Attach Copy B. You should receive two copies of Form 2439, called Copy B and Copy C. (The mutual fund sends Copy A to the IRS.) When your income tax return is completed, attach Copy B to your return. Retain Copy C for your records.

Basis adjustment. There's one more piece of business that's easy to overlook, and it's an important one. When you received a capital gain allocation on Form 2439, you get to increase the basis in your mutual fund shares by 65% of the amount of the allocation. If you overlook this adjustment, you'll pay too much tax when you sell your shares.

Why 65%? That's the amount that's left after you get credit for the 35% tax mentioned above. Be sure to record this basis adjustment in your records for this mutual fund. It'll save you money when the time comes to sell your shares.

If you're using the single-category averaging method to determine the basis of your mutual fund shares, the basis adjustment is simple. Just multiply the allocation amount by 65% and add the result to the total basis of your shares.

If you're using any other method to determine your basis, you'll need to take a few more steps. After finding 65% of the allocation amount, divide by the number of shares to which it applies. This tells you the amount of the basis adjustment per share. Use this per-share adjustment to increase the basis of each separate group of shares you own.

In either case, be sure to retain Copy C of Form 2439 in your tax records as proof that you're entitled to this basis adjustment.

Comment. Overall, this tax treatment is neither good nor bad. It puts you in about the same place you'd be in if you received a capital gain dividend in cash, paid tax with part of that cash, and then bought additional shares with the cash that was left over.

Exempt Interest Dividends

Some mutual funds are established to provide a way to invest in municipal bonds and other securities that produce tax-exempt interest. Dividends from these mutual funds are usually composed mainly of tax-exempt interest. Under the special tax rules for mutual funds, you should treat the tax-exempt interest portion of your dividend the same as if you received the tax-exempt interest directly.

Although these dividends are generally tax-free, you can't simply ignore them:

- Your dividend from this type of mutual fund isn't necessarily entirely tax-exempt. You may have to report part of your dividend as ordinary income or capital gain.

- Exempt interest dividends must be reported on your income tax return, even if they don't affect the amount of tax you pay.

- These dividends may affect the amount of tax you pay on your social security income.

- Exempt interest dividends may affect your deduction for investment interest expense and other investment expenses.

- Exempt interest dividends may be partly or entirely subject to the alternative minimum tax (AMT).

- Some or all of your exempt interest dividend may be subject to state income tax.

Reporting exempt interest dividends. Exempt interest dividends aren't reported in any box on Form 1099-DIV. They're reported in a statement or report from the mutual fund (which may also include a Form 1099-DIV for other portions of your dividend). You should receive this statement shortly after the end of the year.

Find the total of your exempt interest dividends for the year. Add this amount to any exempt interest income you have from other sources and report that amount on the appropriate line of Form 1040.

Federal Interest Dividends

In general, states are not permitted to impose an income tax on interest from federal obligations, even though this interest is subject to federal income tax. For purposes of state income tax, interest on United States savings bonds, United States treasury bills, and various other bonds or obligations of the Unites States and territories are exempt. (The exemption doesn't extend to Ginnie Mae Bonds, Fannie Mae Bonds, or FHLMC securities.) If your state has an income tax and you receive this type of income, look for a line on your state income tax return where you can exclude the interest.

This rule applies to certain mutual funds on a "flow-through" basis. To qualify, the laws of most states say the mutual fund must meet a requirement that at least half its assets consist of obligations that are exempt from state income tax. If this is the case, the portion of the mutual fund dividend that represents exempt interest is excluded from income on the state form.

Reporting federal interest dividends. Information about the amount of federal interest included in your mutual fund dividend won't appear on Form 1099-DIV. Your mutual fund should provide this information in an annual statement or report, which may accompany Form 1099-DIV or may arrive somewhat later. If you believe your mutual fund has this type of income but can't find this information, contact the mutual fund or your broker.

There's nothing special to do on your *federal* income tax return for this type of interest. It's included in the ordinary dividend reported on Form 1099-DIV, and you should report it just like any other ordinary dividend. To determine the proper reporting on your state income tax return, review the form and instructions carefully. Look for information about interest on savings bonds and other federal obligations.

Nontaxable Distributions: Return of Capital

Mutual funds sometimes make dividend payments that don't represent earnings. When you receive this type of dividend, you're considered to be getting back some of the money you invested in the fund. That's why these payments are sometimes called *return of capital distribu-*

tions. But people tend to simply call them *nontaxable distributions* because in nearly all cases that's what they are: nontaxable. In fact, that's what the IRS calls them, although they can be taxable in limited circumstances.

Don't confuse these payments with exempt interest dividends. Those dividends represent interest received by the mutual fund from municipal bonds and similar investments. Return of capital distributions don't come from exempt interest or from any other type of earnings.

It's easy to tell which type of dividend you received. Return of capital distributions—the type we're discussing here—appear on Form 1099-DIV in a box labeled "Nontaxable distributions." If you receive exempt interest dividends instead, those don't appear on Form 1099-DIV, as explained earlier.

Adjusting your basis. Before you can determine how to report your distribution, you have to take care of an important piece of business: adjusting the basis of your shares. Remember, your *basis* is a measure of your investment in the shares. When you receive a return of capital, you're getting part of your investment back, so your basis in the shares goes down.

If you use the single-category averaging method to determine basis in your mutual fund shares, the basis adjustment is simple. All you have to do is subtract the amount of the nontaxable distribution from the total basis of your shares.

If you use any other method, you have to do a little more arithmetic. Divide the nontaxable distribution by the number of shares to which it applies. This tells you the amount of the distribution per share. Then reduce your basis for each share by this amount.

In nearly all cases, the amount of the return of capital distribution is smaller than your basis in the shares. That lets you know the distribution is truly nontaxable. If you receive a return of capital distribution that exceeds the basis in your shares, you have to report capital gain as explained below.

Tax reporting. You don't have to report a nontaxable distribution. That means you have nothing at all to report if the distribution is less than or equal to your basis, which is nearly always the case. But what if the distribution is greater than your basis? You aren't allowed to have negative basis. If your return of capital distribution is larger than your basis, you reduce the basis to zero— and you report the additional amount of the distribution as capital gain on Schedule D.

> **Example:** At a time when your basis in your mutual fund shares is $170, you receive a "nontaxable distribution" of $250. You'll reduce your basis in the shares to zero, and report a capital gain of $80. This amount is taxable as capital gain even though the dividend is called a nontaxable distribution.

Report the gain as short-term or long-term, depending on how long you held the shares to which the distribution relates.

Chapter 10
Investment Interest Expense

If you borrow money in connection with your investing activity, you need to understand the special rules for investment interest expense. You can't deduct investment interest unless you itemize. Even if you itemize, your deduction is limited by the amount of investment income you report. This chapter answers the following questions:

- What interest expense counts as *investment* interest expense?

- How does the investment income limit work?

- What is the special rule if you have long-term capital gains or qualified dividends?

Investment Interest

The tax law divides interest expense into various categories, each with its own tax treatment. It's important to determine how much interest expense you have in each category because different limitations apply in each case. In addition to investment interest, the other main categories are business interest, home mortgage interest, personal interest, student loan interest and passive activity interest.

If you borrow money in connection with a business, the interest you incur is *business interest*. You'll deduct that interest in determining the amount of income or loss you have from that business.

> ■ **Traders.** Investing is *not* considered a business. However, if you're a *trader* as defined in Part V of this book, interest expense you incur in connection with your trading activity is business interest, not investment interest. The limit discussed in this chapter doesn't apply to such interest.

Interest expense that isn't connected with a business or investment is generally considered *personal interest* for which no deduction is allowed. Interest on credit cards typically falls into this category, as does most interest on auto loans and amounts borrowed for consumer items like home appliances. Yet you're allowed to deduct *home mortgage interest* if you itemize, and a limited deduction for *student loan interest* became available beginning in 1998.

Some people confuse *passive activity interest* with investment interest. Don't make this mistake, because the rules for passive activity interest are very different.* Buying and selling stocks is *not* a passive activity. A passive activity is generally a *business* activity (not an *investing* activity) in which you have some ownership without having enough direct involvement to be "materially participating" under the tax regulations.

General rule. *Investment interest* generally includes any interest you pay on money borrowed to buy stock or other investment property. There's one exception, though. Interest you're allowed to deduct as home mortgage interest isn't considered investment interest, even if you used a home equity loan to buy investment property.

Investment property generally includes anything that produces interest, dividends or annuities, and anything that produces capital gain or loss, provided that you don't hold the property as part of a business. Stocks, mutual fund shares and stock options are all considered invest-

---

* Those rules are beyond the scope of this book. See IRS Publication 925, *Passive Activity and At-Risk Rules*, for more information.

ment property. You may also hold other types of investment property, such as land or precious metals.

Margin interest. Many people who buy and sell stocks arrange with their broker to borrow against the investments held in their accounts. This type of loan is called a *margin loan.* Interest on a margin loan is investment interest only if you use the loan to buy stock or other investment property. For example, if you take out a margin loan to buy a home entertainment system, interest on the loan is nondeductible personal interest. You don't get to treat this interest as investment interest merely because the money came from a margin loan.

Straddles. If you buy and sell options, your investment activity may produce *straddles* as explained in Chapter 16. When you pay interest on loans incurred in connection with straddles you have to add the interest to the cost of your investment instead of claiming a deduction for investment interest.

Short sales. If you make short sales of stock, you may be required to make a payment in lieu of dividend to the person from whom you borrowed stock for the short sale. If the payment is treated as investment interest, it's subject to the rules described in this chapter. Chapter 12 explains when these payments are treated as investment interest.

Interest allocation. You may take out a single loan for more than one purpose. When this happens, you have to allocate the interest according to the way you used the money.

> **Example:** You borrowed $12,000, using $9,000 of that amount to by stock and the remaining $3,000 to buy furniture for your home. You used 75% of the loan to buy investment property, so you'll treat 75% of the interest on this loan as investment interest.

Actually, you'll probably end up treating *more* than 75% of the interest on this loan as investment interest. The reason is that as you repay the loan, you're treated as if you paid the *personal* (non-investment) part of the loan first. When you've paid the loan down to $10,000, for example, the remaining debt is 90% investment debt, and at that point you'll treat 90% of the interest payments as investment interest.

Investment Interest Limit

To claim a deduction for investment interest, you must *itemize*. This means you claim specific deductions for items like state taxes, home mortgage interest and charitable contributions instead of the standard deduction. Most taxpayers—roughly 70%—claim the standard deduction, but if your itemized deductions (including investment interest expense) are larger than the standard deduction, it's generally better to itemize.

Even if you itemize, your deduction for investment interest expense is limited to your net investment income. If your net investment income is zero, you can't deduct any investment interest expense. If your net investment income is smaller than the amount of your investment interest expense, you'll be able to deduct some but not all of that expense. If you aren't able to deduct the full amount of your investment interest expense, the part you didn't deduct *carries over* to the next year, when you'll be able to claim the deduction if you itemize and have net investment income.

> **Example:** In 2004 you have investment interest expense of $3,000 and net investment income of $2,000. You deduct $2,000 of investment interest expense and carry $1,000 to the next year. In 2005 you have investment interest expense of $500 and again have $2,000 of net investment income. Your total investment interest expense is $1,500: $500 from the current year plus $1,000 carried over from the previous year. You can claim the entire $1,500 as a deduction because it doesn't exceed your net investment income.

Net investment income. *Net investment income* is your gross income from property held for investment reduced by investment expenses other than investment interest expense. This figure includes interest, nonqualified dividends, annuities and certain royalties, but doesn't include Alaska Permanent Fund dividends. It also includes short-term capital gain, but doesn't include long-term capital gain or qualified dividends unless you make the election described below.

> ▪ **Net capital gain.** Here's a point that confuses many people, including some tax professionals. IRS instructions say net investment income doesn't include *net capital gain*. That makes it sound like you don't include any kind of capital gain, short-term or long-term. But they're using the term *net capital gain* with a special meaning: the excess of long-term capital gain over short-term capital loss. In other words, it's the amount that's eligible to be taxed at the lower tax rate for long-term capital gain. If you have a net *short-term* capital gain, you include that in your net investment income, because that's not part of your *net capital gain* under this special definition.

Election to include long-term capital gain or qualified dividends. If your investment interest expense is greater than your net investment income, you might consider electing to treat some or all of your long-term capital gain or qualified dividends as investment income. The benefit of doing this is that you can claim your investment interest deduction in the current year, instead of carrying it forward to the next year. There's a downside, though: you lose the benefit of long-term capital gain tax rates for the portion of your gain covered by this election.

It's a good idea to make this election if the amount of investment interest is so large you might not be able to deduct all of it in the foreseeable future. On the other hand, if you think you can deduct the investment interest within the next year or two, you might be better off not making the election so you can preserve the benefit of the lower capital gains tax rate.

Example: Normally you have only a very small amount of investment income. This year, you played the market more than usual and ended up paying $10,000 of margin interest, all of which was used to buy stocks. Your only investment income was $500 of interest and $18,000 of long-term capital gain from selling stock you bought a few years ago.

If you don't make this election, your entire $18,000 capital gain will be taxed at a favorable rate, but you'll deduct only $500 of the margin interest. You may not get the full benefit of the investment interest deduction for many years, if ever. In this situation, you elect to treat $9,500 of the long-term capital gain as ordinary income so you can deduct all your margin interest. The remaining $8,500 of long-term capital gain still qualifies for the favorable tax rate.

Example: Change the facts so that your margin interest is $2,000 and you expect to have at least $1,500 of net investment income next year. In this case you don't make the election, even though that means waiting a year before you can get the full benefit of your investment interest deduction. The benefit of the deduction is much greater in the later year because it will reduce your ordinary income, not your long-term capital gain.

The way I think about this is that you deduct the investment interest "against" some other investment income. The greatest benefit comes from deducting it against investment income that's taxed at regular tax rates, not long-term capital gain. Yet deducting it against long-term capital gain is still better than waiting an eternity before claiming the deduction—or failing to deduct it at all.

Chapter 11
Other Investment Expenses

We saw in Chapter 2 that costs of buying and selling your investments, including brokerage commissions and mutual fund loads, are included in the basis of the investments. You aren't allowed to claim a separate deduction for those items. In Chapter 10 we saw that you can claim investment interest expense as a deduction, but only if you itemize, and only to the extent it doesn't exceed your net investment income. Now we turn to other investment expenses: subscriptions to financial publications, account maintenance fees and any other expenses that relate to your investing activity.

> - **Traders.** If you're a trader as defined in Part V of this book, the rules described in this chapter don't apply to expenses incurred in your trading activity.

General Rule

You can claim investment expenses as a deduction only if you itemize. Even then you may not get the full benefit of this deduction. In fact, many investors who itemize receive no benefit from these deductions.

The reason is that these expenses are classified as *miscellaneous deductions*. That may sound innocuous, but deductions in this category are allowed only to the extent that your total miscellaneous itemized deductions exceed 2% of your adjusted gross income.* Many people

---

* *Adjusted gross income* is total income reduced by certain deductions (such as IRA contributions) but before taking out itemized deductions or personal exemptions.

find that their miscellaneous deductions are too small to break through this "2% floor."

> **Example:** Your adjusted gross income is $60,000. Your only investment expense, other than investment interest and brokerage commissions, is $450 you pay to subscribe to investment newspapers and magazines. You don't have any other miscellaneous expenses. You receive no benefit from your $450 expense because it falls below the 2% floor ($1,200).
>
> If you had a total of $1,350 in miscellaneous expenses, either because your investment expenses were larger or because you had other miscellaneous expenses, such as tax return preparation fees and certain legal expenses, your deduction would be $150, the amount above the 2% floor.

Investment Seminars

The cost of attending investment conventions and seminars is not deductible. That may seem like a strange rule, because seminars of this type may be as helpful in learning about investments as books and periodicals. Blame it on people who got greedy back when the deduction was allowed. Ads promising that investment seminars would involve deductible travel to luxurious resorts or aboard cruise ships appeared in prominent financial publications. Congress decided that the best way to handle this situation was to do away with the deduction altogether.

Part III
Capital Gains: Advanced Topics

This part of the book explores topics many investors never encounter because they don't make short sales or trade in stock options. The tax rules for these transactions are complicated, but it's essential to understand them—for both compliance and planning purposes—if you do this type of trading.

Part III Capital Gains: Advanced Topics

Chapter 12
Short Sales

This chapter describes short sales, and explains the general tax rules relating to short sales. It also explains how the wash sale rule applies to short sales. Chapter 15 explains *constructive sales*, which can occur if you sell *short against the box* (see below).

How Short Sales Work

If you've never done a short sale, the concept is likely to seem strange. When you sell stock short, you're selling stock you don't own. You borrow the stock from someone else, promising to "repay" those shares of stock later. You sell the shares you borrowed, receiving cash. When you're ready to close the short sale, you deliver shares back to the person from whom you borrowed them.

As a practical matter, the borrowing takes place automatically. Your broker takes care of that. The fact remains that you owe a debt that has to be repaid in stock. That means there are two ways to close a short sale: you can *buy* shares to repay the loan, or you can deliver stock you owned at the time of the short sale.

If you buy shares to close the short position, you're in exactly the opposite position of someone who owned shares during that period of time: you make a profit if the stock goes *down*, and lose money if the stock goes *up*. For this reason, short sales can be used as a way of betting that the price of a particular stock will decline.

Example: You sell short 100 shares of XYZ at $60 per share. You receive $6,000 in the sale, and have an obligation to replace the 100 shares at some future time. If the stock price declines to $47, you can satisfy your obligation by purchasing 100 shares for $4,700, retaining $1,300 as your profit. On the other hand, if the stock goes up, you may end up having to pay more than $6,000 to satisfy your obligation to repay the stock. In that case you would have a loss on your short sale.

Short against the box. The other way to close a short sale is to deliver shares you held at the time of the short sale. If you hold shares of a particular stock and decide to sell short—instead of selling the shares you own—you are selling *short against the box.* This is a way of neutralizing a stock position without selling the shares you own.*

> **Example:** You hold 100 shares of XYZ. You want to eliminate your risk from a decline in value of the stock, but you aren't ready to sell the stock. You sell short 100 shares while continuing to hold the original shares. In other words, you sell short against the box. Now, if the value of the stock goes down, you'll have a gain on the short sale that exactly matches your loss on the shares you hold.

When you're ready to close the short sale, you can buy shares in the market, but you don't have to do so. You can simply deliver the shares you started out with.

> ▪ Selling short against the box can bring the constructive sale rule into play. See Chapter 15. Also, as noted in Chapter 9, any dividends you receive on stock you've sold short against the box do not get the lower tax rate for qualified dividends.

Simple Short Sales

Special rules apply if you make a short sale and at the same time own substantially identical stock. Before we turn to those rules, let's look at the simpler situation

---

* Some brokers, but not all, permit short sales against the box.

where you don't own the stock at the time you make the short sale, or at any time before you close the short sale. At the time you make the short sale, you borrow shares and sell them, receiving cash. Although you've received cash, you have nothing to report on your tax return at this point. You won't know whether you have a profit or a loss until you close the short sale.

To close the short sale, you'll have to buy shares at the current price. Your broker will return these shares to the account from which you borrowed at the time you made the short sale. If you're able to buy the shares for a smaller amount than you received at the time of the short sale, you have a profit. You'll report that profit as a short-term capital gain. Note that the gain is short-term even if your short position was open more than a year. That's because the thing you sold was stock you held less than a year. If you have to pay more for the stock than the amount you received at the time of the short sale, you'll report a short-term capital loss.

Closing date. The date of sale for a regular sale of stock is the trade date. Yet a short sale isn't closed by the purchase of shares. It's only closed when the shares are *delivered*. As a result, if you close a short sale by purchasing shares in the market, the tax law looks at the settlement date, not the trade date—except when you have a profit on the short sale. So the only time you have to look at the settlement date instead of the trade date is when you're closing a short position at a loss.

> **Example:** You made short sales of the stock of two different companies, A and B. Stock A went down, giving you a profit of $10,000. (Remember, when you sell short, you make money when the stock goes down.) Stock B went up, giving you a profit of $10,000. On December 31 you close both positions by purchasing shares in the market.

You have to report your profit on stock A in the current year, because profits on short sales are recorded on the trade date. Yet the loss on stock B does not get recorded until the following year, when the trade settles. Although you have two transactions that offset each other economically, from a tax standpoint they occur in different years. What's more, you can't carry the loss back to the previous year when you had the profit.

Owning Identical Stock

At some point, you may make a short sale of stock you already own (selling *short against the box*), or you may buy stock at a time when you have a short position in the same stock. In this situation, the general rule is that the holding period for your gain or loss from the sale is determined by how long you held the shares used to close the short sale. Your gain or loss is long-term if you close the short sale using shares you held more than a year; otherwise your gain or loss is short-term. There are exceptions to this rule, though. As described below, you may have to report short-term gain even if you use shares you held more than a year to close the short sale, or you may have to report long-term loss on a short sale closed with short-term shares.

Short-term gain. If you hold substantially identical stock* for one year or less at the time of the short sale, or if you acquire substantially identical stock after the short sale but before you close the short sale, then two rules apply:

- If you have a gain on the short sale, the gain will be short-term, regardless of how long you held the stock that was used to close the short sale.

- Your holding period for the substantially identical stock begins when you close the short sale, or when you sell the stock, whichever occurs first.

Example: You bought 100 shares of XYZ six months ago. You sell short 100 shares of XYZ while continuing to hold these shares. Nine months later

---

* The tax law uses the term "substantially identical stock" with the same meaning here as for the wash sale rule. See Chapter 6.

you use the original shares to close the short sale. If you have a gain on the sale, it's a short-term gain, even though you held the shares a total of 15 months before using them to close the short sale.

Example: Start with the same situation as the previous example, but this time you close the short sale by buying shares in the market. You continue to hold your original shares for another nine months, and then sell them for a gain. The gain is short-term even though you held the shares a total of two years. Your holding period for those shares started over again when you closed the short sale.

Example: You sold short 100 shares of XYZ at a time when you didn't own any shares of that stock. Then, while your short position was still open, you bought 100 shares of XYZ. You hold the shares more than a year, and then sell them for a gain. The gain is short-term unless you held the shares *more than a year after closing the short sale.*

Note that these rules apply to gains, not losses. Any loss from sale of the stock is long-term if you held the stock more than a year before selling it or using it to close the short sale.

If you work through this rule, you'll see that all of the following must be true for you to get a long-term gain on a short sale:

- At the time of the short sale, you hold long-term shares but no short-term shares in the stock you're selling short.

- You don't acquire any shares of that stock while the short sale is open.

- You use your long-term shares to close the short sale.

Long-term loss. On the flip side, there's a special rule for losses. If you held substantially identical stock for more than a year as of the date of a short sale, any loss from closing the short sale is a long-term loss, even if you use stock you held less than a year to close the short sale.

> **Example:** You held 100 shares of XYZ more than a year when you decided to sell short 100 shares of that stock. The price of the stock went up, and you closed the short sale at a loss, using newly purchased shares. Your loss is long-term, even though you used newly purchased shares to close the short sale.

This rule applies to losses, not gains. If you used newly purchased shares to close your short sale at a gain, you would have a short-term gain even though you owned long-term shares at the time you made the short sale.

Larger amount sold short. If you sell short more than the number of shares you hold, the special rules described above don't apply to the excess shares. For example, if you hold 100 shares of XYZ and sell short 150 shares of that stock, the special rules would apply to 100 shares but the rule for simple short sales would apply to the other 50.

> ▪ **Reminder:** If you make a short sale of stock you already own, be sure to understand the constructive sale rules described in Chapter 15.

Stock Becomes Worthless

Sometimes stock becomes worthless. A company may fail and leave nothing but scraps for the creditors to fight over. That's a sad event if you're unlucky enough to own the stock when it happens. If you've made a short sale of that company's stock, however, the company's failure is your success. You'll never be called upon to pay anything to close your short sale because the stock is worthless.

It might be tempting, in this situation, to simply leave the short sale in place indefinitely. After all, you've already received your profit. You received cash at the time you made the wash sale. The longer you delay closing the short sale, the longer you can avoid reporting the gain. That *used* to be the rule. Because of a 1997 change in the law, you have to report gain from a short sale on the date the stock becomes substantially worthless. It may be difficult to determine exactly when that day occurs, but the point is that you can't avoid reporting your gain by simply leaving a short position open indefinitely. If events in a particular year indicate that the stock has become substantially worthless, that's the year when you have to report gain from your short position, even if the position remains open at the end of the year.

Short Sales and the Wash Sale Rule

As explained in Chapter 6, the wash sale rule prevents you from claiming a deduction from selling stock at a loss if you buy replacement stock within 30 days before or after the sale. The idea is that you shouldn't get a deduction because you're maintaining an investment in the stock with at most a small interruption in ownership. The wash sale rule also applies to losses from short sales.

Applying the wash sale rule to short sales is tricky because there are two different ways it can apply. You can have a wash sale as a result of another *purchase*, or you can have a wash sale as a result of another *sale*. Even the IRS gets confused here: their explanation in Publication 550 combines elements of the rule for purchases with the rule for sales, making it difficult to tell what rule actually applies to either situation.

Replacement purchases. The rule applying the wash sale rule to replacement purchases in a short sale situation has been in place for many years. Here's an example, taken from IRS Publication 550, showing why the wash sale rule applies to replacement purchases:

Example: On June 2, you buy 100 shares of stock for $1,000. You sell short 100 shares of the stock for $750 on October 6. On October 7, you buy 100 shares of the stock for $750. You close the short sale on November 17 by delivering the shares bought on June 2.

You have a loss on the short sale because the sale was at $750 and you closed it by delivering stock you bought for $1,000. Yet at the end, after you closed the short sale on November 17, you're in the same position you were in before the short sale: you still own 100 shares. What's more, from October 7 to November 17, you were in an *equivalent* position: you held 200 shares but you were short 100, and that's economically the same as simply holding 100 shares. There was only one day (October 6) when your position was different. The idea behind the wash sale rule is that you have to change your position for at least 31 days if you want to claim a loss, so the wash sale rule applies in this situation.

Notice, though, that you closed the short sale more than 30 days after you bought the replacement shares. We've already learned that your loss from a short sale occurs when you close it, not when you enter into the short position. How can the wash sale rule stretch back from November 17 to October 7?

The answer is a special rule that says *solely for purposes of applying the wash sale rule* a short sale is considered to occur on the date you make the short sale (*not* the date you close it) if both of the following are true:

- On the date of the short sale, you own identical stock, or an option or contract to acquire identical stock, and

- You later deliver the stock you owned (or stock acquired using the option or contract you owned) to close the short sale.

That's exactly what happened in the example above. That means we determine whether you have a wash sale by looking at October 6, not at November 17. You made a replacement purchase within 30 days before or after October 6, so the wash sale rule applies. You can't deduct the loss from closing the short sale on November 17.

Instead, you have to add that loss to your basis for the replacement shares you bought on October 7.

A questionable case. The regulation laying out how the wash sale rule applies to replacement purchases seems to imply that if the two conditions described above are *not* both true, you apply the wash sale rule by looking at purchases made within 30 days before or after the date you close the short sale. The result could be to apply the wash sale rule in situations where it doesn't make sense.

> **Example:** You sell short 100 shares without owning any of the same stock (a "naked" short sale). Contrary to your expectations, the stock rises (which means you're losing money on your short sale). You buy stock in the market to close the short sale and, because you're so impressed with the way the stock's price is rising, you buy 100 more shares (a "long" position) to hold as an investment.

Clearly the wash sale rule shouldn't apply here. The loss arose from a short position, and the 100 shares you bought did not replace that short position. I think there's a good chance the IRS would agree that the wash sale rule doesn't apply here, but there's no official pronouncement to that effect, and if you read the regulation literally, it seems as if the wash sale rule might apply.

Replacement sales. Prior to 1984, the wash sale rule applied to replacement *purchases* but did not apply to replacement *sales.* Congress amended the law that year to bring replacement sales within the scope of the wash sale rule. The Treasury has never issued regulations providing details on how this rule works. That's unfortunate, because the language in the law is somewhat vague. It says simply that "rules similar to" the regular wash sale rule apply to losses from closing short sales.

The rule applies if, within 30 days before or after closing a short sale at a loss, you sell substantially identical stock, or enter into another short sale of substantially identical stock. Here are examples of the two different situations.

Example 1: You sell short 100 shares of XYZ at a time when you don't own any XYZ (a "naked" short position). You're betting that the stock price will fall, but instead it rises, leaving you in a losing position. At this point you're more certain than ever that the stock is overpriced and you want to hang on to your short position to profit from the inevitable fall. Yet you want to deduct your loss on this year's tax return. So you close your short position at a loss, and then open another short position the next day. This is a wash sale because you replaced your losing short position with an identical short position within the wash sale period.

Example 2: You buy 100 shares of XYZ and at the same time make a short sale of 100 shares (short against the box). Just before the end of the year, the price of the stock is up, so you have a profit in your long position and a loss in your short position. You close the short position at a loss on December 29. On January 2, you sell the stock for a profit equal to your loss from the short position. Overall you have no profit or loss, but you want to claim a deduction for your loss in the year you closed the short position. The wash sale rule prevents this deduction, because you made an additional sale of stock within 30 days after closing the short sale at a loss.

Another questionable case. Consider the following sequence of transactions. On February 1, you buy 100 shares at $45. On March 10, you make a short sale of 100 shares at $38 (a short sale against the box). On April 15, you close the short sale by delivering the stock you bought on February 1 (a loss of $7 per share). On April 20, you make another short sale (a "naked" short).

You have a short sale at a loss, followed within 30 days by another short sale. Under the literal language of the Internal Revenue Code, it appears this would be a wash sale. Yet this shouldn't be a wash sale because the loss was from the *long* position, not the short position, and you didn't replace the long position. Possibly you avoid having a wash sale by referring to the rule in the regulations that says you look to the date you made the wash sale, not the date you closed it, if you close it using stock you owned at the time you made the wash sale. The result isn't clear, however, because the regulation was written for the replacement purchase rule, not the rule for subsequent sales (which didn't exist when the regulation was written).

Short Sale Expenses

Consider what happens when a company pays a dividend while you have a short position in that stock. The dividend will go to the person who bought the shares from you. Meanwhile, the person who loaned the shares to you expects to be reimbursed for the dividend. After all, that person merely loaned you the shares, she didn't sell them.

That's why you're required to reimburse the lender for the dividend she would have received if you hadn't borrowed shares for your short sale. That's part of the promise you make when you borrow the shares: you'll not only replace the shares, but also make up for any dividends lost prior to closing of the short sale. This is sometimes called a *payment in lieu of dividend.* If you make such a payment, you need to know how to treat it on your tax return.

General rule. In general, you treat these payments the same way you treat interest on money you borrowed to make an investment. You claim a deduction, but only if you itemize, and only to the extent of your net investment income, with any excess carried over to the following year. See Chapter 10 for an explanation of the investment interest expense deduction.

"Short short" exception. If you close the short position by the forty-fifth day after the date of the short sale, you can't deduct your payment in lieu of dividend. Instead, you have to add that amount to the basis of the stock you used to close the short sale. That way, it either decreases your gain or increases your loss from the short sale. The reason for this exception is to prevent you from using short sales to convert capital losses into ordinary deductions.

Extraordinary dividends. A period of forty-five days is long enough to prevent tax planning for normal dividends, but not long enough if you make a short sale of stock in a company that pays a very large dividend. In that situation, the tax benefit from claiming an ordinary deduction from making a payment in lieu of dividend might be large enough to justify the risk of holding the short position open more than forty-five days. If a company pays an *extraordinary dividend,* you aren't allowed to deduct the payment in lieu of dividend unless you keep the short sale open more than a year. You've received an extraordinary dividend if the total amount of dividends received during the time the short sale was open is greater than 10% of the amount you received in the short sale (5% if you sold short preferred stock).

Example: You sold short XYZ at $45 per share. While the short sale was open, XYZ paid a dividend of $5 per share. You're required to pay $5 per share to the lender of the shares. If you hold your short position open more than a year you can deduct this amount as investment interest. Otherwise, you have to treat it as a reduction in the amount you received in the sale.

Chapter 13
Stock Options

Options give you the right to buy or sell stock or other property at a specified price during a specified period of time. In this book we're concerned primarily with options to buy or sell stock. (A brief discussion of index options appears in Chapter 14.) If you trade options on other kinds of property, such as commodities or foreign currencies, you should be aware that additional rules may apply.

You should also be aware that the rules described here don't apply to options received as compensation for services. For an explanation of nonqualified stock options, incentive stock options and other forms of equity compensation, refer to my book on that subject: *Consider Your Options.**

> ▪ Option trading can involve a high degree of risk. Before trading options, be sure to read and understand *Characteristics and Risks of Standardized Options*, and read books on principles of option trading. See *Books on Personal Finance and Investing* in the Appendices at the end of this book.

Option Terminology

A *call option* is an agreement or contract that permits the holder to buy stock at a specified price for a specified period of time. For example, if you hold a call option on XYZ stock at $45, you can use that option to buy XYZ at

---

* *Consider Your Options: Get the Most from Your Equity Compensation*, 2004 ed., Fairmark Press Inc. See ordering information in the back of this book.

that price even if the stock is trading in the market at a much higher price. In other words, you can force someone to sell you the stock at a bargain price.

A *put option* permits the holder to *sell* stock at a specified price for a specified period of time. If you hold a put option on XYZ stock at $45, you can use that option to sell XYZ at that price even if the stock is trading in the market at a much *lower* price. In other words, you can force someone "overpay" for the stock.

> ▪ The standard size for a stock option trading in the market is 100 shares. If you buy three call options, you're acquiring the right to buy 300 shares.

The price specified in the option agreement is the *strike price* (also called the *striking price* or the *exercise price*). The last day to exercise the option is called the *expiration date.*

There are two sides to each option agreement. The person who has the right to exercise the option is the *holder* of the option. The person who must buy or sell the stock if the holder exercises the option is the *writer* (also called the *grantor*) of the option.

Example: You hold XYZ stock and decide to sell a call option on this stock. You don't own an option on the stock, so you're creating a new option. That's why you're called the *writer* of the option. The purchaser is the *holder* of the option.*

A call option is *in the money* if the stock is trading at a price higher than the strike price. It's *at the money* when the trading price of the stock is the same as the strike price of the option. When the trading price of the stock is below the strike price of the option, the option is *out of the money* (or *under water*).

---

* Technically it isn't possible to identify a particular person who holds the option you sold. When someone exercises an option, the obligation to perform is assigned to a particular option writer according to procedures established by the Options Clearing Corporation.

The opposite relationships hold for a put option. These options are in the money when the stock trades at a price below the strike price of the option, and out of the money when the stock trades above the strike price. In each case, saying that an option is *in the money* means the option has value built into it, given the price at which the stock is trading.

An option is *deep in the money* when it's in the money to a large extent. Most of the time the term is used loosely, so there's no precise measure of how much difference you need between the market price of the stock and the strike price of the option before the option is deep in the money. The usual notion is that the option is so far in the money that it is almost certain to be exercised.*

Straddles, Constructive Sales

Option traders and investors may run into special rules that are covered in other chapters. The discussion in this chapter assumes your options are not part of a *straddle* (Chapter 16) and that your options don't create a *constructive sale* (Chapter 15). Generally, these special situations arise when you hold different positions that are related (such as holding XYZ stock and, at the same time, holding a put option on XYZ stock or selling a call option on XYZ stock).

Holders of Call Options

If you buy a call option, you acquire the right to buy stock. You can't claim a deduction at the time you purchase the option. Instead, your call option has a basis equal to the amount you paid for it (including brokerage commissions and other costs, if any). There are three different ways your option may terminate:

You exercise the call option. In this case, you're using the option to buy stock. Your basis for the option is added

---

* Under the straddle rules described in Chapter 16, there's a special definition of the term "deep in the money" that doesn't correspond to this general usage.

to the amount paid for the stock. Your holding period for the stock begins when you exercise the option: it does *not* include the time you held the option.

> **Example:** You buy a call option on XYZ with a strike price of $45, paying $500 for the option to buy 100 shares at this price. Later, when the stock is trading at $60, you exercise the option, paying $4,500 to buy 100 shares. Although you have a built-in profit (you paid a total of $5,000 to buy stock worth $6,000), you don't report gain or loss at this time. Instead, you hold XYZ stock with a total basis of $5,000 ($4,500 paid for the stock plus $500 paid for the option).

Your call option expires. You may hold the call option until it expires unused. In this case you're treated as if you sold the option for $0 on the expiration date. You'll report a capital loss, which may be short-term or long-term, depending on whether you held the option more than a year.

> **Example:** You pay $500 to buy a call option on 100 shares of XYZ at $45 per share. Two months later, the stock is trading at $42 and you allow the option to expire unused. You'll report a capital loss of $500 on the expiration date.

> **Note:** You may find yourself holding a worthless option that won't expire until after the end of the year. For example, you paid $500 for an option on XYZ at $45 and the stock has declined to $12 with only a few weeks until expiration. You want to claim the loss this year, but there's no way to sell the option and it won't expire until the following year. In theory you should be able to abandon your rights under the option and claim the loss, but to the best of my knowledge there's no mechanism for doing so.

You sell the call option. The third possibility is that you sell the option you purchased earlier. Treat this situation the same as if you sold any other capital asset. You report a gain or loss based on the difference between the amount you received in the sale and the amount you paid for the option. The gain or loss is long-term if you held the option more than a year.

Holders of Put Options

If you buy a put option, you acquire the right to sell stock. As in the case of a call option, you can't claim a deduction at the time you purchase the option. Instead, your put option has a basis equal to the amount you paid for it (including brokerage commissions and other costs, if any). Here again, there are three different ways your option may terminate:

You exercise the put option. If you exercise the put option, you're using it to sell stock. You don't report gain or loss on your option, but you reduce the amount you received in the sale by the cost of the option.

> **Example:** You paid $500 for a put option to sell 100 shares of XYZ at $45. Later, you exercise the put option, selling 100 shares at the strike price of $45. You received $4,500 in the sale, but the option cost $500, so the net amount you received is only $4,000. You'll report that you sold the stock for $4,000.

Your put option expires. You may hold the put option until it expires unused. The tax treatment here is the same as if you hold a call option until it expires: You'll claim a capital loss as if you sold the option for $0 on the date of expiration. The loss is long-term if you held the option more than a year before it expired.

You sell the put option. If you purchase a put option and subsequently sell it, you'll report capital gain or loss on the sale equal to the difference between the amount received in the sale and the amount paid for the option. The gain or loss is long-term if you held the option more than a year before the sale.

Writers of Call Options

You can sell a call option even if you don't own one. In this case you're creating a new option, and you're the *writer* of the option. If the purchaser of the option exercises it, you're obligated to sell stock at the strike price.

Although you receive cash at the time you sell the option, you don't report gain or income at that time. Instead, you wait until your option position terminates to report the consequences. There are three ways your option position may terminate:

The call option is exercised. If the option is exercised, you're required to sell stock at the strike price. You don't report any gain or loss on the option, but you increase the amount reported on the sale of the stock by the amount you received when you sold the option.

Example: You sell (write) a call option for 100 shares of XYZ with a strike price of $45, receiving $500 in the sale. The option is exercised, and you're forced to sell the stock at $45. In addition to the $4,500 you received in the sale of the stock, you received $500 in the sale of the option. You'll report that you sold the stock for $5,000.

The call option expires. The holder of the option may permit it to expire unused. If this happens, you get to keep the amount you received when you sold (wrote) the option. You'll report this amount as short-term capital gain on the date the option expired. Note that this gain is short-term even if the option was outstanding more than a year.

> ▪ **It ain't true.** There's a persistent myth that if you sell a call option on stock you hold (a *covered call*), you don't report gain when the option expires, but instead merely reduce your basis in the stock. That isn't true, and never has been. See Chapter 16 for more details on covered calls.

Closing transaction. Your option position may terminate because of a *closing transaction*. In essence, you're buying back the option you sold. You'll report a short-term capital gain or loss determined by the difference between the amount you received when you sold (wrote) the option and the amount you paid in the closing transaction.

Example: You sell (write) a call option for 100 shares of XYZ with a strike price of $45, receiving $500 in the sale. Later, when this option is trading at a lower price, you pay $300 to close your position. You report a capital gain of $200. The gain is short-term, regardless of how long the option was outstanding.

> • **Caution:** If you hold stock at the same time you write a call option on the same stock, you've written a *covered call*. Special rules described in Chapter 16 apply to covered calls.

Writers of Put Options

As in the case of a call option, you can sell a put option even if you don't own one. In this case you're creating a new option, and you're the *writer* of the option. If the purchaser of the option exercises it, you're obligated to buy stock at the strike price.

Although you receive cash at the time you sell the option, you don't report gain or income at that time. Instead, you wait until your option position terminates to report the consequences. There are three ways your option position may terminate:

The put option is exercised. If the option is exercised, you're required to buy stock at the strike price. You paid money for the stock, but you received money when you sold the option. You don't report gain or loss at this point, but you reduce your basis in the stock by the amount you received for the put option.

Example: You received $500 when you sold (wrote) a put option permitting the holder to sell 100 shares of XYZ at $45. The holder exercises the option, forcing you to buy the stock for $4,500. You received $500 for the put option, so your net cost for the stock is $4,000. When you sell the stock, you'll report gain or loss relative to a basis of $4,000.

The put option expires. The holder of the option may permit it to expire unused. If this happens, you get to keep the amount you received when you sold (wrote) the option. You'll report this amount as short-term capital gain on the date the option expired. Note that this gain is short-term even if the option was outstanding more than a year.

Closing transaction. As in the case of a call option, you can close your position in the put option, in effect buying it back for the current trading price of the option. You'll report a short-term capital gain or loss determined by the difference between the amount you received when you sold (wrote) the option and the amount you paid in the closing transaction.

Example: You sell (write) a put option for 100 shares of XYZ with a strike price of $45, receiving $500 in the sale. Later, when this option is trading at a higher price, you pay $750 to close the option. You report a capital loss of $250. The loss is short-term, regardless of how long the option was outstanding.

Wash Sales and Options

Chapter 6 covers the wash sale rule in general. Options present two different types of problems in connection with the wash sale rule. First, if you sell stock at a loss, you can turn that sale into a wash sale by trading in options. And second, losses from the options themselves can be wash sales.

Buying call options. If you sell stock at a loss, you don't have to buy replacement stock within the wash sale period to have a wash sale. You can have a wash sale merely by entering into a contract or option to buy replacement stock.

Example: On March 31 you sell 100 shares of XYZ at a loss. On April 10 you buy a call option on XYZ stock. (A *call option* gives you the right to buy 100 shares.) The sale on March 31 is a wash sale.

It doesn't matter whether the call option is in the money. This is an automatic rule. If you buy a call option during the wash sale period (from 30 days before the sale until 30 days after the sale), you have a wash sale. That's true even if you never exercise the option to acquire the stock. The disallowed loss is added to your basis for the call option.

Selling put options. You can also turn a sale of stock into a wash sale by selling put options. This rule is *not* automatic. It applies only if the put option is deep in the money—and there's no precise standard as to when a put option is *deep enough* in the money for the rule to apply. The rule applies if it appears, at the time you sell the put option, that there's no substantial likelihood it will expire unexercised. When that happens, selling the put option can be roughly equivalent to buying the stock.

Example: On March 31 you sell 100 shares of XYZ at a loss. On April 10 you sell a put option giving the holder the right to sell to you 100 shares of XYZ at a price substantially higher than the current market price of the stock. The sale on March 31 is a wash sale.

As seller of a put option that's deep in the money, you participate in the upward and downward movement of the stock price, unless the price moves higher than the strike price. If the strike price is high enough, the chances of that happening are small, and you've simply found a different way to continue your investment in the stock.

Holding period questions. For technical reasons, the law isn't crystal clear how the rules for holding periods work when the wash sale rule applies because of trading in options. One knowledgeable commentator has suggested that the wash sale rule doesn't affect the holding period of a call option. I have my doubts, though, because it would be easy to convert a long-term loss to a short-term loss if you didn't add the holding period of the stock to the holding period of the option. The tax law contains elaborate rules designed to prevent this type of conversion, and all those rules would be pointless if you could defeat them through the use of wash sales involving options.

To prevent this type of conversion, it would be necessary to apply the extended holding period not only to a call option, but also to any stock acquired by exercise of that option. That's contrary to the usual rule for determining the holding period of stock acquired by exercising an option. You would also have to extend the holding period of a short call position, if the wash sale rule applied because you sold a call that was deep in the money. That's a very strange rule because short positions are always considered to be short-term: their holding period is zero because you don't hold an asset.

The IRS has never told us the extended holding period applies in these situations. If you can benefit from converting long-term loss to short-term loss, you may want to consider using stock options and the wash sale rule to accomplish this result.

Example: You have a large, long-term loss on XYZ stock. In the same year you have long-term gains and short-term gains. If you simply sell the stock, the loss will reduce your long-term gains. A short-term loss would be better, because it would reduce your short-term gains.

To get the better result, you sell the stock and immediately buy a call option for the same number of shares of XYZ. Shortly thereafter, you sell the option. The wash sale rule prevents a deduction for the loss on sale of the stock. The loss is added to your basis for the option, and you claim a short-term loss on sale of the option.

Will the IRS accept this result? If not, will you win if you fight the IRS in court? There's no way to know for sure. If you're willing to venture into a gray area, be my guest, but don't say I didn't tell you it was gray.

Losses on options. Congress amended the wash sale rule in 1988 so that it applies directly to contracts or options to buy or sell stock or securities. That means you can have a wash sale when you close an option position at a loss, if you establish a replacement position within the wash sale period. The Treasury has yet to issue regulations under this rule, and a host of questions remain unanswered. Foremost among these is the question of when one option is substantially identical to another option.

Until the Treasury decides to issue regulations or other guidance, neither I nor anyone else can say exactly how the wash sale rule applies to losses on options. But there's a pretty good rule of thumb that should tell you when you're safe and when you're on thin ice. If the positions you acquired within the wash sale period permit you to participate in the same up and down market swings as the position that produced the loss, there's a chance the IRS will say you have a wash sale. If that's not the case, you should be safe.

Suppose you've sold a call option at a loss. Buying another call option on the same stock within the wash sale period may be viewed as a wash sale even if the new call option has a different expiration or a different strike price. The new option isn't identical, but perhaps it can be considered *substantially* identical, which is enough to invoke the wash sale rule.

The IRS also might assert that you have a wash sale if you buy XYZ *stock* after selling a call option at a loss, especially if the call was in the money when you sold it. Similarly, you could also have a wash sale if you write a deep-in-the-money put option during the wash sale period after selling a deep-in-the-money call at a loss. All of these are ways of continuing to participate in the up and down motions of the price of the same stock.

By contrast, you shouldn't have a wash sale if you sell a call option at a loss and also write a put option that's at the money or out of the money. The long call option and the short put option are both bullish positions, but the short put option doesn't let you participate in the upside of the stock. You haven't preserved your overall position relative to the stock.

These remarks are simply my ideas of how the IRS might interpret the wash sale rule in connection with options. Until we have further guidance, we won't be able to say with certainty what transactions will or will not produce wash sales. Unfortunately, there's no sign that guidance on these issues will be forthcoming in the near future.

Chapter 14
Section 1256 Contracts

For the most part, the subject of section 1256 contracts is beyond the scope of this book. Most people encounter this subject in connection with trading commodities, and this book doesn't cover rules for commodity trading. Yet there's one category of section 1256 contracts—index options—that's close enough to our subject matter to deserve at least brief coverage.

The tax treatment of section 1256 contracts is different from any other kind of financial asset. There are two special rules:

- Your holdings in section 1256 contracts are *marked to market* at the end of each year.

- Any gain or loss you have from section 1256 contracts is 60% long-term gain or loss and 40% short-term gain or loss, without regard to how long you held them.

We'll look at details for these rules in a moment. First, let's look at the one type of section 1256 contract we're interested in here: index options.

Index Options

There are several categories of section 1256 contracts, but only one that falls within the scope of this book. *Index options* are a way of making a bet on which way a particular stock index is going to move—or hedging a bet you've already made.

Suppose you think the S&P 500 index is going to rise in the near future. There are various ways you can bet on that result. You can buy shares of the stocks that make up the S&P 500, but that wouldn't usually be practical. A more likely choice would be to buy shares of a mutual fund that seeks to mimic the performance of the S&P 500 index. An index option provides a third possibility. You could buy an option on the S&P 500 index. If the index is higher than the strike price on the expiration date, you'll receive cash equal to the difference.

Not all index options are section 1256 contracts. Only those that meet certain technical requirements qualify. Generally, they must be considered "broad-based" under criteria of the Securities and Exchange Commission, and they have to *settle in cash*. That means you don't get shares of stock when you exercise the option; instead, you get an amount of cash determined by the difference between the value of the index on the exercise date and the strike price of the option. Further details concerning which index options qualify as section 1256 contracts are available from the exchanges on which the options trade.

> ▪ Don't confuse index options with options on exchange-traded index funds. While I'm not aware of any ruling on this point, I suspect that options on exchange-traded index funds won't be considered section 1256 contracts because they settle in shares of the fund, not in cash.

The 60/40 Rule

The most remarkable thing about the tax treatment of section 1256 contracts is that gain or loss from short or long positions in these investments will be treated as 60% long-term capital gain or loss and 40% short-term gain or loss. It doesn't matter how long you hold them. You get the long-term part even if you sell the same day you bought them, and you get the short-term part even if you hold them more than a year. In effect, you get a blended tax rate on gain from section 1256 contracts: somewhere between the rate you pay on long-term capital gain and the rate you pay on ordinary income (which is the rate that applies to short-term capital gain).

Mark-to-Market Rule

Under the mark-to-market rule, you're treated as if you sold (or closed) all your section 1256 contracts for their fair market value on the last day of the year. You'll report gain or loss from that deemed sale just as if it were an actual sale. Your basis for the section 1256 contracts is adjusted to reflect the gain or loss you reported.

> **Example:** At the end of the year, you hold a section 1256 contract you bought for $4,000. The value of the contract at the end of the year is $4,250, so you report gain of $250 ($150 of long-term capital gain and $100 of short-term capital gain). Your basis in the section 1256 contract is adjusted to $4,250. If you later sell it for $4,300, you'll report only $50 of gain ($30 of long-term capital gain and $20 of short-term capital gain).

> **No wash sales.** The wash sale rule (Chapter 6) is designed to prevent you from claiming losses that otherwise wouldn't be allowed while you continue to hold an investment. When it comes to section 1256 contracts, all your gains and losses are reported each year because of the mark-to-market rule. For that reason, the wash sale rule doesn't apply to section 1256 contracts.

Mixed Straddles

When you start combining section 1256 contracts with other investments, you can run into rules for *mixed straddles*. For example, if you hold a put option on the S&P 500 at the same time you hold shares of a mutual fund that mimics the performance of the S&P 500, you have a straddle because one investment position protects you from loss in the other. This is a *mixed* straddle because gain and loss on one part of the straddle is 60/40 gain or loss, while gain or loss on the other position is subject to the normal rules for capital gains and losses. There isn't room here to go into the technicalities for mixed straddles. I mention them so you'll be aware that such rules exist if you do this kind of trading. These rules may require you to report long-term loss when you would expect to report short-term loss, or you may have to report short-term gain when you would normally report long-term gain. The idea behind these rules is to prevent people from creating unfair tax advantages from combining different types of investment positions, but you can have negative effects from these rules even if you aren't seeking any special tax advantage in your trading.

Chapter 15
Constructive Sales

This chapter covers a rule, adopted in 1997, under which you may be treated as having sold an asset even when you continue to own it. This *constructive sale* treatment applies when you have other transactions that neutralize your market position. The most common example is a situation where you hold stock and at the same time make a short sale of the same stock—in other words, sell *short against the box.*

The constructive sale rule doesn't apply to all short sales, or even to all sales that are short against the box. For an explanation of short sales, and rules that apply to short sales *other than* constructive sales, see Chapter 12.

Background

What do you do when you make a winning investment? It's a nice problem to have, but a problem nonetheless. If you continue to hold the stock, it may continue its ascent—but it may fall back, eliminating your gains. Yet if you sell it, you're volunteering to pay taxes you could have avoided, at least for the time being, by standing pat.

Until 1997, there was a third alternative. You could make a short sale of that stock while continuing to hold your appreciated shares—a sale *short against the box.* The short sale neutralized your market position without requiring you to report any gain.

Example: You bought XYZ at $24 and it has soared to $68. You believe this stock's run is over and it's time to consolidate your gain. Before 1997 you could accomplish this by making a short sale of XYZ while continuing to hold the stock. You wouldn't report any gain on the sale because you haven't sold the shares that went up in value. You don't lose anything if the stock goes down after you've made the short sale, because your short position gains by the same amount as your long position (the shares of stock) loses.

Congress decided in 1997 that you shouldn't be able to neutralize your position this way without reporting gain. Under the constructive sale rule, you're treated as if you sold the appreciated stock, even though you continue to hold it, if you keep the short sale position open too long. You can also have a constructive sale if you trade options in such a way as to neutralize your stock position.

Constructive Sales in General

Selling short against the box doesn't necessarily create a constructive sale. For one thing, the rule applies only to appreciated positions (stock that has a value higher than your basis). If you make a short sale against the box for stock that hasn't gone up in value, the rules described in Chapter 12 apply.

The rule also doesn't apply if you close the short sale soon enough—and leave it closed long enough while continuing to maintain your position in the appreciated stock. To avoid having a constructive sale, you have to close the short position no later than 30 days after the end of the year, then continue to hold the appreciated stock without protection for at least 60 days. If you establish a new short position within 60 days after closing the first one, you can still avoid having a constructive sale if you meet these requirements for the *second* position. In other words, you would have to close the second position no later than 30 days after the end of the year of the original short sale, and continue to hold the appreciated stock without protection for at least 60 days.

These time periods refer to calendar days, not trading days. For the vast majority of taxpayers—everyone who reports on a year that ends December 31—the deadline for closing a short position to avoid a constructive sale is January 30.

> **Example:** On June 17, while holding shares of XYZ that went up in value, you make a short sale of XYZ stock. You're protected against any loss in the value of this stock for as long as you hold the short position open. On January 10 you buy shares in the market to close the short sale, and continue to hold your shares of XYZ, without making any further short sales or establishing other protective positions, for at least 60 days. You have satisfied the conditions to avoid a constructive sale.

Notice that in this example you're protected against market loss on your stock for an extended period of time, without having a constructive sale.

Effect of a Constructive Sale

If you have a constructive sale, you're treated as if you sold the appreciated stock on the date of the short sale. That's true even though we don't know whether you have a constructive sale until the following year.

> **Example:** You hold appreciated shares of XYZ and sell short against the box in February 2004. On January 25, 2005, you close the short position and continue to hold the XYZ stock. On March 10, 2005 you make another short sale against the box.

You have a constructive sale because your second short sale, in March 2005, comes less than 60 days after you closed the first short position. As a result, the short sale that occurred in February 2004, more than a year earlier, is a constructive sale. You have to report gain from that constructive sale on your tax return for 2004. The same would be true if you simply sold the XYZ stock (instead of selling short against the box) on March 10, 2005.

When you have a constructive sale, you're treated as if you sold *and repurchased* the stock at its fair market value on the date of the constructive sale. The stock takes a basis equal to the value used for the constructive sale, so you don't get taxed twice on the same gain. The stock also takes a new holding period: you're treated as if you acquired it on the date of the short sale.

> ▪ Although you're treated as acquiring the stock on the date of the short sale, the holding period for purposes of determining gain is presumably suspended under the rules explained in Chapter 12 until such time as you close the short position. You would have to hold the stock at least a year and a day after closing the short sale to get a long-term capital gain.

Options and Other Protective Positions

You don't have to sell short against the box to have a constructive sale. You can have the same result if you use stock options or other protective positions to neutralize your position in appreciated stock.

The Treasury hasn't issued regulations telling us exactly what positions (other than short sales against the box) will give rise to a constructive sale. When the regulations come out, they should be prospective, applying only to transactions that occur after the regulations are issued. The Treasury has informally indicated, however, that the regulations may apply retroactively to transactions that obviously fall within the intended reach of the constructive sale rule.

Meanwhile, we can glean some guidance from the legislative history of the constructive sale rule. It's clear that you don't have a constructive sale if you establish a position that provides only "one-way" protection for your stock position. For example, if you buy a put option on shares you own, you're protected against a decline in the value of your stock, but you can still benefit from further appreciation. Likewise, if you sell a call option, you lose the benefit of further appreciation in the stock price, but you can still suffer from a decline in value.

Buying a put option or selling a call option would not be safe from application of the constructive sale rule, however, if the option is deep in the money at the time of the transaction. For example, if you hold appreciated shares of XYZ and buy a put option at $150 when the stock is trading at $110, it's likely that you'll be treated as if you made a short sale for purposes of this rule. The wide disparity between the value of the stock and the strike price of the option creates a situation where you have not only protected yourself against loss if the market price of the stock declines, but also transferred to the writer of the option the economic benefit of any appreciation in the value of the stock up to a price of $150.

Similarly, you can have a constructive sale from a *combination* of options, where either one of the options by itself would not cause a constructive sale. For example, if your appreciated XYZ stock is trading at $98, you could buy a put option at $95 and simultaneously sell a call option at $100. This combination of option positions is called a *collar*, because it limits both your profit and loss from the stock position. A collar this "tight" is almost certain to be considered equivalent to a short sale for purposes of the constructive sale rule.

A "looser" collar should be permitted without a constructive sale, however. It has been suggested that a collar is loose enough if the spread between the strike prices of the put and call options is at least 15% of the current value of the stock. In the example where the stock is trading at $98, you shouldn't have a constructive sale if you buy a put at $90 and sell a call at $105.*

In Short

The constructive sale rule leaves us with opportunities to control risk without reporting gain. We can eliminate all risk for a limited period of time by selling short against the box. If we need protection for a longer period of time

---

* Although this "15% rule" hasn't been adopted by the Treasury, it has some vague support in the legislative history of the relevant tax law. More conservative commentators suggest using a "20% rule."

but can accept risk within certain limits, we can use a collar that meets the standards mentioned above. The constructive sale rule doesn't do away with tax-wise risk management, but success now depends on the planner's ability to adopt more sophisticated tax planning approaches.

Chapter 16
Straddles

We come now to an intricate and esoteric subject, but one you can easily bump up against if you buy and sell stock options. A *straddle* is a set of two or more *offsetting positions*—that is, positions that reduce risk because they normally move in opposite directions. There's nothing wrong with trading in such a way as to create straddles. If you do, though, you'll encounter rules that are designed to prevent people from using straddles to obtain unfair tax advantages. These rules apply even if you created the straddle without any improper tax motive. The rules for straddles have three main effects:

- They may require you to delay claiming some or all of your loss from selling or closing one position in the straddle.

- They may turn a long-term gain into a short-term gain, or turn a short-term loss into a long-term loss.

- They may require you to treat certain expenses as part of the cost of the straddle instead of claiming an ordinary deduction.

This chapter falls short of being a complete explanation of the straddle rules. The subject is simply too large—and too technical—for a full explanation here. Yet you'll learn enough to identify straddle issues and handle the situations that are most likely to arise. We'll also explain how you can avoid some of the straddle rules if you write *qualified covered calls*.

Definition of Straddle

The term *straddle* comes from the notion of someone who can't make up his mind which side he wants to be on. He has one leg on one side of the fence and one leg on the other, so he straddles the issue. In fact, we sometimes refer to a pair of financial positions as the *legs* of a straddle. The straddle rules apply to many types of financial positions, including futures contracts, forward contracts, and options on currencies and commodities. In this book we're concerned only with positions in stocks, and in options on stocks.

> ▪ The term *straddle* has a specific meaning to option traders. The definition in the tax law is broader. It includes combinations of positions an option trader might call a *spread* rather than a straddle, for example.

Position. You hold a position if you have an interest in the stock or option, which may be a positive or negative interest. If you hold shares of XYZ stock, you have a position (specifically, a *long* position) in that stock. You also have a position in that stock if you don't hold any shares, but you have sold the stock short. Likewise, you can establish a position by buying or selling a call option or a put option.

Straddle. Generally speaking, the term *straddle* is used in the tax law to refer to a combination of two or more financial positions that offset one another. When one position goes down in value, the other one will rise. It isn't necessary to have a perfect correlation, though. It's enough if one position protects, at least partially, against loss from another position. Positions are *presumed* to create a straddle if they relate to the same stock, and the value of one or more positions ordinarily varies inversely with the value of the other.* In other words, if one goes down, you expect the other to rise.

Example: You hold 100 shares of XYZ, and you buy an option to sell 100 shares of XYZ (a *put* option). When the value of the stock rises, the value of the put option will normally fall. This combination of positions is a straddle.

Straddles often consist of a stock position and a position in options on that stock. A straddle may also be made up entirely of options.

Example: A straddle might consist of a short position in January calls on XYZ and a long position in April calls on the same stock. Another possible straddle would be a long position in puts at $95 and a short position in puts at $105.

Short against the box. Based on the general definition, you would expect the straddle rules to apply if you hold stock in a company and also have a short position in the same stock—in other words, you're short against the box. This combination of positions is *not* a straddle, however. There are special rules, explained in Chapter 12, to cover the situation where you're short against the box. The straddle rules don't apply to stock unless you also hold a position in an option on that stock.†

Covered calls. We'll see below that if you engage in the common practice of selling calls on stock you own, these *covered calls* may or may not result in straddles. Even if they don't result in straddles, you may be subject to some of the rules that apply to straddles.

---

* There are other combinations of positions that create presumed straddles. The one mentioned here is of primary interest for our purposes.
† In some circumstances you may be treated as if you have an option on a stock because you have an option on a related stock, such as the stock of a company that is about to be acquired by the company whose stock you hold.

Interests owned by others. You can have a straddle because of an offsetting position owned by your spouse, or by a partnership or other entity you own. For example, if you hold shares of XYZ and your spouse holds an option to sell XYZ (a *put* option), the two of you collectively hold a straddle, and the rules described here will apply.

Loss Deferral

If you have a loss from selling or closing one position of a straddle, you have to determine whether that loss is allowed under the special rules that apply to straddles. The first step is to apply the wash sale rule explained in Chapter 6. If the regular wash sale rule disallows your loss, then that's the rule that applies and you don't have to go any further. You look at the special rule for straddles only if you have a loss that isn't disallowed by the regular wash sale rule.

The special rule reduces your remaining loss deduction (the part that isn't affected by the regular wash sale rule) by the amount of unrecognized gain you have in certain other positions as of the end of the year. You have *unrecognized gain* if selling or closing the position at fair market value would produce a gain. For example, if you made a short sale of XYZ at $60 and the stock is trading at $70 at the end of the year, you have unrecognized gain of $10 per share in your short position if it remains open.

There are three types of positions that can have unrecognized gain:

- Offsetting positions,
- Successor positions, and
- Offsetting positions to successor positions.

Offsetting positions are the positions that caused you to have a straddle in the first place. These are positions you held at the same time as the position that produced the loss, where the value of the position normally changes in the opposite direction to the position that produced the loss.

Example: You sold short 100 shares of XYZ and also bought a call option permitting you to buy 100 shares of XYZ. You close the short position at a loss of $800. The value of the call option normally changes in the opposite direction of the short stock position, so it's an offsetting position.

At the end of the year you still hold the call option and it's trading at $5 per share more than the amount you paid. That means the call option has $500 of unrecognized gain. You can report only $300 of your loss from the short position. The rest is deferred until next year.

Here's where things get really technical. A *successor position* is a position (P) that meets all of the following requirements:

- P was at any time offsetting to another position (the "second position").

- The second position was offsetting to any position you sold or closed at a loss.

- You entered into P within 30 days before or after you sold or closed the loss position.

- You entered into P no later than 30 days after the loss position was no longer included in a straddle.

If you're an ordinary mortal, that's enough to make your head swim. The basic idea, though, is to extend the wash sale rule to cover situations where you trade in and out of positions that offset the same position.

Example: You hold 100 shares of XYZ stock, and also hold an option to sell 100 shares of XYZ stock (a put option). These are offsetting positions, so you hold a straddle.

You sell your put option at a loss and, within 30 days after that sale, sell a call option on your XYZ stock. As the seller of a call option, you once again hold a position that is offsetting to the stock, which you continue to hold.

If you still have the position in the call option at the end of the year, and you have unrecognized gain in that position, the loss you can claim from selling the put option will be reduced by the unrecognized gain in this position.

The third situation where your loss is reduced or eliminated is when you have a unrecognized gain in a position that's offsetting to a successor position. The definitions above for offsetting and successor positions apply to this rule.

Example: You hold shares of XYZ and also an option to sell XYZ, creating a straddle. You sell the put option at a loss on June 10. On June 20 you sell the stock at a gain. On June 30, you again buy stock in XYZ. The stock purchase doesn't create a wash sale because your previous sale of the stock was at a gain, not a loss. Yet the new stock position is a *successor position* to the previous stock position—and that position was offsetting to the put option, which created the loss. As a result, your loss will be reduced or eliminated if you have an unrecognized gain in the new stock position at the end of the year.

Treatment of disallowed loss. If you have a loss that's disallowed under this rule, it's carried over to the next year. To claim the loss, you have to dispose of the position that caused it to be disallowed. You also have to apply the rule described above to make sure the loss you carried over isn't disallowed because of unrecognized gain at the end of the second year in an offsetting position, a successor position, or a position that's offsetting to a successor position.

Loss Treated as Long-Term

Even if your loss isn't disallowed under the rules described above, the straddle rules may require you to treat a short-term loss as a long-term loss. This rule applies to any loss from disposition of a position in a straddle if both of the following are true:

- You held one or more offsetting positions when you acquired the position that produced the loss, and

- You would have had long-term gain or loss if you sold any offsetting position on the day you acquired the position that produced the loss.

Example: You've held XYZ stock more than a year when you buy an option to sell XYZ stock. Two months later you sell the put option at a loss. Although you held the put option less than a year, you have to treat the loss as a long-term loss, because you held an offsetting position (the stock) more than a year before you acquired the put option.

Holding Period Rule

Here's a rule that trips people up fairly often. If you hold a position as part of a straddle, and you didn't have a long-term holding period for the position before it became part of a straddle, your holding period for that position doesn't begin until you no longer hold an offsetting position. In other words, if you want long-term gain when you sell a position that was part of a straddle, you have to hold it for at least a year and a day after you terminate the straddle.

Example: You made a good investment when you bought XYZ stock ten months ago: it has doubled in value. You want to hold the stock long enough for a long-term gain, but you're afraid the market in this stock is ready to pull back. If you aren't aware of the straddle rules, you might buy a put option, to protect against a decline in the price of the stock, then sell both positions when you've held the stock more than a year. The put option creates a straddle, so this strategy leaves you with a short-term capital gain.

What's more, if you sell the put option and continue to hold the stock, you won't get credit for the 10 months you held the stock before you created the straddle. To get a long-term gain, you have to start over again, holding the stock more than a year after you sold the put option.

Carrying Charges

If you incur interest or other costs with respect to a position in a straddle, in excess of any taxable income you have from a straddle (such as dividends on stock that's part of the straddle), you aren't allowed to deduct that amount. Instead, you have to add it to the basis of the straddle position.

> **Example:** You take out a margin loan to buy XYZ stock, and you also buy an option to sell that stock, creating a straddle. Interest on the margin loan (reduced by dividends paid by this stock, if any) is not deductible. Instead, you have to add the interest expense to the amount you paid for the stock when you sell it.

Covered Call Options

There's one straddle-like transaction that's often used by professional investment managers and others with market savvy: covered call options. The idea is to sell call options on stock you already own. You receive a cash payment—the option *premium*—when you sell the call option. If the option expires unexercised, as is often the case, you get to keep the premium, which increases your overall investment return. At the same time, you set the strike price of the option high enough so that if it *is* exercised, you'll be happy with the profit you receive on the sale.

> - This brief description may make it sound as if it's easy to enhance your investment return by selling covered calls. It isn't quite that easy though, so you should make certain you have good knowledge of this area before venturing forth.

The people who wrote the straddle rules were aware that there's a legitimate investment practice that involves selling covered calls. They didn't want the straddle rules to punish people who engaged in that practice, so they wrote an exception for *qualified covered calls*. This exception doesn't apply to *all* covered calls. It applies only to *qualified* covered calls, as defined below. What's more, even if you sell only qualified covered calls, some aspects of the straddle rules described above may apply to you.

General rule. In general, your positions aren't treated as a straddle if you sell options that are *qualified covered call options* on stock you hold, provided that those positions aren't part of a larger straddle. Subject to exceptions below, this rule for qualified covered calls avoids all the problems described above: loss deferral, loss treated as long-term, the holding period rule and the rule for carrying charges.

Special year-end rule. There's one situation where the loss deferral rule described above applies, even if your investment positions consist of stock and qualified covered calls. It's designed to prevent you from claiming a loss from one position just before the end of the year, when you plan to dispose of the other position just after the end of the year. The loss deferral rule applies to a straddle that consists of stock and a qualified covered call if all of the following are true:

- You dispose of either position (the stock or the call position) at a loss.

- You have gain on the other position in a different taxable year.

- You held the other position less than 30 days after disposing of the loss position.

Definition of qualified covered call. There are five requirements for an option position to be a qualified covered call, but you only have to worry about two of them:

1. You sell the option more than 30 days before its expiration date, and

2. The option is not *deep in the money.**

The first part is easy, but the definition of *deep in the money* is highly technical. What's more, we'll see at the end of this section that even if the option you sell isn't deep in the money, certain aspects of the straddle rules can apply if your option is even *slightly* in the money.

First you have to know what we mean when we say an option is in the money. There's a very precise definition that applies just for purposes of these rules. An option is in the money if the strike price is lower than the *applicable strike price.*

Generally, the *applicable stock price* is the closing price on the day before you sold the option. But if the stock opened on the day you sold the option at a price greater than 110% percent of the previous day's closing price, then the opening price is the applicable stock price.

Before we go on, let me point out that you'll save yourself a lot of brain damage if you never sell call options with a strike price below the applicable stock price. When you do that, you don't have to worry about whether your option is deep in the money, because it isn't in the money at all. You also don't have to worry about the special rules, described later, for qualified covered calls that are in the money when issued.

---

* The other requirements are: (3) the option is traded on a national securities exchange, (4) you aren't an options dealer, and (5) your gain or loss on the option is capital gain or loss.

Deep in the money. Unless you have a perverse love of complexity, you're going to just *hate* the definition of *deep in the money.* Here it is, in all its glory:

An option is deep in the money if its strike price is lower then the lowest qualified benchmark. Generally, the lowest qualified benchmark is the highest available strike price that's less than the applicable stock price (as defined above). However, the lowest qualified benchmark for an option with a term of more than 90 days and a strike price of more than $50 is the *second* highest available strike price that's less than the applicable stock price. Also, if the applicable stock price is $25 or less, the lowest qualified benchmark can't be less than 85% of the applicable stock price. Furthermore, if the applicable stock price is $150 or less, the lowest qualified benchmark can't be more than $10 below the applicable stock price.

Got that? We'll have a quiz in the morning.

Qualified covered calls that are in the money. Apart from avoiding having to deal with that horrible definition, there's another reason to avoid selling call options that are in the money. Two special rules apply to qualified covered call options that are in the money when issued:

- If you held the stock long-term before selling the call option, then any loss you have on the option will be long-term capital loss. This is the same rule that applies to straddles in general.

- Your holding period for the stock doesn't include the time the option was outstanding. This is *not* the same as the usual rule for straddles. Under the usual rule, your holding period *starts over* when you no longer have a straddle. In this case, the holding period is interrupted while the straddle is in place, but then resumes.

Part IV
Asset Transfers

This part of the book covers topics that easily could be the subject of an entire book. Here are the main things you need to know about tax rules for gifts, custodial accounts for minors, and charitable gifts of stock.

Part IV Asset Transfers

Chapter 17
Tax Rules for Gifts

This chapter tells what you need to know if you make or receive what I call *financial gifts*—in other words, gifts of cash, stock or other financial assets. Actually, the rules here apply to non-financial gifts as well. For example, you may have to file a gift tax return if you give your child an automobile. In this chapter you'll learn:

- How gifts are treated under the income tax.

- How the "unified transfer tax" applies to gifts and estates.

- How the annual gift tax exclusion works, and what other exclusions are available.

Gifts and Income Tax

Before we turn to gift tax, let's take a look at how gifts affect your income tax.

Recipient doesn't report income. Gifts you receive aren't considered income. You don't report them on your income tax return in any way. There are two important qualifications on this simple rule.

- **True gifts.** This rule applies only to true gifts. You can't avoid paying income tax by calling something a gift when it isn't. For example, a "gift" you receive in exchange for services or some other consideration isn't a gift.

- **Income after gift.** If you receive a gift of property that produces income, you must report any income produced after the gift. For example, if you receive stock as a gift, you must report any dividends paid on that stock after the gift.

No deduction except for charitable gifts. Some people hear that you can make an annual gift to a child "tax-free" and wonder if this means they can claim a deduction for such gifts. I'm afraid the answer is no. There is no deduction for gifts—except gifts to qualifying charities as explained in Chapter 19. The annual exclusion allows you to avoid paying *gift tax*. It does not affect your *income tax*.

Basis and holding period. If the gift consists of property other than cash, it's important for the recipient to know the basis and holding period of the property. That way the recipient knows how much gain or loss to report on a sale, and whether the gain or loss is short-term or long-term. Chapter 7 provides an explanation of the rules for determining basis and holding period for property received as a gift.

The Unified Transfer Tax

Federal estate and gift tax work hand in hand. Gifts you make during your lifetime can affect the amount of estate tax that's owed at your death.

To understand this, begin with the estate tax. This tax generally doesn't kick in until you leave more than $1,500,000 to someone other than your spouse or a charity.* The way this works is there is a *credit* that applies against the estate tax, to wipe out the tax that would otherwise apply to the first $1,500,000 of taxable estate.

This same credit is used against the gift tax.† If you make a taxable gift, you don't actually pay tax on the gift unless the total amount of taxable gifts in your lifetime is greater than $1,500,000. Because the same credit is used

---

* This is the dollar amount for deaths occurring in 2004 and 2005. If the tax law remains unchanged, the amount will increase to $2,000,000 in 2006 and $3,500,000 in 2009. What happens after that is anyone's guess.

† However, the $1,500,000 gift tax credit is not scheduled to increase when the estate tax credit rises above $1,500,000.

for both taxes—it's called the *unified credit*—any part of the credit that gets used up because of taxable gifts will reduce the amount of credit that's available for your estate when you die.

For wealthier individuals, it often makes sense to use the unified credit during their lifetime. But you don't want to use it unnecessarily if you think there's any chance your taxable estate will be more the $1,500,000. That's where the annual gift exclusion comes in.

Gifts Tax Annual Exclusion

Under the gift tax you can give an annual amount to each donee each year without reporting a taxable gift. The amount is adjusted for inflation in $1,000 increments. As of 2004 the annual amount is $11,000. If you're married, you and your spouse can jointly give twice that amount per donee each year, even if the entire gift comes from just one of you. (To do this, you and your spouse must file gift tax returns and elect "gift-splitting.") You can use this rule to remove a large dollar amount of assets from your estate without incurring any gift tax or reducing your unified credit.

> **Example:** Suppose you're married and have three adult children, each of whom is married. Each year, you can give $22,000 to each child, and the spouse of each child, for total gifts of $132,000 per year without any gift tax implications.

This exclusion applies only to gifts that take effect right away, called gifts of *present interests*. If you want to make your gift through a trust, you need to have an expert make certain the trust contains provisions that will prevent your gift from being a *future interest*. Trusts that meet this requirement are often called *Crummey trusts*, named after a case that clarified the tax treatment of this type of trust.*

---

* A lawyer I know brags that his trusts are the crummiest you'll ever see.

You can also make gifts of present interests through a custodial account under the Uniform Transfers to Minors Act. These gifts are considered present interests (and therefore qualify for the annual gift tax exclusion) even though the minor does not gain control until age 18 or 21. See Chapter 18 for more about custodial accounts.

Other Exclusions

The annual exclusion isn't the only way to make gifts without incurring gift tax. There's an unlimited exclusion for gifts to your spouse. (An annual limit applies if your spouse is not a United States citizen, but it's about ten times the usual gift tax exclusion.) There's also an unlimited exclusion for the payment of medical expenses or educational costs, provided you make these payments directly to the service provider or educational institution.

Chapter 18
Custodial Accounts for Minors

People with children (or other young relatives) sometimes think of setting up investment accounts for kids. State laws make it easy to set up *custodial accounts* for minors and relatively simple to administer them. A custodial account can be an excellent way of introducing a minor to the world of investing, or establishing a fund that helps a young adult get started. These accounts have drawbacks, however, so you should make sure you understand what you're getting into before putting a lot of money in a custodial account.

Custodial Account Basics

A minor child can't maintain a brokerage account, even with the permission of his or her parents. Only persons who have reached the *age of majority*—18 in most states—can buy and sell stocks. Many years ago, the only way to transfer stock ownership to a child was to establish a trust. Custodial accounts are designed to provide a simpler and less costly way of transferring stock and other assets to a child.

Each state has its own law for custodial accounts. The laws are based on a model called the Uniform Transfers to Minors Act, and custodial accounts are often called UTMA accounts.* The laws are uniform in the sense of being based on the same model, but they differ in various details. In particular, not all states use the same age of maturity to transfer control of assets to the child. In some

---

* Nearly all states have replaced the earlier Uniform *Gifts* to Minors Act with the more modern Uniform *Transfers* to Minors Act, but some people still refer to *UGMA* accounts from force of habit.

states, the child gets the assets at age 18, in others at age 21, and in some states the person who sets up the account can choose between these two ages. Comments here about the "Act" refer to the model on which the state laws are based. Your own state's law may differ.

Ownership. The first important thing to understand about custodial accounts is that *the child owns the assets.* Even though control of the assets has not yet passed to the child, *ownership* has passed as soon as you put money or other assets into a custodial account. *Custodial assets belong to the child.* That simple fact answers many of the questions people have about custodial accounts:

Q: *Can I take back the money I transferred to the account?*

A: No, the child owns that money now.

Q: *Can I move money from an account set up for one child to another child's account?*

A: No, because the money in a child's account belongs to that child.

Q: *Who pays tax on the account's income and gains?*

A: The child does, because the child is the owner of the account's assets.

Custodian. Although the child is owner of the account, control of the assets is in the hands of the *custodian.* The custodian can be, but doesn't have to be, the person who transferred cash or other property to the account.* The custodian has several responsibilities:

- The custodian must prudently invest the custodial assets.

- The custodian must maintain records of all transactions and provide tax information to the child

---

* If estate planning is a concern, someone transferring property to an account for his or her child should not be the custodian.

or, if the child is too young, to the person responsible for filing the child's tax return.

• The custodian determines what expenditures to
make on behalf of the child from account assets.

• When the child reaches the age specified by the
relevant state law, the custodian must turn the
account over to the child.

When Custodial Accounts Are Suitable

Custodial accounts are a wonderful convenience when
used for suitable purposes. Yet many people who set up
these accounts end up regretting that they did. Here are
some of the main reasons for what I call *UTMA regret*:

• The account was intended for the child's education, but the child has other ideas about how to
use it, and will obtain full control at age 18.

• Parents who contributed to the account find that
they need cash to buy a new house or for some
other reason, but can't use this account because it
belongs to their child.

• The account established for the first child made
some fortunate investments and is now far larger
than the account established years later for a
younger sibling, and there's no way to equalize the
accounts.

• The account reduces the amount of student financial aid the child qualifies for in college, to a much
greater extent than if the parents held the same
assets.

Before you set up a custodial account, ask yourself *why*.
There are certainly some good reasons to do this. You
may want to introduce the child to principles of investing
by letting him or her participate in investment decisions
and see how the account grows. You may want to provide
the child with a nest egg with which to be "launched" into

adulthood—bearing in mind that the child may not be mature enough to handle this sum of money well, and may have to chalk up a waste of these funds to experience.

What's more, custodial accounts can produce tax savings by shifting income into the child's tax bracket. You can shift capital gains to the child, too, even when the property increased in value before you made the gift. We'll see in Chapter 29 that the tax savings from shifting income and capital gains are quite limited for children under age 14. Once your child reaches that age, the tax savings from having investment income and capital gains taxed at your child's tax rate can be quite substantial, adding to the other joys of having a teenage child.

You should think twice before accumulating large amounts of money in a custodial account, however. These accounts are not well designed for estate planning. They adversely affect eligibility for student financial aid. They place the child in complete control of financial assets at an age when the child may have foolish ideas about how to handle them.

There are better alternatives for setting aside larger dollar amounts. Trusts are a little more complicated than custodial accounts but provide protections in terms of how and when the money is used, and also can be far better vehicles for estate planning. If you simply want to save for college in a way that makes more sense than using a custodial account, consider using one of the many 529 plans* that have sprung up in recent years, or a Coverdell education savings account. Then again, you can simply keep the assets in your own name, perhaps in a separate account that you intend to turn over to your child or use for the child's benefit.

Let me emphasize that I'm not *anti-UTMA*. I have custodial accounts for my own children. Yet I'm amazed at the number of messages received at my web site from

---

* The best information available on these plans can be found at www.savingforcollege.com.

people who regret setting up these accounts. It's a lot easier to get into that situation than to get out of it.

Using Custodial Accounts

UTMA accounts are not just for investing. The custodian is allowed to use money in the account for the benefit of the minor. Specifically, the Uniform Act says:

> A custodian may deliver or pay to the minor or expend for the minor's benefit so much of the custodial property as the custodian considers advisable for the use and benefit of the minor, without court order and without regard to (i) the duty or ability of the custodian personally or of any other person to support the minor, or (ii) any other income or property of the minor which may be applicable or available for that purpose.

That's a pretty liberal standard! An earlier version of the Act contained the words, "for the support, maintenance, education and benefit of the minor," leading some people to believe custodial property could be used only for items that would constitute *support*. The current version, which is in effect in nearly all states, uses the more generous words, "for the use and benefit of the minor." Official commentary on the Act says this change was "intended to avoid the implication that the custodial property can be used only for the required support of the minor."

> • **Note:** As custodian, you're supposed to be able to account for where the money went. If you pulled money from the account to buy a computer for your child, make a permanent record of this fact.

Here are some of the questions that come up most often:

Support. Some people have the idea you can't use a custodial account to cover expenses that fall within a parent's support obligation. If you read the language quoted above, you'll see that it clearly permits use of the account *without regard to the duty of any person to* *support the child.* We'll see below that there's at least a theoretical tax issue if you use the account to satisfy a support obligation, but the Uniform Act says that if the custodian uses the account for the minor's benefit, it doesn't matter if the custodian or someone else has a support obligation.*

Costs of education. *Of course* you can use these accounts to pay for the child's education. That's probably the biggest single use. For reasons explained above, I don't think this is the best way to save for college, but if you want to use a custodial account for college costs (or costs of primary or secondary education) that's clearly proper.

Car for the child. Your child needs an auto? Why not? It's an expenditure for the benefit of the child.

Paying taxes on the child's income. The child owns the account, and is liable for tax on any income the account generates. Since the child owes the tax, a withdrawal from the account to pay the tax is a payment for the benefit of the child.

Transfer to another child. Sometimes one child ends up with an account that's larger than the parent can provide for a sibling, due to a later start or a difference in the way the account was invested. Can you make a transfer from one account to the other to "even things up"? As a parent I sympathize with the motive, but I can't see how that's proper under the Act. The child with the larger account *owns* the account. Taking money from that account to transfer to a sibling's account may, in some philosophical way, be for the benefit of both children. Yet I believe the Act requires a more direct benefit to the child who owns the account.

Paying family expenses. You can get into some tough issues here. Suppose tapping the account is the only way the parent can afford to live in a nice neighborhood. Sup-

---

* Using the account to make child support payments to a former spouse might be considered improper, however.

pose further that the reason the parent wants to live in the nice neighborhood is better schools and environment for the child. Can you charge rent from the child and pay it from the account? Use the account for part of the down payment on a home? If push came to shove I would have to say these types of expenditures are probably improper under the Act, but others may disagree.

Tax Treatment of Custodial Accounts

In nearly all cases, a transfer to a custodial account is a gift.* The tax treatment of gifts is discussed in Chapters 7 and 17. Apart from tax consequences that apply to gifts in general, there are no special tax rules for transfers to custodial accounts. There is no limit on the amount that can be transferred in this way.

As mentioned briefly earlier, you have to report income and gains from custodial accounts as income of the minor. The tax law treats the child exactly as if he or she had direct control of the assets, with no custodian intervening.

Generally, withdrawals from custodial accounts have no significance at all. Of course, if you sell assets to make the withdrawal, gain or loss from the sale will appear on the child's tax return for the year of the sale. Also, the custodian should maintain records of all amounts withdrawn from the account and how those amounts were used. There's no tax reporting for the withdrawals per se, though.

Many years ago, the IRS issued a ruling saying that if custodial assets are used to satisfy a support obligation, income of the account is taxable to the person having the support obligation. How much do you need to worry about this? Not much, I believe. The Act specifically says that payments made from a custodial account for the benefit of the minor don't affect the support obligation of any person. This language was included specifically to

---

* A custodial account may also be used to hold assets the child inherits, or even money the child earns.

prevent attribution of income. While the issue hasn't been tested in court, it appears unlikely that income from a custodial account would be taxed to a person other than the minor under this old ruling.

Chapter 19
Charitable Gifts of Stock

At some point you're likely to hear that charitable gifts of stock can provide better tax benefits than charitable gifts of cash. (I hear this all the time from my law school alumni association.) There are a few things you should know if you're planning such a gift.

Overview

If you give cash to a qualified charity, and you choose to claim itemized deductions on your tax return, you can deduct your charitable contribution up to a limit: 50% of your adjusted gross income.

> **Example:** You contribute $20,000 to charity in 2004. Assuming your adjusted gross income is greater than $40,000, you can claim the entire $20,000 as a deduction. If your adjusted gross income for the year turned out to be $36,000, you would deduct $18,000 in 2004 and "carry forward" the remaining $2,000 as a possible deduction in 2005.

If you give stock instead of cash, you may be able to deduct the full value of the stock, even though you bought the stock at a lower value and never paid tax on the gain.

> **Example:** You bought 200 shares of XYZ in 1998 for $8,000. The shares are now worth $20,000. If you contribute the shares to charity, you can claim a charitable contribution deduction of $20,000 even though you never paid tax on your $12,000 gain.

That's an important advantage. If you sold the stock instead of contributing it to charity, you would probably pay federal income tax of about $1,800. Then you would have only $18,200 left to contribute to charity. You would contribute a smaller amount to charity, and receive a smaller charitable contribution deduction. Giving the stock allows you to provide a larger benefit to the charity *and* claim a larger tax deduction.

Important Details

Giving shares of stock to charity is a perfectly legitimate way of obtaining a tax benefit from your contributions. In planning such a contribution, keep the following points in mind:

- **It's still a contribution.** This form of contribution gives you more bang for your charitable buck—but the tax benefits are not so great that you come out ahead of where you would be if you didn't make the contribution. If you're inclined to make a charitable contribution, it makes sense to get the best possible tax result from that contribution, but don't forget the value of what you're giving away is still greater than the tax benefits.

- **Appreciated stock only.** There's no special tax advantage in giving away stock that hasn't gone up in value. In fact, if stock has gone down in value, it's generally better to sell the stock and make a gift of the proceeds. That way you can claim a deduction for your capital loss on the stock.

- **Long-term shares only.** This is an important point that some financial advisors forget: you get a tax benefit only if you held the stock more than a year before making the contribution. In the example above where you bought the stock for $8,000 and contributed it when it was worth $20,000, your deduction would be only $8,000 if you held the stock a year or less at the time of the contribution.

- **Stock from options.** If you acquired stock by exercising an incentive stock option, a charitable gift of this stock may not be good tax planning, even after you've satisfied the special holding period for this type of stock. The reason is that a sale of this stock may help you recover a credit for the AMT you paid when you exercised the option.

- **Lower limit applies.** The limit on charitable contribution deductions is lower for property than for cash. As mentioned earlier, your deduction for cash gifts is limited to 50% of your adjusted gross income. For gifts of property, the limit is 30% of your adjusted gross income. If you make $100,000 and give more than $30,000 worth of stock or other property, you'll have to claim only part of your contribution as a deduction and carry the rest forward for possible deduction in a later year.

Unfortunately, the tax rules for charitable contributions are just as complicated as tax rules for anything else. The summary above would change, for example, if you were making a contribution to a *private foundation* instead of a public charity. There are many other rules relating to charitable contributions. If you're planning to make a very substantial gift, it may pay to have a tax professional with expertise in this area review your plans.

Part V
Taxation of Traders

We turn now to the tax treatment of those individuals who qualify as *traders* under the tax law. You may be a trader if you engage in a large enough volume of short-term trades, consistently enough over a long enough period of time. People who qualify as traders avoid some of the rules that restrict tax benefits of investors, and as a result may end up paying less tax on the same amount of income.

Part V Taxation of Traders

Chapter 20
Introduction to Trader Status

Almost from the very beginning of the income tax, the courts and the IRS have divided taxpayers who buy and sell stocks into three categories: investors, dealers and traders. *Investors* generally seek to profit by *holding* stocks: they look for dividends or rising stock prices, or both. *Dealers* seek to profit from transactions in which they sell securities to customers: they buy stock to sell it as inventory, not for the purpose of obtaining investment returns.

Traders make up the third category. They seek their profits in short-term price swings. They may have little or no interest in the outlook for the company they're trading because they don't hold shares for long periods. Traders have been known to trade a stock without knowing anything at all about a company except the stock symbol and the recent trading patterns. Yet traders aren't dealers because they don't have customers. They buy and sell to secure the profits they can from the stock market's zigs and zags.

Trader Definition

You're a trader if your activity of buying and selling stocks meets two requirements. First is the *trading activity test*. This test looks at the type of buying and selling you do. As outlined above, you pass this test if your trading approach is designed to capture short-term swings in stock prices. See Chapter 22 for more details on this test.

The second requirement is the *substantial activity test*. Here we're looking at how serious you are about trading. Do you consistently do enough trading over a long enough period of time so we can consider your activity a business? Or is it merely something you do on the side, albeit with a hope of scoring some big profits? Chapter 23 provides details on this test.

You aren't a trader unless you pass both tests. We'll see later that there are a number of cases where taxpayers engaged in very substantial market activity, yet failed to qualify as traders because their activity was investing, not trading. Likewise, there are cases where the taxpayer may have done some trading, looking for short-term market swings, but wasn't considered a trader because the volume of trading wasn't large enough over a long enough period of time.

Someone who fails either test is considered an *investor*. The term makes sense when you fail the trading activity test, because that means you're seeking investment returns, usually by making relatively long-term investments. Yet the term also applies when you fail the substantial activity test. This is a strange use of the term, because it may apply to someone who never holds stock more than an hour at a time. If that's your approach, you're not much of an investor in the normal sense of that word. Under the tax law, though, if you don't pass the substantial activity test you're not a trader, and that means you're treated as an investor.

Tax Treatment of Traders

The tax law treats traders in some ways the same as investors, and in other ways better than investors. They are the same as investors in the following respects:

- Profits and losses from buying and selling stocks are capital gain or loss, not ordinary income or loss.

- Brokerage commissions are used in computing gains and losses, not as a separate business deduction.

- Traders are subject to the wash sale rule.

- Traders don't pay self-employment tax on profits from trading stocks.

Yet there are important ways in which traders are treated differently from investors:

- Interest expense (usually margin interest) is a business expense, so it isn't subject to the investment interest limitation.

- For investors, many other investment expenses are limited or not allowed at all as a deduction. Traders may be able to claim these expenses as business deductions.

See Chapter 24 for more details on the tax rules for traders.

Mark-to-Market

Beginning in 1997, securities traders have been allowed to elect a special tax treatment called "mark-to-market" accounting. *You don't have to make this election to be considered a trader.* If you make the election, the following special tax rules apply:

- Any shares you hold at the end of the year are treated as sold on that date for an amount equal to the fair market value of the shares. You report any gain or loss that results from this deemed sale.

- The wash sale rule doesn't apply to your trading activity.

- Profits and losses from your trading activity are treated as ordinary income and loss, not capital gain and loss. Although your trading profits are ordinary income, they still are not subject to self-employment tax.

Chapter 25 provides details on the consequences of this election and how you make it.

Explaining Trader Taxation

The tax treatment of traders is unusual to the point of being almost unbelievable. Knowledgeable tax professionals who have never studied trader taxation are likely to look at the tax treatment described above and say it simply can't be right. So before we get into details of what the rules are, we'll look at details of how the rules came to be. Chapter 21 provides a complete explanation, and legal citations tax professionals can use to confirm that the treatment described here is correct.

Chapter 21
The Trader and the Platypus

When the first platypus was brought from Australia to England, people figured it had to be a hoax. Here was an animal that had to be considered a mammal because it had fur and fed its young on breast milk—yet it had a flat bill and webbed feet like a duck, and laid eggs. The idea was preposterous, and the more you knew about biology, the more likely it was you would refuse to believe such an animal existed.

At the risk of offending traders, I compare them to the duck-billed platypus, at least when it comes to taxes. The tax treatment of traders is a unique mixture of rules for investors and rules for businesses:

- Traders don't sell goods or services to customers, yet they're considered to have a business.

- Despite having a business, traders don't pay self-employment tax on their income.

- Traders report deductions on Schedule C (used for businesses) but report their trading income on Schedule D (used for capital gains and losses). As a result, Schedule C nearly always shows a loss, even when the trading activity is profitable.

The more you know about taxes, the stranger these characteristics seem. Like a mammal that lays eggs, trader taxation simply doesn't fit anything we know about the world. Many experienced tax professionals who lack specific knowledge of trader taxation simply refuse to believe the statements above can possibly be true.

What's worse, the specific knowledge needed to believe these statements isn't widespread. Trader taxation isn't part of the curriculum for any tax course I've seen. Very few texts even mention the subject. The only guidance available from the IRS appears in the instructions for certain forms, and even that wasn't available before they released forms for the year 2000. As a result, both within the IRS and without, misunderstanding and misinformation concerning traders is widespread, and we frequently see absurdly incorrect statements coming from sources that are normally quite reliable:

- For many years, the web site of one of the top accounting firms includes a statement that "according to recent cases" you can't be a trader unless you perform transactions for others. In reality the opposite is true: if you perform transactions for others, you aren't a trader as that term is used in the tax law.

- An individual who has many years of experience hosting the tax message board of a popular investment web site insisted the income of traders should be treated as ordinary income, not capital gain. Yet the law for more than 60 years has been that trading profits and losses are capital.

- A tax professional in New York City requests clarification of trader taxation from the IRS. The request goes to someone who lacks knowledge of trader taxation, and a letter comes back saying traders can't report gains and losses on Schedule D while taking expense deductions on Schedule C. According to this letter, "Such 'best of both worlds' treatment is clearly not allowed under the [Internal Revenue] Code and Regulations." At the same time the IRS was preparing this letter, another group within the IRS was preparing form instructions correctly stating that trader gains and losses go on Schedule D, while trader expenses go on Schedule C.

The people who made these blunders are not fools. In fact, they're highly trained professionals who normally provide accurate information—just like the biologists who confidently proclaimed that an egg-laying mammal must be a hoax. They are reacting to claims that seem absurd in light of their training.

Endangered Species

One reason for so much neglect of this subject is that most of the rules of trader taxation don't appear in the Internal Revenue Code and regulations. Instead, they appear in opinions issued by judges who decided scores of cases involving trader classification. When you need an answer about trader taxation, there's no convenient way to look it up.

There's another reason so few people have knowledge of trader taxation. Until recently, very few people were traders. In fact, it was almost impossible to be a trader without trading on the floor of an exchange. By definition, traders are people who buy and sell rapidly. That's a recipe to go broke in a hurry if you're paying high commissions, burdened with large spreads, and relying on outdated information, all of which were likely not long ago.

In recent years we've seen commissions fall to a small fraction of what they once were. The bid-ask spread is also much smaller than it was at one time. Real-time quotes and other current information are as close as the nearest Internet connection. It's still hard for someone other than a floor trader to make money trading in and out of stocks rapidly, but it's no longer impossible.

The result was an explosion in the number of people engaged in short-term trading during the bull market of the late 1990's. Not all of these people qualify as traders, but it's a safe bet that the number of people with a legitimate claim to that status in 2000 was many times the number in 1990. The IRS has provided us with some basic guidance in the instructions for tax forms, beginning in the year 2000. Yet we're still faced with a situation where many skilled tax practitioners are puzzled by the seemingly bizarre tax rules that apply to traders. The remainder of this chapter explains how these rules came to be as they are. We'll also look at the frequently made comment that these rules can't be correct because they're "too good to be true."

The Bike Man Cometh

From the very beginning of the income tax we've had to distinguish between business activities and non-business activities. For example, you can deduct expenses if you raise dogs as a business, but if you raise dogs as a hobby your deductions are limited to income from that activity. Sometimes it's hard to draw the line between business and non-business, but the line must be drawn because it determines how much tax you pay.

Early decisions by the Board of Tax Appeals (predecessor of today's Tax Court) established that buying and selling stock for your own account can be a business. A good example is the *Ignaz Schwinn* case,* decided in 1928. Schwinn's last name is well known because he organized a successful bicycle manufacturing company. Yet during a number of years when that business was in low gear he spent more time playing the market (both stocks and commodities) than running the bicycle business. In 1924 he had a loss of nearly $70,000 on a sale of 2,300 shares of Anaconda Copper stock he bought in 1919. Under the law then in effect, Schwinn was entitled to a full deduction for this loss if it was connected with a business. The loss wasn't connected with the bicycle business, but the court found that Schwinn's trading activities were a business and allowed the loss.

Schwinn's loss wouldn't be allowed today. For one thing, he probably wouldn't be considered a trader, because his trading wasn't short-term (see Chapter 22). In addition, traders are now subject to the same capital loss limitations as investors, unless they make the mark-to-

---

* *Schwinn v. Commissioner*, 9 BTA 1304 (1928).

market election. We'll return to capital gain in a few moments. First, though, let's focus on an issue that gives fits to many tax professionals.

Trading for Your Own Account

The Board of Tax Appeals found that Ignaz Schwinn's market activity was a business, even though he was trading for his own account—in other words, not on behalf of his bicycle company or anyone else. He wasn't providing goods or services to anyone else: he was simply trying to make trading profits for himself. Some tax professionals will tell you this type of activity can't be a business. They believe you must have *customers*, or trade for others, to have a business.

Perhaps that notion comes from *Deputy v. duPont,** a famous tax case in which the United States Supreme Court denied deductions connected with the stock dealings of Pierre duPont. The Court said duPont incurred the expenses for the benefit of the corporation (not for his own benefit) and also that they weren't "ordinary and necessary" expenses, as required to claim a business deduction. In a concurring opinion, though, Justice Frankfurter said there was another, simpler reason to deny the deduction: to have a business, you must "hold [yourself] out to others as engaged in the selling of goods or services."

Justice Frankfurter's comment was strange because it was already firmly established, in cases like *Schwinn*, that trading for your own account can be a business. It doesn't seem likely that he intended his brief remarks to suggest that all those cases were incorrect. As we'll see shortly, Congress had recognized six years earlier, in connection with a change in the definition of capital assets, that a "stock speculator" may have a business for tax purposes. In any event, the courts never adopted the approach Justice Frankfurter suggested in his concurring opinion.

---

* *Deputy v. duPont*, 308 US 488 (1940).

The IRS made at least one attempt to apply the Frankfurter approach to a trader, but seemed to abandon that effort after losing the *Fuld* case in the Court of Appeals in 1943.* Some years later, the IRS tried to use this theory on professional gamblers, saying they can't claim business deductions because gamblers don't provide goods or services to customers. The IRS won some of these cases but lost others, and in 1987 the United States Supreme Court decided the *Groetzinger* case† to resolve the issue. The result was a resounding defeat for the IRS.

The opinion pointed out that the Supreme Court as a whole had never endorsed Justice Frankfurter's idea that a business had to have customers. Furthermore—and most important for our purposes—the opinion noted that traders, like gamblers, have no customers, yet they have long been considered to have a business. In fact, the IRS conceded as much in oral argument. The Court decided to "formally reject the Frankfurter gloss which the Court has never adopted anyway."

The *Groetzinger* case eliminates all argument on this issue. The Supreme Court could not have been more definitive in concluding that you can have a trade or business without having customers. What's more, although the case involved a gambler rather than a trader, it discusses trader cases and cites them with approval.

Too good to be true? What all this means is that traders—individuals who meet the requirements described in the following chapters—treat their expenses as business deductions. They avoid the limitations that apply to "miscellaneous" deductions of investors, and also avoid the investment interest expense limitation. To some tax professionals this seems too good to be true, if a trader is simply someone who buys and sells stock for his own account, as an investor does.

---

* *Fuld v. Commissioner,* 139 F2d 465 (2d Cir 1943), affirming 44 BTA 468 (1941).
† *Groetzinger v. Commissioner,* 480 US 23 (1987).

Yet that's what it *means* to be a trader. A trader is someone whose activity qualifies as a business under the tax law. That means a trader's expenses are business deductions, not investment deductions. If you believe traders shouldn't be permitted to claim business deductions, you're missing the entire point of trader classification: determining that the activity should be treated as a business.

Traders and Capital Gain

Tax professionals are used to the idea that business profits are ordinary income, not capital gain. If trading is a business, then the profits from trading can't be capital gain, right? Wrong.

In the early days, traders (or "speculators," as they were usually called then) did *not* have capital gains and losses. That was the point of the *Schwinn* case discussed earlier: the taxpayer wanted to avoid the limitation on capital losses. By establishing that his trading activity was a business, Ignaz Schwinn was able to claim a business deduction, not a capital loss, on his stock sale.

Congress decided the capital loss limitation should apply to traders, and accomplished this by changing the definition of *capital asset*. Before 1934, capital assets did not include "property held by the taxpayer primarily for sale in the course of his trade or business." The new definition used almost the same words, but now an asset was excluded only if it was held for sale *to customers*. The specific purpose of this change was to prevent stock speculators from avoiding the capital loss limitation.*

In making this change, Congress recognized that stock speculation—trading—can be a business, but specified that the profits and losses from the business would be treated as capital gains and losses. That fundamental approach to trader taxation remained unchanged for more than six decades, and is still in force except for

---

* For a discussion of this change in the law, see *Fuld v. Commissioner*, 139 F2d 465 (2d Cir 1943), affirming 44 BTA 468 (1941).

traders who make the mark-to-market election as explained in Chapter 25.

Too good to be true? Traders are treated as having a business, so they can claim business deductions, yet their profits are treated as capital gain. At first blush, this result seems too good to be true. If you stop and think for a moment you'll see that this isn't so. Trader profits are nearly all *short-term* capital gain, taxed at the same rates as ordinary income, so there's no benefit there. Yet trader losses are subject to the $3,000 per year capital loss limitation—a limitation that doesn't apply to other types of business losses. Capital gain treatment of trader profits is more harm than benefit because of the capital loss limitation. Avoiding this disadvantage is one of the main reasons for making the mark-to-market election (Chapter 25).

Self-Employment Income

Here's another place tax professionals—including some of the tax professionals who work for the IRS—sometimes go wrong. Normally, if you carry on a business, the net income from that business is subject to self-employment tax. This tax replaces the usual social security tax that applies when you work as an employee. It can be a heavy hit, because employers and employees each pay half of the social security tax. When you're self-employed, you're both the employer and the employee, so the self-employment tax is roughly double the social security tax you would pay as an employee.* It would potentially be a significant disadvantage of trader status if you had to pay that tax.

Yet the self-employment tax doesn't apply to trader income. This has always been true for traders whose income consists of capital gain, because the law quite plainly excludes capital gain from the definition of self-

---

* For technical reasons having to do with the deduction allowed for the employee portion you pay a little less than double when you pay self-employment tax.

employment income.* It's possible that a trader could have some incidental income that isn't capital gain. In the rare case where such income exceeds deductible expenses, the net amount would be subject to self-employment tax.

When Congress changed the law to provide the mark-to-market election for securities traders, there was some question as to whether traders who made the election would be subject to self-employment tax. That's because the election converts trading profits and losses into ordinary income or loss. Yet Congress didn't intend the self-employment tax to apply, even when traders make the mark-to-market election, so an amendment was adopted to clarify that even in this case, the income of a trader is not self-employment income.†

Too good to be true? The law is now perfectly clear that traders don't pay self-employment tax on their trading profits, regardless of whether they made the mark-to-market election. To many people it will seem as if traders are getting away with something. Yet there's a flip side to this rule. If trading profits aren't self-employment income, then traders can't use those profits to qualify for social security benefits. Those benefits are determined in part by the number of years worked and the amount paid in social security tax or self-employment tax, so a trader may end up with lower benefits than someone in a different type of business.

Perhaps more important, a trader can't use his or her trading profits as a basis for contributing to IRAs and other retirement plans. The generous tax treatment of retirement savings is one of the best deals available under the tax law. Many traders would be much better off if they could treat their trading profits as self-employment income and sock away money in a tax-qualified retirement plan. That's an opportunity traders simply don't have.

---

* Internal Revenue Code section 1402(a)(3)(A).
† Internal Revenue Code section 475(f)(1)(D).

Chapter 22
The Trading Activity Test

Many books on investing will tell you the best way to accumulate wealth is to buy good stocks and hold them long-term. Avoid "churning"—the frequent buying and selling that eats away at investment accounts. When you hold long-term, your expenses are lower, your taxes are lower, and you make a lot fewer mistakes.

If that's the way you operate, you may be a good investor but you aren't a trader under the tax law. The cases firmly establish that trader status is available only if your primary focus is the small zigs and zags that happen over minutes, hours and days. If your goal is to benefit from price changes that occur over months and years—or from other forms of investment income, such as interest and dividends—then you're an investor, not a trader. That's true no matter how much time you devote to your investments.

History

In the earliest cases, courts didn't always apply the trading activity test. The *Schwinn* case, described in Chapter 21, is a good example. The court found that the taxpayer's buying and selling of stocks and commodities was a business without seeming to focus on whether the trading was short-term. In fact, the issue in that case was how to treat a loss from stock held more than two years.

Not long after these early cases, the IRS began to assert that the activity of investing should not be considered a business even when people devote a great deal of time and energy to that activity. Taxpayers won some cases and lost others. In 1941, the Supreme Court decided to clear the air.

Eugene Higgins* had extensive investments in real estate, bonds and stocks, and devoted "a considerable portion of his time" to the oversight of these financial interests. In fact, he rented offices and hired others to help him by keeping records, receiving securities, interest and dividend checks, making deposits and so forth. The IRS said Higgins should not be allowed to deduct these expenses because they didn't arise in a business. The Supreme Court agreed:

> The petitioner merely kept records and collected interest and dividends from his securities, through managerial attention for his investments. No matter how large the estate or how continuous or extended the work required may be, such facts are not sufficient as a matter of law to permit the courts to reverse the decision [against the taxpayer].

After *Higgins*, it was reasonably clear that long-term investors could not qualify as traders. Every now and then someone would try to get around this requirement, but the courts stood firm.

The *Yaeger* case† provides a good example. Louis Yaeger's stock trading was so extensive that he maintained an office at his brokerage firm. He spent a full day at the office, then "returned home to read more financial reports late into the night," working every day of the week, right up until the day before he died.

Yet his activity was clearly investing, not trading. He had over 1,000 securities transactions per year, but nearly all of them were purchases with only a few sales. His investment strategy involved the purchase of distressed companies whose underlying value was not recognized. He had some short-term capital gains, but a far greater portion of his income was from dividends and long-term capital gains. Under the rule established in the *Higgins* case, Yaeger couldn't be considered a trader, so the court ruled for the IRS.

---

* *Higgins v. Commissioner*, 312 US 212 (1941).

† *Estate of Yaeger v. Commissioner*, 889 F2d 29 (2d Cir 1989).

How Short Is Short?

Many day traders sell all their holdings at the end of the day. Clearly their activity is trading, not investing. Yet you don't have to be a day trader to be a trader. Someone who often holds stocks several days at a time should still be considered a trader, not an investor.

Beyond this, though, there isn't a lot of guidance in the cases. The courts sometimes look at how much gain is long-term (more than a year), but my sense is that this is simply a convenient fact to mention in the opinion. I doubt that someone with an average holding period of nine months would be considered a trader, even though that's less than a year. A court is likely to conclude that when you hold stock that long, you're looking for an investment return, not a trading profit.

Does Strategy Matter?

In a doubtful case, the court might look beyond the holding period to consider the strategy. An average holding period of six weeks might come from following a short-term trading strategy based on technical analysis— or simply be the result of impatience or market turbulence affecting someone who is engaged in investing, not trading. Until we see cases of this nature, though, we can't be certain how the courts will approach them.

Other Investment Income

Some courts have noted the amount of other investment income the taxpayer had, as a way of indicating that his activity was investing, not trading. If the income from an activity was mostly interest, dividends and long-term capital gain, it might seem reasonable to conclude that the activity was investing, not trading.

I would suggest, though, that courts should distinguish between the amount of short-term capital gain and the amount of short-term *trading activity*. It's possible for a trader to end up with a very small profit (or even a loss) despite making over a hundred million dollars in trades. In this situation, the fact that interest income happened to be greater than the income from short-term trades should not be viewed as an indication that the individual is primarily an investor.

Traders as Investors

Can you be *both* an investor and a trader? There's no question that you can. It would be perfectly reasonable to set aside some of your assets as an investment fund that isn't part of your trading activity. If you otherwise qualify as a trader, you shouldn't lose that status because you also hold stocks as an investment.

If you fail to keep the two activities separate, though, you could cast doubt on whether you qualify as a trader. It might appear that your short-term trading is part of your investing, rather than a distinct activity. Furthermore, if you commingle the activities it may be difficult to allocate your expenses between investing and trading in a way that will satisfy the IRS.

For that reason, if you maintain investments at the same time you're trading, you should take care to keep the two activities separate. Your investments should not be in the same account you use for trading, and any expenses relating to your investment activity should be recorded as investment expenses, not trading expenses. If you make the mark-to-market election, you're required to *identify* your investment securities, as described in Chapter 25.

Chapter 23
The Substantial Activity Test

The late 1990's saw an explosion of interest in day trading: buying and selling stock within the same day, often within the same hour, in the hope of capturing very short-term movements in stock prices. There should be little doubt that day traders pass the trading activity test described in the preceding chapter. Yet they aren't considered traders for tax purposes unless they also pass the *substantial activity test*.

Frequent, Regular and Continuous

The substantial activity test is most often stated as a requirement that the trading activity be *frequent, regular and continuous*. These words don't establish a precise standard. Most of the cases dealing with this test are no-brainers—for example, situations where the taxpayer was obviously not a trader because he made fewer than 20 sale transactions per year. These cases give us only a limited amount of help in deciding where to draw the line between trading activity that does or does not qualify you as a trader. I've studied the cases, and here's what I make of them.

Number of Trades

Probably the most important factor in this test is the number of trades. If you trade only a few times per month, your trading probably isn't frequent enough to qualify you as a trader. For example, in the *Boatner* case,* 75 trades in a year fell short of this standard.

---

* *Boatner v. Commissioner*, TC Memo 1997-379.

How many trades are enough? There's no way to say with certainty. I imagine that 75 trades per *month* would easily qualify, although I can't point to a case that establishes this as a "safe" level for a trader. Assuming we could all agree that 75 trades per month qualifies as "frequent" trading, what about 50? Or 30? The cases provide no guidance on where to draw the line.

I heard one tax lawyer say that even a thousand trades per year probably isn't enough. She was probably thinking of the *Yaeger* case mentioned in the previous chapter. The taxpayer in that case wasn't a trader even though he had more than a thousand trades per year. Yet he failed to qualify because his primary activity was long-term investing. More than 90% of his trades were purchases. If he had made over a thousand short-term trades, I'm confident he would have been considered a trader. Don't confuse the trading activity test with the substantial activity test!

Consistent Activity

Remember that "frequent" is only one of the words used to describe activity that passes this test. Even if your trading is frequent, you may not qualify as a trader if your activity isn't "regular and continuous."

Although the courts have used these words repeatedly, I'm aware of only one case that illustrates how they may be applied. In the *Paoli* case,* the taxpayer made over 300 sales within a year. Most of the sales were stock held less than a month, and more than 100 were day trades: stock bought and sold the same day.

Possibly this level of activity would have qualified the taxpayer as a trader if he traded consistently throughout the year. Yet nearly 40% of the trades occurred in a one-month period, and the number of trades per month fell off sharply in the following months, with only one trade occurring in the last quarter of the year. The court con-

---

* *Paoli v. Commissioner*, TC Memo 1991-351.

cluded that this pattern of trading was inconsistent with trader status.

The *Paoli* case is important because it reflects a pattern that arises frequently. Many would-be traders launch their activity with gusto, engaging in a large number of trades only to find that they are rapidly losing money. A trader in this position may pull back and regroup, perhaps trying to trade more selectively in hopes of finding a more profitable approach. Eventually this person may drop out of the game altogether, and wonder whether he or she can at least salvage a good tax result by filing as a trader.

Arguably it would have been more appropriate in *Paoli* to conclude that the taxpayer was a trader *for part of the year*. Another court faced with similar facts might come to that conclusion.* If you find yourself in such a situation, though, you have to be prepared for the possibility that the IRS and the courts may find that you never qualified as a trader at all.

Part-Time Traders

It's hard to imagine someone failing the substantial activity test while trading on a full-time basis. Yet many people trade during only part of the day, while holding a full-time job that does not involve trading. It seems clear enough that trading can be "frequent, regular and continuous" even though it's carried on by someone who holds another job. I can't point to many recent cases where part-timers were found to be traders,† but there are cases where courts considered whether part-timers were traders and rejected their claims for other reasons.‡ If you can't be a trader on a part-time basis, these cases wasted a lot of time looking at other issues.

---

* *Paoli* was a "memorandum" decision of the Tax Court. This type of decision may be persuasive to another judge, but is not considered to be binding authority.

† In the *Carmel v. United States*, 134 BR 890 (Bkcy Ct ND Ill. 1991), the court found that a lawyer who was also a compulsive gambler was a trader.

‡ The *Paoli* and *Boatner* cases cited earlier are two recent examples.

Although it's clear that you can be a trader on a part-time basis, you have to expect greater skepticism regarding your status if trading isn't your main activity. To overcome that skepticism, you need to show you spend enough time at trading to indicate that you take the activity seriously as a business. I can imagine someone failing to qualify as a trader despite frequent trading if the amount of time devoted to the activity was negligible, perhaps because all trades were based on a tip sheet to which that person subscribes. Someone who trades less frequently but devotes a great deal of time to the activity might have better luck in securing trader status.*

Dollar Amount

A large dollar amount of trading isn't likely to qualify you as a trader if your trades are infrequent. This is likely to be a minor factor if it is considered at all. Yet a small dollar amount may indicate that you aren't serious about trading as a business, and could be a negative factor in a borderline case.

Professional Approach

You have a better shot at qualifying as a trader if you take a professional approach to the activity. It should be helpful if you can show that you made a careful study of trading before plunging in; that you keep good records; that you trade based on analysis of some kind, not mere hunches. Of course these factors are also likely to contribute to your success as a trader, so you should follow these procedures in any event.

---

* In the *Paoli* case the taxpayer tried to support his claim to trader status by saying he spent four hours per day on the activity throughout the year. The court rejected this testimony, perhaps finding it difficult to believe anyone could spend this much time on an activity that produced only one trade in a three-month period.

Chapter 24
How Traders Are Taxed

The tax rules for traders are unusual—unique, in fact. Yet for the most part they follow from two simple principles:

- A trader is considered to be carrying on a business, so traders are entitled to business deductions (rather than the deductions allowed for investors).

- Although traders carry on a business, their trading profits and losses are capital gain and loss, not ordinary business income and loss.

Chapter 25 describes the mark-to-market election, which changes some of the rules described here. Be sure to read that chapter if you've made this election. Chapter 21 explains how the rules described here came to be as they are and provides references tax professionals can use to confirm that the rules stated here are correct.

Declaring Trader Status

People ask how they declare to the IRS that they intend to be taxed as a trader. Sometimes they ask how they *elect* to be a trader for tax purposes. Actually, no election is required. In effect, you declare that you're a trader by filing a Schedule C (used to report business income and expenses), and indicating the type of business as "securities trader."

Business Deductions

When we call someone a trader, we're really saying his or her activity of buying and selling stock is a business. This is a simple point, but it's one where a lot of people, including knowledgeable tax professionals, get hung up.

To some people it simply seems illogical that this type of activity can qualify as a business. Yet that's exactly what we're looking at when we determine whether someone is a trader. *By definition*, a trader is someone whose trading activity is considered a business for tax purposes.

Investment deductions are allowed only if you claim itemized deductions on Schedule A. Even if you itemize, various restrictions may deny you some or all of the value of your investment expense deductions. See Chapter 11 for more about investment expense deductions.

These rules don't apply to the deductions a trader incurs in his or her trading activity. This activity is a business, so the trader claims business deductions on Schedule C.* Some important restrictions that apply to investment expense deductions don't apply to business deductions:

- A trader can claim business deductions without itemizing.

- A trader's expenses are not subject to the "2% floor" that applies to most investment expenses.

- A trader's interest expense isn't subject to the investment interest limitation described in Chapter 10.

- The rule against deducting investment seminar expenses does not apply to trading seminars if you're a trader.

- A trader who uses a computer or other equipment mainly for his or her trading business may be entitled to a deduction for the cost of that equipment.

- If a trader devotes part of his or her home to the trading activity, a home office deduction may be allowed.

---

* Beginning in the year 2000, a statement to that effect appears in the instructions for Schedule D.

230 Capital Gains, Minimal Taxes

Bear in mind that brokerage commissions and other costs of buying and selling shares are not considered business expenses. Instead, these costs figure into the gain or loss you have when you sell shares.

A full discussion of all the tax deductions you may be able to claim in connection with your trading activity would fill an entire book. See the Appendices at the end of this book for places you can look for more information.

Trading Profits and Losses

Your trading profits and losses are treated as capital gain or loss, even though your trading activity is a business. Way back in 1934 Congress changed the law to require this result, and it holds to this day unless you make the mark-to-market election as discussed in the following chapter. That means you report gains and losses from stock sales on Schedule D.

As a trader who hasn't made the mark-to-market election, you also have to deal with the wash sale rule (Chapter 6). At one time the wash sale rule didn't apply to individual traders. Unfortunately, Congress decided to change the law. The regulations still reflect the old law, but that's because they're out of date. It's clear that the wash sale rule applies.

Some traders engage in thousands of transactions per year, often trading the same stocks over and over again. Reporting each individual trade, and working through the application of the wash sale rule in each instance, is a colossal problem. The mark-to-market election provides a partial solution because it eliminates the wash sale rule. The only other solution I'm aware of is to maintain good records and use the best available software. The IRS may accept a computer printout in lieu of a stack of Schedule D-1 extension forms, but one way or another they expect to see the gain and loss on each individual transaction reported.

Self-Employment Income

Traders don't pay self-employment tax on their trading income because this tax doesn't apply to capital gains. In theory, a trader could generate enough incidental income other than trading gains to incur some self-employment tax liability, but I've never seen that happen. This is one of the unique and surprising aspects of trader taxation: although your activity is a business, the income isn't considered self-employment income.

IRAs and Retirement Plans

You may be happy about avoiding self-employment tax, but there's a flip side you won't like as much. You can't contribute to an IRA or a retirement plan unless you have compensation income or self-employment income. Your trading income isn't self-employment income, so you can't use it to support an IRA or retirement plan contribution. Unless you have some other source of compensation income, you'll have to save for retirement without the benefit of one of these arrangements.

Chapter 25
The Mark-to-Market Election

Since 1993, securities *dealers* have been required to use the *mark-to-market* system of accounting. Beginning in 1997, securities *traders* have been *permitted to elect* to use this system. If you're a trader and you make this election, your tax treatment will change:

- Any trading positions you hold at the end of the year will be treated as sold at fair market value on the last business day of the year, with the gain or loss reported just as if an actual sale occurred. This is what is meant by the term "mark-to-market."

- Gains and losses from your trading activity are treated as ordinary income and loss, not capital gain or loss.

- The wash sale rule does not apply to losses incurred in your trading activity.

You can probably tell right away that there are advantages and disadvantages to making the election. Avoiding the wash sale rule is certainly an advantage. What about the other two points?

Marking to Market

For a true day trader, the requirement to treat year-end positions as sold is meaningless. If you sell all your positions at the end of each day, you certainly aren't going to be holding any positions at the end of the year. Day traders should consider the mark-to-market election because of the other tax consequences, but the actual process of marking to market won't apply to them.

You don't have to be a day trader to be a trader under the tax law, however. If you make this election and hold positions at the end of the year, this rule will affect you. In particular, you lose the ability to defer the gain from a winning position into the following year by delaying a sale of that position. Losing this flexibility can be a disadvantage for some traders, but for most traders this rule is of little or no consequence.

Ordinary Income and Loss

We usually think of capital gain as a more desirable form of income than ordinary income. Yet for a trader, treatment of profits and losses as capital gains and losses is more likely to be a disadvantage. On the upside, gains are all or nearly all short-term capital gain (if not, you won't qualify as a trader), and that means paying tax at the same rate that applies to ordinary income. No advantage there to capital gain. On the downside, losses are subject to the capital loss limitation. This is a big disadvantage, because even good traders can have losing years. If you lose $50,000 and have to treat it as a capital loss, you can deduct only $3,000 in that year. You can carry the rest of your loss forward, but you can't carry it back. Unless you have capital gains in future years, it will take 17 years to make full use of your loss.

Avoiding the limit on capital losses is the main reason for considering the mark-to-market election. Eliminating the wash sale rule is important too, but the really big savings are in moving your losses from Schedule D to Form 4797. We'll see below that you have to make the election early in the year—before you know whether you have a loss for the year. You might say the election is an insurance policy against getting a bad tax result if you find yourself with a losing year.

Trapping Capital Losses

An important point to consider in making the election is whether you'll end up trapping capital losses you had from an earlier year. Suppose, for example, you lost

$30,000 during your first year as a trader. Because of the capital loss limitation, you were able to deduct only $3,000 of that loss. The remaining $27,000 carried forward to the present year. Now you're trading profitably, and considering the mark-to-market election for this year.

If your profitable trading continues, you might be better off *not* making the election. That way your profits will be capital gain, and you can absorb the $27,000 loss that was carried forward from the previous year. If you make the election, your profits will be ordinary income, and you'll be able to use only $3,000 of your loss carry-over. You'll carry the remaining $24,000 to the next year, but it may take another eight years to use the entire loss.

Of course, at the time you make the election you can't be certain how your year will turn out. (As you'll see below, you have to make the election early in the year.) If you have further losses, you may be glad you made the election, because it's easier to use ordinary losses than capital losses.

Self-Employment Income

Strangely enough, although the election converts your trading profits to ordinary income, you still don't have self-employment income. Congress felt that traders should be able to make this election without changing the status of their income for purposes of the self-employment tax, so a special exception provides that trading gains aren't self-employment income even if the trader makes this election and converts those gains to ordinary income.

Of course this means a trader who makes the election still can't use trading profits to support a contribution to an IRA or retirement plan. The two concepts go hand in hand. You avoid self-employment tax, but also lose the tax advantages of retirement plans.

Permanent Election

The mark-to-market election is permanent. It applies for the year you make the election *and all subsequent years*, unless the IRS grants permission to change the election. If your reason for wanting to terminate the election is to get a better tax result—for example, to absorb trapped capital losses—it's unlikely that the IRS will grant this permission.

Making the Election

Most accounting elections are permitted at the time you file your tax return for the year of the election. For example, if you want to make an accounting election for the year 2004, you're normally allowed to do that when you file your tax return in April of 2005. That's not the case for the mark-to-market election, though.

The IRS requires this election by the due date, *without extensions*, of the tax return for *the year before* the year for which the election is effective. For example, if you're making the election for the year 2004, you have to make it by April 15, 2004, which is the due date for your tax return for the year 2003. If you file your tax return on or before that date, you have to attach the election to your tax return. If not, you have to file a request for extension of time to file your return, and file the election with your extension request. *If you miss this deadline, you have to wait until the next year to file the mark-to-market election.*

The election itself is a simple statement that looks something like this:

John Doe
SSN 123-45-6789
2001 Form 1040

The taxpayer elects under section 475(f) of the Internal Revenue Code to use the mark-to-market method of accounting for his securities trading business beginning with the tax year commencing January 1, 2005.

The identifying information at the top should include your name and social security number, and the form number and year. If you file the election with your extension request, the form number is 4868, not 1040.*

Reporting Change of Accounting Method

In addition to filing the election as indicated, you may have to file Form 3115. This form is used to show a change of accounting. You don't file this form at the time you make the election, though. You have to make the election by the due date of the *previous* year's return, but you file Form 3115 with the return for the *current* year. For example, if you're making the election for the year 2004, you file the election by April 15, 2004 (the unextended due date of your 2003 tax return) and you file Form 3115 with your 2004 tax return in April, 2005.

Form 3115 is a delightful concoction of arcane questions, many of which only a tax professional can answer. The good news: only the first three pages of this eight-page monster apply to you. Here are some tips in grappling with Form 3115:

- The IRS recently did away with district directors, so it appears you'll have to leave a blank where the form asks about that.

- The type of accounting method change is "financial products."

- The answer to question 1 in Part 1 is "yes," and the citation is "Rev. Proc. 99-17." Note that because you're filing under an automatic procedure, you don't have to pay a user fee with this form.

- The answer to question 2 is *no.*

- Question 8 asks if you're changing your overall method of accounting. As of this writing it isn't completely clear, but I believe the answer is *yes.*

---

* For years prior to 1999 the rules for making the election were more liberal in terms of both the deadline and method of making the election. See Rev. Proc. 99-17.

Section 481(a) adjustment. The section 481(a) adjustment (page 3 of Form 3115) is the amount necessary to eliminate duplications or omissions that result from a change in methods of accounting. It appears that the IRS interprets the adjustment as follows. For the year before the election is effective, you account for your trades in the normal way. For the first year the election is effective, you account for your trades as if you had been using the mark-to-market method all along. As a result, when you sell or close any trading positions you held at the end of the last year before the mark-to-market election took effect, you treat them as if they had been marked to market the previous year (with basis equal to the year-end value). The difference between the actual basis of these positions and the year-end value is the amount of the adjustment.

Example: At the end of 2003 you held shares with $24,000 basis but value of $26,000. You made the mark-to-market election effective beginning in 2004, and ended up selling these shares for $30,000. You report $4,000 of gain on the sale of the shares, and in addition you have a $2,000 section 481(a) adjustment.

If the adjustment is under $25,000 you can elect to take it in a single year; otherwise you spread it over four years beginning with the year the election took effect. If you didn't hold any trading positions on December 31 of the year before the election took effect, the section 481(a) adjustment is zero.

Attach a statement. You need to attach a statement something like this:

John Doe
SSN 123-45-6789
Attachment to Form 3115

In accordance with Rev. Proc. 99-17 and section 475(f) of the Internal Revenue Code, the taxpayer filed an election with his 2001 income tax return to use the mark-to-market method of accounting in connection with his trade or business of trading securities, effective beginning with the taxable year commencing January 1, 2002. This method of accounting will be used for the taxpayer's books and records and financial statements.

Sign the form and attach it to your tax return. In addition, *no later than the date you file your tax return*, send a *copy* of Form 3115 and the attached statement to:

Commissioner of Internal Revenue
Attn: CC:DOM:IT&A (Automatic Rulings Branch)
P.O. Box 7604
Benjamin Franklin Station
Washington, D.C. 20044

If you use an approved private delivery service (FedEx, Airborne, UPS) instead of the post office, the address is:

Commissioner of Internal Revenue
Attn: CC:DOM:IT&A (Automatic Rulings Branch)
1111 Constitution Ave., N.W.
Washington, D.C. 20224

Reporting Gains and Losses

Prior to year 2000, the IRS did not provide any guidance as to how traders who made the mark-to-market election should report their gains and losses. Many traders reported their gains and losses on Schedule D (capital gains and losses), then made an entry on Schedule D to zero out the effect of those gains and losses, with a notation that the gain or loss was being moved to Schedule C (business income and losses) in accordance with the rules for traders who have made the mark-to-market election. The reason for putting the gains on Schedule D in the first place was to make that schedule match up with the sales reported by the broker on Form 1099-B.

Beginning with tax returns for the year 2000, the IRS has clarified that you are to report your trading gains and losses on line 10 of Form 4797. This makes sense because Form 4797 is used to report sales that produce ordinary income or loss rather than capital gain or loss.* There's no need to file amended returns for prior years when you didn't use this procedure, provided that you figured the correct amount of tax.

There's one point on which many traders will be disappointed. The IRS says they want all transactions listed on an attachment to this form. It isn't good enough to put an aggregate number on the form. If you have 5,000 trades in the course of the year, the IRS wants a listing showing gain or loss from each individual trade! The listing doesn't have to be on a particular form, so it can be a computer spreadsheet that provides the necessary information. The mark-to-market election saves you plenty of paperwork by eliminating the wash sale rule, but it doesn't eliminate the need to report individual trades.

Identifying Investment Securities

Before you make the mark-to-market election, you need to think about identifying any stocks you hold as an investment. Failure to do so could be costly.

What's at stake. Suppose you're a trader and you make the mark-to-market election. In addition to stocks you trade, you have some stocks you hold as investments. You've held some of these stocks for years, and they've gone up in value a great deal. If these stocks are considered part of your trading business, you'll report ordinary income, not capital gain, when you sell them. Even if you don't sell them, the gain will be treated as ordinary income when you mark to market on December 31. Depending on how much gain you have in your investment stocks, this could be a real disaster.

What you can do. The rules permit you to maintain investments that are not part of your trading business. To do this, though, you have to identify those investments. In other words, you have to make it clear, up front, which

---

* Some practitioners believe it's best to report trading transactions first on Schedule D, and then move them to Form 4797, but I see no indication the IRS wants you to do that.

stocks are part of your trading business and which are not. You can't decide later to treat the losers as trading stocks (for ordinary losses) and the winners as investment stocks (to avoid marking to market and get capital gain treatment).

Early in 1999, the Treasury Department issued proposed regulations addressing the identification issue. As of this writing, final regulations have still not been issued. Here is what the proposed regulations tell us:

- If you make the mark-to-market election, you must identify any securities held other than in connection with your trading business.

- Your identification isn't effective unless you can demonstrate by clear and convincing evidence that the securities have no connection to your trading business.

- If you hold an investment security and also trade the same security, or substantially similar securities, your identification isn't effective unless you hold the investment securities in a separate, non-trading account maintained with a third party.

The Treasury asked for commentary on whether these proposed rules are too strict, so it's possible the final regulations will soften these rules somewhat. Until that happens, you should assume that these strict rules will apply.

When to identify. The proposed regulations provide that if you want to identify securities as not being part of your trading business, you must do so on the same day you acquire the security (or enter into or originate your position in the security, in the case of short positions or options). If you hold any investment securities at the time the mark-to-market election becomes effective, presumably you can identify them at that time.

How to identify. Regulations for securities dealers provide two ways to identify securities for purposes of these rules. One is to establish a separate account for investment securities, and the other is to clearly indicate on your own records which securities are not part of your trading business.

These rules also apparently apply to securities traders. There's some question in my mind, however, whether the procedure of identifying shares on internal records makes sense for an individual trader. It will be difficult to establish factually that the identification occurred at the proper time, rather than being made up later. For this reason, I recommend that anyone who makes the mark-to-market election and holds some securities for investment should establish separate accounts for trading and investment activities, taking care never to mix the activities of the two accounts.

No connection to trading business. Even if you identify securities as investment securities, the IRS can disregard your identification unless you demonstrate by "clear and convincing evidence" that the security has "no connection" to your trading activity. If the IRS rejects your identification, you'll be required to mark the securities to market at the end of the year, and report any gain as ordinary income. It isn't clear to me what is meant by "no connection" to the trading business. In particular, it isn't clear whether investment securities can be used as collateral for trading margin without being drawn into the mark-to-market regime.

Until we receive further clarification from the Treasury or the IRS, the only sure way to avoid problems is to keep your investment securities in a separate account from your trading securities, and avoid using the investment securities as collateral for margin in the trading account. If it's important for you to use your investment securities as collateral in connection with your trading activities, you should consider whether the benefits of the mark-to-market election are great enough to justify taking the risk that the IRS will treat those securities as trading securities.

Part VI
Many Happy Returns

These chapters deal with tax calculation, filing and payment issues that are likely to be important to people who buy and sell stocks and mutual funds. Chapter 26 covers specifics of reporting capital gains and losses. Chapter 27 points out that you can incur liability under the alternative minimum tax from having a large long-term capital gain. Chapter 28 explains the rules for making estimated tax payments, and Chapter 29 covers special rules for children.

Part VI Many Happy Returns

Chapter 26
Reporting Sales of Stock

When you sell stock through a broker you'll receive a form reporting the results of that sale: Form 1099-B. This form does *not* tell how much gain or loss to report. It merely tells how much you received from the sale. It's up to you to figure how much gain or loss you report from the sale, and whether the gain or loss is long-term or short-term. If you don't report your full basis in the stock, you may inadvertently pay tax on the same income twice.

Throughout this book you've learned how to determine your *basis* and your *holding period* in various situations. You need those two pieces of information, in addition to the amount of *proceeds* from the sale, to report the sale on your return. Generally, sale proceeds are equal to the sale price of the stock minus any brokerage commissions and other selling expenses.

Schedule D

You report capital gains and losses on Schedule D, which is an attachment to Form 1040. The front of that form is in two parts, one for short-term gain or loss and one for long-term gain or loss. So the first thing you need to know is whether your holding period is a year or less (short-term) or at least a year and a day (long-term). If you sell exactly on the first anniversary of the day you acquired the stock, your gain or loss is short-term. Once you have the right part of the form, proceed as follows:

- In column (a) write a simple description of what you sold. There's an example right on the form: "100 sh XYZ Co."

- In column (b) write the date acquired. Use the date that measures your holding period, rather than the date you literally acquired the stock. For example, if you received shares in a stock split, the new shares have the same holding period as the old shares. If you made a single sale of shares that were acquired on more than one date, write "various" in this column. But don't combine long-term and short-term shares in a single group, even if you sold them all at once.

- In column (c) write the date of sale. For stock sold on a stock exchange, this is the *trade date*, not the settlement date.

- Column (d) on the form is labeled "sales price." If you received a Form 1099-B for the sale (as you should have if you sold your stock through a broker) you should report the same number here as appears on the Form 1099-B. Otherwise, report the proceeds from the sale minus any selling expenses.

- Column (e) is where you report your cost or other basis. Be sure to include any appropriate adjustments, such as the disallowed loss from a previous wash sale. Also, if your broker didn't subtract the brokerage commission and other selling expenses when reporting your sale proceeds on Form 1099-B, you have to add those items to your basis.

- Subtract the number in column (e) from the number in column (d), and write the result in column (f).* If the number is positive, you have a capital gain. If the number is negative, indicate this by writing it in parentheses. Some software programs use a minus sign instead of parentheses

---

* Because the rates for long-term capital gain changes as of May 6, 2003, the 2003 version of Schedule D has an extra column. If you're preparing your return by hand, follow the instructions for column (g) carefully.

and that's okay too, but easier to miss when reading a return quickly.

Follow the rest of the instructions for this form to combine your gain or loss with any other capital gains and losses, then transfer the number to the appropriate line on Form 1040.

▪ **Long-term gain? Caution:** Many people forget they need to do a special rate calculation if they have a long-term capital gain. This is where you get your tax savings from the special capital gains rate, so don't make this mistake! If you're preparing the return yourself without the aid of tax software, you'll have to follow instructions carefully. It's worth the effort, because this rate calculation lowers your taxes.

The IRS wants you to attach an explanation if you use something other than the actual cost of the stock as your basis. You might attach a statement that looks something like this:

John Doe
SSN 123-45-6789
2000 Form 1040, Schedule D

The basis used for 1000 shares of XYZ stock includes $850 of disallowed loss from a prior wash sale.

Chapter 27
Alternative Minimum Tax

The alternative minimum tax affects a small but growing percentage of taxpayers. When it applies, the cost can be substantial. What's worse, this tax is so complicated that it's often difficult to predict when it will apply. This tax typically doesn't come into play for people who buy and sell stocks and mutual funds except in one situation: it can apply when you have a large long-term capital gain.

Background

The basic idea behind the alternative minimum tax is a good one: people with very high levels of income shouldn't be able to completely avoid paying income tax while the rest of us pony up each year. The AMT is a poor reflection of that idea, however. Many high-income individuals escape its reach—and every year it ensnares more and more people who were never intended to be affected.

Whatever its merits or demerits, the AMT is a potential problem if you have a large long-term capital gain. Congress never intended to apply the AMT to people in this situation, but the interaction of different provisions can cause the AMT to apply. In fact, President Clinton had to pay AMT because of capital gains in his blind trust.

In some circumstances, you get a credit in later years if you pay AMT. For example, people who pay AMT because they exercised incentive stock options usually recover some or all of the tax in a later year, in the form of an *AMT credit*. Unfortunately, if you incur AMT liability because of a long-term capital gain, you aren't eligible for the AMT credit. You won't get this tax back in a later year.

The AMT Exemption

Why pay AMT when you have a long-term gain? The major reason is elimination of the *AMT exemption*. This is a special deduction that's designed to prevent the alternative minimum tax from applying at lower income levels. The problem is that the AMT exemption is *phased out* when your income goes above a certain level. Capital gain is income even though it's taxed at a special rate, so it can reduce or eliminate your AMT exemption.

When your income is in the range where the exemption is being phased out, each dollar of long-term capital gain adds $1.25 to your AMT income. That means the effective rate of tax on capital gain under the AMT can be much higher than the rate under the regular tax, even though the "official" AMT rate for long-term capital gain is 15%, the same as under the regular tax.

You don't automatically pay AMT when you have a long-term capital gain. Whether you end up in that situation depends on various factors, including the size of your income, the size of the gain, and the number of items on your return that are affected by the AMT. There are no good rules of thumb, other than to check the AMT calculation if you have a large capital gain.

What You Can Do

There isn't an awful lot you can do about this situation. I often hear people offer ideas for reducing AMT liability, but most people have limited ability to take advantage of those ideas, and sometimes the ideas are simply unsound. Still, there are a few things you should consider.

Take a close look at deductions that are allowed under the regular tax but not under the AMT. An example would be the deduction for state and local taxes. If you can schedule some of your payments of such taxes so they don't fall in the same year you have an AMT problem, you may get a greater benefit from the deduction.

On the flip side, you may find that you pay a lower rate of tax on income you receive in an AMT year. For example, if you're paying AMT because of a long-term capital gain, you might choose that year to exercise nonqualified stock options. At least some of the income from exercising your options may end up being taxed at the AMT rate (26% to 28%) rather than your regular income tax rate, which may be as high as 35%.

> ▪ **Caution:** Accelerating income into an AMT year may not be a good idea if you're eligible for the AMT credit (for example, because you exercised an incentive stock option). This planning idea produces the best results when at least some of your AMT isn't eligible for the AMT credit.

Chapter 28
Estimated Tax Payments

If you're an employee, you may have never had to worry about making estimated tax payments. The amount of income tax withheld from paychecks may be enough to cover the tax you owe and then some, providing a refund. Even if you owe some tax on April 15, estimates aren't required unless you owe more than $1,000.

When you invest in stocks and mutual funds, there's a good chance you'll end up with a tax bill of more than $1,000 in one or more years. In that situation, it's possible that you'll incur a penalty if you don't make quarterly payments of estimated tax.

First Things You Should Know

If you've never had to deal with estimated taxes before, the whole idea can seem foreign and uncomfortable. There are two things you should know right away to put your mind at rest.

- **It's easy.** In most cases, the process of figuring out how much to pay isn't hard at all. And paying the tax is a snap.

- **No jail time.** You won't go to jail if you make a mistake and pay too little. In fact, the penalty isn't exactly a killer. It's just simple interest on the amount you underpaid, and the interest rate isn't terribly high. If you somehow blow it and under-pay by $400, and correct the underpayment with your next payment three months later, your penalty will be less than $10. It's better to avoid the penalty, but really, this is nothing to lose sleep over.

General Rule: 90%

The general rule is that your estimated tax payments, when added to your withholding and credits, must add up to 90% of the current year's tax liability. If your withholding and credits already add up to 90% of your tax liability, you don't have to make estimated tax payments. Yet in many cases you don't have to make estimated tax payments even if your withholding and credits fall short of the 90% figure, for reasons described below.

> • When we talk about the *tax due*, we mean the total amount of tax you owe—including any self-employment tax and the dreaded alternative minimum tax (AMT).

Tax Due Less Than $1,000

Here's a rule that makes it easy for many people who have withholding that falls just a bit short to avoid dealing with estimated tax payments. No payment is required if the amount due after subtracting withholding and credits will be less than $1,000. (The amount used to be $500, but Congress increased it to $1,000 beginning in 1998.)

> **Example:** Suppose you expect your wage withholding to be just enough to cover your income tax liability. Then you have a $4,000 long-term capital gain you didn't plan on. This gain will be taxed at 15%, so the added tax is $600. You can make an estimated tax payment if you feel more comfortable doing so, but there won't be a penalty if you wait until April 15 of next year to send in the payment because it's less than $1,000.

The only problem with this rule is that sometimes it's difficult to know what your tax liability will be. But $1,000 is a reasonable amount of leeway for the majority of taxpayers.

Prior Year Safe Harbor

Most people can avoid paying estimated tax if their withholding and credits equal 100% of the tax shown on the *prior year's* income tax return. I call this the *prior year safe harbor*. This rule often permits taxpayers to avoid making estimated payments if they receive a large sum of income on a one-time basis.

> ■   For purposes of this rule, your prior year tax isn't the amount of the check you sent in, but the total amount of tax you had to pay, including withholding. For example, if your withholding was $12,000 and you had to pay another $250 when you filed your return, your prior year's tax was $12,250—*not* $250.

Example: In a normal year withholding is enough to cover your income tax—in fact, you usually get a small refund. This year you sell stock with a capital gain of $200,000. Despite this huge increase in income, you don't have to make estimated tax payments if your withholding will be at least equal to the tax shown on the prior year's tax return.

Similarly, you normally don't have to make estimated tax payments if you had no tax liability at all for the previous year. Remember, "no tax liability" doesn't just mean your withholding was enough to cover your tax. It means even if you didn't have any withholding at all you wouldn't owe any tax.

> • **Higher income, higher percentage.** There's a rule that requires taxpayers with adjusted gross income above $150,000 on the prior year's return ($75,000 if married filing separately) to pay 110% of the prior year's tax (not just 100%) when applying the prior year safe harbor. Congress has been known to tinker with this percentage, so check the form instructions.

Even if the prior year safe harbor doesn't allow you to completely avoid making estimated tax payments, it permits you to determine an amount that will avoid a penalty without making an accurate estimate of the current year's taxes.

> **Example:** Your income tax for 2003 was $24,000. You expect your withholding for 2004 to be $21,000. You don't know how much income you'll have for 2004, though, because you may sell stock at a gain. Because of the prior year safe harbor, you can safely cover your estimated tax requirement by paying $3,000 ($750 per quarter). When added to your $21,000 of withholding, you'll have total payments that equal your prior year's tax.

There are situations where it doesn't make sense to use the prior year safe harbor. You may have a year in which you had an unusually large amount of income. When the next year rolls around, you would be paying estimates that are larger than necessary if you pay based on that banner year. In this case you'll want to estimate the current year's tax and try to pay at least 90% of that number.

> **Example:** In 2003 you made a killing in an IPO and reported an extra $80,000 of income. In 2004 you won't have that extra income, but still need to make estimated tax payments. If you base the payment amount on your 2003 tax, you'll pay a lot more than necessary. It makes more sense to use a realistic estimate of your 2004 tax.

Estimating Your Tax

As you've seen above, there are plenty of situations where it isn't actually necessary to do any estimating when you make estimated tax payments. But sometimes you need to make an estimate of the current year's tax. Otherwise you'll either pay way too much, or come up short and end up with a penalty.

Form 1040-ES (the form used to pay estimated tax) comes with a worksheet you can use to estimate how much tax you'll owe for the current year. There's certainly nothing wrong with using this worksheet—but most people don't. The reason is that the worksheet takes you through more detail than may be necessary, but still leaves you with nothing better than an educated guess about your tax liability. You don't file the worksheet with the IRS, and there's no requirement to justify how you came up with the amount of your estimated tax payment. So most people use a somewhat simplified method to figure their estimated tax:

- Look at each number on the prior year's tax return and ask yourself if this year's number is likely to be significantly different. Ignore differences in wages because there will be a corresponding difference in withholding. Use rounded numbers and don't worry about minor changes.

- Add up all the differences to see how much larger or smaller your taxable income will be for the current year.

- Apply the tax rates to see how much difference this will make in your income tax. (If the difference results from a long-term capital gain, apply the capital gain tax rates.) Round the number up or simply tack on an added amount if you want to increase your comfort level about avoiding a penalty.

Many people using this method don't bother looking up the changes in the tax rates that result from inflation adjustments. These changes will decrease your tax slightly, so that's one way of providing a cushion of extra payments.

Voluntary Payments

Depending on your situation, the amount of estimated tax you're *required* to pay could be quite a bit less than your true estimate of the amount of tax you'll owe. That's because you're allowed to pay estimates based on the previous year's tax, even if you know this year's tax will be higher. When that happens you have a choice. You can pay the minimum amount required—and pay the rest on April 15. Or you can pay something close to the true estimate so you won't owe a lot on April 15. Which is better depends on your comfort level and money management skills.

Pay now and relax. Some people choose to make estimated payments even when the payments aren't required. The reason? Perhaps they're concerned that the money won't be there when they need it to pay taxes. Perhaps they're simply more comfortable knowing that they won't have a huge tax bill in April. There are a variety of good reasons to make estimated tax payments even if the payments aren't legally required. The biggest one is peace of mind.

Pay later and earn. The main reason *not* to pay more than you have to is that you lose the use of your money between the time you pay the estimate and the time you would have sent payment with your return. You should be able to earn at least a little bit of interest during that time. So there's at least one good reason to pay later, even though there are good reasons to pay sooner.

Which is better. Which approach is better—making voluntary payments, or paying the minimum—depends on your personality and your circumstances. Consider the following example:

Example: You normally don't pay estimates because almost all of your income is from wages subject to withholding. In January, 2004 you sell stock and have a capital gain of $40,000. You expect to owe $6,000 of tax, but you don't have to pay estimates because your 2004 withholding will be at least equal to your 2003 tax.

You have several choices, including the following:

- You can put $6,000 aside in an interest bearing account until April 15, 2005 when the tax is due. This way you can make a little profit on the money before sending it to the IRS. If you have the discipline to leave the money alone, you come out ahead using this approach. There's a danger, though. If you start with this intention, but end up spending the money on a trip to Aruba, or losing it when you try to cash in on an IPO, you may wake up with a headache on April 15, 2005.

- You can send in a single estimated payment of $6,000. This approach is easy, and may seem relatively painless if you do it at a time when you're flush with money from the stock sale. It's also very safe: this approach assures that you won't somehow lose or spend the money before you file your tax return. It doesn't allow you to earn interest on the $6,000, though.

- You can send in four quarterly estimates of $1,500 each. You may prefer this approach if you don't like the idea of writing a single check for $6,000 to the IRS (who does?). And this approach gives you the flexibility to reduce later payments if you have a capital loss or other reduction in taxable income later in the year. There's a little more paperwork involved in this approach though, and more opportunity to lose or spend the money before you file your return.

There's nothing illegal or immoral about any of these approaches. They're all equally acceptable to the IRS. (They won't be upset if they receive a $6,000 payment for one quarter and no payment in later quarters.) If you find yourself in a situation like this, choose the approach that works best for you.

Increasing Your Withholding

There's a way you may be able to cover your extra tax liability without making estimated tax payments: increase the amount of tax withheld from your paycheck. You get a special benefit with this approach: *extra withholding that comes late in the year is treated the same as if it was spread evenly over the year.* You can use this approach to avoid late payment penalties.

How to do it. To increase the amount of federal income tax withheld from your paycheck, ask your employer for a new Form W-4. You're required to fill out this form when you start working for an employer. You can fill out a new one whenever your circumstances call for a change in the amount of withholding.

This form contains several worksheets, and the instructions tell you to "complete all worksheets that apply." But the worksheets are there mainly to make sure you don't *reduce* your withholding more than you're supposed to. There's never a problem when you want to *increase* your withholding. You can fill out the worksheets if you want, but you're not required to do so. And there's no particular need if the only thing you're doing is increasing your withholding to cover tax on your investment income.

There are two ways to increase your withholding on this form. One is to reduce the number of allowances you claim on the form. This can be a little tricky, because you don't necessarily know how much your withholding will change when you change your allowances. The amount depends on your income level and the withholding method adopted by your employer.

> ▪ Some people are confused by *allowances*. You get one allowance for each exemption you can claim on your tax return (yourself, your spouse and your dependents), but an allowance isn't the same as an exemption. There are allowances for other items, such as deductions and certain credits. Reducing your allowances doesn't mean you'll claim fewer exemptions when you file your tax return. The number of allowances is used *only* to determine how much tax is withheld from your paycheck.

There's another approach that's simpler: request an "additional amount" to be withheld from your paycheck. Do this on line 6 of the form. This makes it fairly easy to determine the amount of the increase when you file Form W-4.

Check with your employer to find out when the change will go into effect. Normally there's a time lag between the day you fill out this form and the day it's processed, so you may not see the change in your very next paycheck. Keep an eye on your paycheck stubs to confirm that the change was properly made, and had the effect you anticipated.

Avoiding late payment penalty. The nice thing about using withholding to cover your estimated tax liability is that it can get you out of a late payment penalty. Withholding is presumed to be received evenly throughout the year.

Example: Suppose you realize in May that you need to pay $6,000 estimated tax for the year, and you've already blown the first $1,500 payment that was due April 15. It won't be a big deal if you send in the payment a few weeks late because the penalty isn't all that terrible. But you can avoid the penalty altogether by increasing your withholding for the rest of the year by $6,000. The IRS will assume the withholding occurred evenly throughout the year, with $1,500 coming in the first quarter. You get the benefit of this assumption even if all of the added withholding comes in December!

Making Estimated Payments

Estimated payments for any year are due on April 15, June 15 and September 15 of that year, and January 15 of the following year. Whenever one of these dates falls on a legal holiday or on a weekend, the due date is the next day that isn't a holiday or weekend day. Here are some points to keep in mind:

- If you owe money with your tax return, *and* have to make an estimated tax payment, you have *two* checks to write on April 15. Be prepared!

- Although the payments are "quarterly," they aren't three months apart. The second payment sneaks up on you, just two months after the first one.

- Like your tax return, estimated payments are considered "on time" if you *mail* them by the due date.

- Most states that have an income tax require estimated payments on the same schedule as the federal payments. If you itemize deductions, it may be to your advantage to make your fourth quarter state estimated tax payment in December, not January, so you can deduct it a year earlier.

- A small number of individual taxpayers use a fiscal tax year that ends with a month other than December. Their payment schedule is different (but equivalent): the fifteenth day of the fourth, sixth and ninth months of their fiscal year, and the fifteenth day of the first month of the following fiscal year.

What to file. When you make estimated tax payments you need to enclose Form 1040-ES, Estimated Tax Voucher. This form is about as simple as they get. It asks for your name, address and social security number—and just one other item: the amount you're paying.

If you've previously made estimated tax payments, the IRS will send forms with your name, address and social security number pre-printed. Even if this is your first year paying estimates, the IRS will send pre-printed forms after they receive your first payment. You're not *required* to use these forms—don't panic if you lose them—but the IRS *prefers* that you use them to help assure that your payment will be processed promptly and correctly.

Form 1040-ES comes from the IRS as part of an intimidating package that includes lengthy instructions and detailed worksheets. As mentioned earlier, you don't have to fill out the worksheets unless you think they'll be helpful. And you should *never* send these worksheets to the IRS.

Other important tips. *Estimated tax payments don't go to the same address as your return!* Don't enclose an estimated tax payment with your Form 1040. Check the instructions for Form 1040-ES for the proper address.

Enclose your check. Write your social security number on the check and a notation of what it's for, like this: 2001 2Q Form 1040-ES. If you're doing this before your first cup of coffee in the morning, double check to see that you *signed* the check.

You don't have to justify your estimated tax payments. In fact, there's no place for a *signature* on the form. When you send it in, you're not promising that this is the correct amount. All you're saying is, "Here's a payment on account."

Be sure to keep an accurate record of your estimated tax payments so you can claim credit for them when you file your return.

Joint payments. If you're married, you can make joint estimated tax payments with your spouse. (There's an exception if either spouse is a nonresident alien.) Paying joint estimated payments does *not* mean you have to file a joint return. But if you end up filing separately, you'll have to sort out who gets credit for what amount.

Chapter 29
Special Rules for Children

If your children are investors—or you're investing money for them through a custodial account—you need to know a few special rules that apply to children. One requires a child under 14 to pay tax at the parents' tax rate when investment income exceeds a minimum amount. Another permits a parent to report the child's income on the parent's return in certain circumstances. First, though, let's answer one of the most frequently asked questions about children's income tax.

Who Files the Return?

If a child has investments, who files the tax return? Here's what the IRS says, in Publication 929:

> Generally, the child is responsible for filing his or her own tax return and for paying any tax, penalties or interest on that return. If the child cannot file his or her own return for any reason, such as age, the child's parent or guardian is responsible for filing a return on his or her behalf. If the child cannot sign his or her return, a parent or guardian can sign the child's name in the space provided at the bottom of the return. Then, he or she should add: "By (signature), parent (or guardian) for minor child."

Note that the child doesn't have to be of legal age to sign the return. The IRS doesn't tell us when a child is "old enough" to sign. Your five-year-old can sign the return and it would be perfectly legal. You should be aware, though, that if a question (or audit) arises on the return, the IRS has to deal directly with the child, not the parent, if the child signed the return—at least until there's a power of attorney permitting the parent to act on the child's behalf.

Custodial account information. As explained in Chapter 18, assets in custodial accounts under the Uniform Transfers to Minors Act—*UTMA accounts*—are owned by the child. Income from those assets belongs on the child's return (except as explained later in this chapter for parents who elect to include the child's income on their own return). The Uniform Act requires the custodian to supply relevant information to the child or the person responsible for filing the child's tax return.

Standard Deduction and Exemption

Taxpayers who don't itemize deductions claim the *standard deduction*. This amount is much smaller for a dependent child than it is for an independent taxpayer. For the year 2004, the standard deduction for a minor child is the *greater* of the following two amounts:

- $800, or

- The child's earned income plus $250, but not more than the regular standard deduction for a single person ($4,850).*

It's frequently said that if you shift investment assets to a child, the first $800 of income will be tax-free. That's generally true, but it should be noted that as soon as the child begins earning money, the amount of investment income that escapes taxation shrinks to as little as $250— or zero, if the child earns more than the regular standard deduction amount for a single person. The standard deduction grows as the child earns more money, but the amount that applies against investment income shrinks.

> **Example:** Suppose your child's only income is $1,000 of investment income. The child will have a standard deduction of $800 and pay tax on $300. If

---

* These amounts are adjusted for inflation periodically. For 2003 the numbers were $750 and $4,750 instead of $800 and $4,850.

the child earns $1,000 in addition to the investment income, the standard deduction is $1,250 and the child pays tax on $750. Without the investment income, the child would pay zero tax, so only $250 of the investment income is sheltered by the standard deduction.

Exemption. If you can claim your child as an exemption, the child doesn't get to claim an exemption. That's true even if you decide not to claim the child.*

Applying the Parents' Tax Rate

Now we come to the infamous *kiddie tax.* This is the informal name for a rule that requires children under 14 years of age to pay their parents' rate of tax on certain investment income. Before Congress imposed this rule, wealthy families could save many thousands of dollars in income tax by transferring investment assets to minor children. This kind of asset transfer can still produce income tax savings, but the savings for younger children are much more modest because of the kiddie tax.

The rule applies to children who are under 14 at the end of the year† if they have investment income above a threshold amount. That amount is adjusted for inflation periodically. For 2004 the threshold is $1,600.

Example: In year 2004 your child has $2,600 of investment income and no other income. The first $800 of investment income escapes taxation: your child's standard deduction takes care of that. The next $800 is taxed at the child's rate of 10%. That leaves $1,000 to be taxed at whatever rate would apply if this income were added to the income reported on your return.

Suppose you're in the 28% tax bracket. The

---

* In some cases it's better not to claim the child, to make it possible for the child to claim an education credit that's more valuable than the parents' exemption.
† For obscure reasons, a child is considered to be 14 at the end of the year if the child turns 14 on January 1 of the following year.

total tax on your child's return would be 10% of $800 plus 28% of $1,000, or $360. If the investment assets were in your own name, the entire $2,600 would be taxed at your 28% rate, for a tax of $728. Shifting this income to your child's tax return saved $368.

- **Comment:** For some people, that $368 in tax savings is worth pursuing, but I urge caution. To shift $2,000 of investment income to your child, you may have to transfer $20,000 or more in investment assets. That's fine if an asset transfer fits within your plans. If you end up regretting the asset transfer, though, the tax savings won't be much consolation.

How to report. There are two ways to apply the parents' rate to the child's income. One is to include the income on the parents' return, as explained below. This option isn't always available, or you may decide it isn't best for you even if it is available. In that case you'll need IRS Form 8615. If you need even more in the way of grimy details, you may want to request (or download) IRS Publication 929, *Tax Rules for Children and Dependents*.

Reporting Your Child's Income on Your Return

If your child was under 14 at the end of the year, you may be able to report the child's investment income on your tax return. This may cause your taxes to be higher or lower, but most people think about doing this mainly because of the convenience: it means preparing and filing one less tax return.* You're never required to do this, so you shouldn't make this election if it will cost you more than the benefit you get from avoiding paperwork.

Not everyone can make this election. Requirements in addition to the age limitation include:

---

* You need to attach Form 8814 to your return if you choose to include your child's income on your return.

- Your child had income only from dividends and interest. For this purpose, dividends include capital gain distributions and Alaska Permanent Fund dividends.

- The dividend and interest income was less than $7,000.

- The child has no credits for estimated tax or a prior year overpayment.

The requirement that trips people up most often is the limit on the types of income. Sometimes people make stock investments with their children's assets, and then have a capital loss. They see that the capital loss won't produce any tax benefit on the child's tax return, and wonder if they can benefit from this loss by electing to include the child's investment income on their own tax return. Unfortunately this isn't possible. The only items you can move to your own tax return are dividend and interest income.

Effect of the election. If you elect to include your child's income on your tax return, you still get the benefit of the child's standard deduction. What's more, the child's tax rate still applies up to the same threshold as if the income were reported on the child's tax return. That means most people won't pay much additional tax if they make the election. You can even gain an advantage by making the election, because the child's investment income counts when determining the limit on your investment interest expense deduction (see Chapter 10).

The election can cost you money, though. For that reason, it's a good idea to take a close look at the return, or perhaps even prepare it both ways, before committing yourself to reporting your child's income on your return. If you're not sure about the election, don't make it. In most cases it isn't that hard to prepare a separate return for the child.

- When there's a capital loss in your child's UTMA account, and your child doesn't have enough income to pay any tax, it seems like a shame for the capital loss to be wasted. Yet there's no way to claim the capital loss on the parents' return. The election to include your child's income on your return doesn't apply if your child has capital gains—or capital losses.

Part VII
Planning for Lower Taxes

It's one thing to understand the rules, and another thing to use those rules to lower your taxes. Here are the most important tax planning techniques in connection with buying and selling stocks and mutual funds.

Part VII Planning for Lower Taxes

Chapter 30
Tax Planning for Capital Gains

One nice thing about capital gains and losses is that you have some control over them. You can sell your stock now or later, depending on which choice produces better tax results. You can choose which stock to sell and even choose *which shares* of that stock to sell if you bought shares at different times or different prices. Choose intelligently and you can reduce your tax bite.

Remember, tax considerations shouldn't control your choices. Overall, a sound investment strategy is more important than tax savings. You'll achieve the best results if you let tax planning influence the details of how you operate within your overall strategy.

Three Tax Planning Goals

Most tax planning is aimed at one or more of three goals. Sometimes you can achieve more than one of these goals at the same time. In other situations, you may find that you can achieve one only at the expense of another. The three main goals of tax planning are:

- *Reducing taxable income.* Of course, it's easy to reduce taxable income by earning less. The trick is to have income that isn't *taxable*. For example, interest on municipal bonds is tax exempt, and earnings in a Roth IRA escape tax permanently if you wait long enough before taking distributions.

- *Paying lower tax rates.* If you can't eliminate tax on your income, the next best thing is to reduce the tax rate. The main way to do this is to maximize your use of the lower rates for long-term capital gains and qualified dividends.

- *Deferral.* That's a dull-sounding word for a mundane but powerful concept: other things being equal, it's better to pay taxes later rather than sooner. The principal tax benefit from most retirement savings arrangements comes from deferral. Often it's possible to defer capital gains simply by holding winning stocks for a longer period of time.

The power of tax deferral. If you've never stopped to think about it, you may not realize what a powerful benefit you can achieve by deferring taxes until a later year. There's a tendency to think you haven't really saved much because you're simply paying the same amount at a different time. Yet deferral, especially over long periods of time, can have a significant multiplier effect on your investment return even without any reduction in tax rates.

> **Example:** You put $2,000 in a taxable account, and another $2,000 in a nondeductible IRA. Both investments earn 10% per year, but in the taxable account you pay tax each year. In the IRA, you don't pay any tax until you pull the money out. After 25 years your taxable account has grown to a little over $10,000, assuming you pull money out each year to pay tax at the rate of 33% (federal and state). Your IRA has grown much faster because you haven't pulled tax money out each year. If you pull the money out at the end of 25 years and pay tax at the same 33% rate, you end up with over $15,000.

In this example, you've increased the after-tax money available for your retirement by about 50% without reducing your taxable income or your tax rate. You did it with *tax-free compounding.* That's the power of deferral.

Winners and Losers

The most powerful tax planning techniques for people who buy and sell stocks and mutual funds are also the simplest. They're so simple that it almost seems foolish to mention them. Yet they're so powerful that it would be foolish *not* to mention them. To achieve better tax results in investing—*are you ready?*—you must do two things:

- Hold your winners.

- Sell your losers.

When you're tempted to sell a winner, consider holding it a little longer. Then a little longer still. Then keep holding it. Holding for more than a year allows you to pay tax at the lower rate for long-term capital gains. Holding until January allows you to delay paying tax until the following year. You might find that you can hold on until the *following* January and delay tax for yet another year. If you *never* sell the stock, the basis will be adjusted at your death, and no one will *ever* pay tax on the gain.

Exactly the opposite consideration applies to losses. Sell before you have a long-term loss and you may get a greater benefit from your deduction. Sell before the end of the year and you'll get to claim the loss earlier. If you don't sell during this lifetime, neither you nor anyone else will enjoy the benefit of a deduction for the loss.

What about investment concerns? As I stressed earlier, you shouldn't let tax planning concerns push you into an unsound investment approach. Sometimes there's a very good reason to sell a winner, even if that means paying tax now on a gain that might otherwise be deferred. But consider this:

> ▪ Studies show that investors tend to sell their winners too soon and hold their losers too long.

There's a natural tendency, when you buy a stock that rises, to think about harvesting that profit. *I'll feel awfully dumb if the stock goes back down before I sell,* you tell yourself. Somehow the possible mistake of losing a profit by selling too late seems more important than the possible mistake of losing *future* profits by selling too soon. Time and again, investors give up future profits by selling winners that still have a lot of wind in their sails. That's bad investment planning *and* bad tax planning.

At the same time, most investors are reluctant to sell losers. They don't want to admit they made a mistake. They hold on, thinking the stock or mutual fund is sure to recover, but often that recovery is a long way down the road. Meanwhile your money is tied up in an investment that isn't going anywhere. If you sell the loser, you can move to a better investment *and* reduce your tax for the year with a loss deduction.

It isn't always right to hold a winner, and it isn't always right to sell a loser. When you find yourself resisting these maxims, though, ask yourself whether you have good reasons. You may find that you're responding to the psychology of investing in a way that increases your tax bill without increasing your income.

Build Your Own Tax Shelter

Sometimes I hear from people who have saved the maximum in their 401k or IRA and wish they had some other way to shelter their savings from taxation. There's a way to do that, and it's right under your nose: *buy stocks and hold them.*

Not sexy enough for you? Consider the example of the nondeductible IRA earlier in this chapter. Using this method to obtain deferral resulted in a 50% increase in the after-tax profit from investing. Yet if you adopted a buy-and-hold strategy *without* the IRA, you would achieve an even *better* result. Profits from the IRA are taxed as ordinary income even if they come from stocks that increased in value. If you buy and hold in a regular brokerage account, you get the same benefit of tax deferral and tax-free compounding—and when you're done, your profit is taxed as long-term capital gain.

There are some potential speed bumps on this road to riches. If you invest in stocks that pay dividends, you'll pay at least some tax even with a buy-and-hold strategy. It's also possible that you'll have to pay tax because of a forced sale. Often that's a mixed blessing: you received a nice premium on your shares when Bigco swallowed the company, and that can take the sting out of being forced to pay tax you would have preferred to defer.

Despite these potential problems, the buy-and-hold strategy remains as a powerful, do-it-yourself tax shelter. It may seem like a boring way to accumulate wealth, but sometimes boring is good. There are less expensive ways to amuse yourself than paying tax on gains from stocks you didn't have to sell.

When Holding Periods Matter

It's important to know your holding period for shares of stock and other assets you may sell for a capital gain or loss. Specifically, you need to know if the holding period is long-term and, if not, when it will become long-term. Generally speaking, if you have a gain, you want it to be long-term, and if you have a loss you want it to be short-term. Yet there are situations where the holding period doesn't matter.

Example 1: Earlier in the year you had $10,000 of short-term capital gain and $10,000 of long-term capital gain. Now you're ready to sell stock at a $5,000 loss. Assuming no other transactions, you prefer to have a short-term loss, because that will net out against your short-term gain, preserving the $10,000 long-term gain that qualifies for special, lower tax rates.

Example 2: Change the previous example so all your gains earlier in the year were short-term. Now it doesn't matter whether your loss is short-term or long-term. Either way, the loss will apply against your short-term gain. The holding period for the stock you sell at a loss also wouldn't matter if all your earlier gains were long-term.

Example 3: Earlier in the year you had a $10,000 short-term capital loss. Now you're ready to sell stock at a $5,000 gain. Assuming no other transactions, it doesn't matter whether this gain is short-term or long-term. Either way it disappears because of the loss.

These examples show that it's useful to have a current picture of your overall capital gain and loss situation when you do tax planning for capital gains and losses. There's no point doing back flips to make sure your losses are short-term and your gains are long-term if it won't make any difference on your tax return. Of course, you might be in a situation where you don't know how your year is going to turn out, and in that case you want to make reasonable efforts to have your gains and losses fall in the proper categories.

Managing the Capital Loss Limitation

It's important to keep the $3,000 capital loss limitation in mind if you may be reporting large losses. Remember, any unused loss carries forward but you can't carry it back to previous years.

Example: Earlier in the year, you sold stock for a gain of $40,000. Another of your holdings has done poorly, and if you sell now you'll have a loss of $30,000. You don't know if you'll have gains in future years.

In this situation, you should seriously consider taking the $30,000 loss in the same year as the $40,000 gain. If you postpone that loss until a later year, perhaps hoping for the stock to recover, you may find that you end up having to deduct it at the rate of $3,000 per year—a process that will take ten years. If you sell the stock now, you can claim the entire $30,000 loss as a deduction against your $40,000 gain.

Sometimes you have to make a judgment call in a trade-off between the detriment of the $3,000 capital loss limitation and the benefit of the lower tax rate for long-term capital gains.

> **Example:** Earlier in the year you had a long-term capital gain of $5,000. Late in the year you have stock you plan to sell at a $5,000 loss, and you have to choose which year to sell it. If you sell it this year, you'll deduct the entire $5,000 in one year, but it will reduce long-term capital gain, so the benefit will be relatively small. If you wait until next year to sell, you may have to wait two years to get the full tax benefit of this loss, but it may apply against short-term gain or ordinary income, producing a larger overall tax benefit.

Holding for Qualified Dividends

Before making a short-term sale of shares of stock, check to see whether you can gain tax savings from qualified dividends by holding a little longer. You need to hold the shares at least 61 days (counting the day of sale but not counting the day of purchase) to benefit from this rule.

> **Example:** You bought shares of XYZ and received a dividend. Now you're thinking of selling, after holding the stock 57 days.

If you hold the shares just four more days, your dividend will qualify for the lower tax rate. Sell now and you'll have a nonqualified dividend that's taxed as ordinary income.

Chapter 31
Tax Planning for Mutual Funds

If you invest in mutual funds, you may be able to improve your after-tax investment return by paying attention to some tax issues specific to this form of investment. In this chapter we'll look at the following:

- Allocation issues

- Investing before the annual dividend

- Tax efficiency in mutual funds

- Averaging methods for sales of shares

Allocation Issues

Mutual fund investors face two allocation issues. One is how to allocate their investments among different types of mutual funds: stock funds, balanced funds, bond funds, money market funds, and all the variations on these themes. The other is how to allocate different types of investments between taxable accounts and retirement accounts.

Allocation among types of funds. The best place to turn for guidance on the first issue is an investment book (or advisor), not a tax book. You should allocate your investments among different types of funds in accordance with your investment goals and risk tolerance. The only comments I have on this topic have to do with funds that invest in tax-free bonds or federal securities.

Briefly, tax-free bond funds may be suitable for people in higher tax brackets (especially 33% and higher) but usually are less attractive for people in lower tax brackets.

The reason is that these funds receive a lower rate of interest, relative to the risk involved, than funds that invest in taxable bonds, such as those issued by corporations. To justify this lower rate you should receive a substantial tax benefit, and your benefit is substantial only if you are in one of the higher tax brackets.

To a lesser extent the same consideration applies to funds that invest in federal securities. These funds may be able to pay dividends that are at least partly exempt from state income tax. That means they're more attractive to people who live in states that impose income tax at relatively high rates. For most people this isn't an overwhelming concern as they decide how much to invest in this type of mutual fund, but it's a point worth considering.

Taxable vs. retirement accounts. Once you've determined what mix of funds meets your overall investment objectives, you may face a further issue: how to allocate those investments between your taxable investment account and your retirement account. The tax characteristics of these accounts are very different. You have to pay tax on income earned by the taxable account on an annual basis, even if you don't withdraw the earnings. Earnings in the retirement account aren't taxable until you withdraw them—but when you do, the earnings will be ordinary income, even if they arose from capital gains within the retirement account.

These considerations make it appear that if you have investments that produce ordinary income—nonqualified dividends and interest—the best place for these investments is your retirement account. You get the significant advantage of deferring tax on these investments for an extended period of time. Investments that are intended to produce mainly capital gains and qualified dividends would be held in your taxable account. Remember, you can often defer tax on your capital gains simply by continuing to hold an asset that has increased in value. When the time comes to report the capital gain, you'll pay tax at favorable rates.

There have been some studies that suggest a contrary approach. Under certain sets of assumptions, it's better to keep growth stocks in your retirement account and interest-bearing assets in your taxable account. The reason is that growth stocks have historically produced a significantly higher investment return than interest-bearing assets, so in the long run, the amount of income you're deferring in your retirement account is greater with this strategy.

I haven't examined these studies, but I'm skeptical of the result. For one thing, I don't know if the studies have been updated with the lower capital gains rates that came into effect recently. For another, there are reasons to doubt that the stock market will continue to outstrip other investments to the same extent it did in the late 1990's. You need a crystal ball to know which will work out best, but I'm inclined to believe it's best to keep income-producing assets in the retirement account.

Investing Before the Annual Dividend

As a general rule, it's better to avoid investing in a mutual fund just before it pays its annual dividend. To understand why this is so, you need a few facts about the way mutual fund dividends work.

Many regular stocks pay no dividend at all, or pay dividends quarterly. Mutual funds can pay quarterly dividends, but often pay a large dividend late in the year. The reason is that tax rules require mutual funds to pay out nearly all their earnings as dividends. Many mutual funds don't know how much earnings they have until at or near the end of their year, so that's when they pay their largest dividends (or in some cases, *all* their dividends).

When a mutual fund pays a dividend, cash flows out from the fund. That means the fund's assets are reduced, and the share price goes down. Receiving a dividend from a mutual fund doesn't make you richer. It simply changes the form of your assets.

Example: You own 1,000 shares of XYZ mutual fund with a value of $20 per share. The mutual fund pays a dividend of $2 per share. After the dividend, the shares are worth $18 per share. Instead of $20,000 worth of mutual fund shares, you now have $18,000 worth of mutual fund shares and $2,000 cash.

Many people choose to reinvest their mutual fund dividends. If you made that choice, the dividend still reduces the value of the shares you hold—but is used to buy new shares. In the example above, your old shares would be worth $18,000 and you would have $2,000 worth of new shares. The end result is that you hold $20,000 worth of shares, and there's the rub: your wealth hasn't increased, yet you have to report (and pay tax on) a dividend.

Compare two investors: one who invested just before the dividend and another who invested just afterward. After the dividend, both hold $20,000 worth of shares in the mutual fund. The one who invested before the dividend is worse off, though, because she had to pay tax on the dividend.

It isn't all bad for the earlier investor. As a result of the reinvested dividend, she bought additional shares for $2,000. That means the basis for her investment is $22,000. If both investors now sell for $20,000, the one who bought before the dividend will claim a $2,000 loss. In the end, other things being equal, the two investors should come out the same.

Unfortunately, other things *aren't* equal. For one thing, the dividend may be partly or entirely ordinary income, while the loss will be a capital loss. Often, the tax benefit of a capital loss is smaller than the tax cost of reporting ordinary income. More importantly, you can't claim the tax benefit of the added basis from reinvesting a dividend until you sell your shares in the mutual fund. Normally you buy shares in a mutual fund with the intention of holding that investment for a period of time. Until you sell those shares, you're out of pocket for taxes from the unfortunate timing of buying shares shortly before the dividend.

What about selling? Does this mean you should try to time your sales so they occur just before a dividend? In most cases this isn't necessary. If you sell before the dividend, you avoid having to report the dividend but you have a larger gain (or smaller loss). These two effects will often cancel each other out.

> **Example:** Nine months ago, you invested $10,000 in XYZ mutual fund. Now your shares are worth $12,000 and the mutual fund is about to pay a $750 dividend. If you sell before the dividend, you'll report a short-term capital gain of $2,000. If you wait until after the dividend, you'll report a $750 dividend but your gain will be only $1,250, assuming no change in the mutual fund's value other than the dividend payment.

Although these effects often cancel out, there are times when you get an advantage by selling before the dividend—and other times when you're better off if you wait. In the example above, you might benefit by selling before the dividend if the mutual fund pays an ordinary dividend and you have large capital losses for the year. Because of the large capital losses, you would rather report $2,000 of capital gain (even though it's short-term gain) than report $1,250 of capital gain and an ordinary dividend of $750. You prefer the larger capital gain because it will absorb more of your capital loss.

On the other hand, it might be better to wait until after the dividend if a significant portion of the dividend is capital gain. When a mutual fund pays a capital gain dividend, you report it as long-term capital gain even if you held your shares in the fund less than a year.* In the example above, if $500 of the dividend is capital gain, you can convert part of your profit from short-term gain to long-term gain if you hold the shares until after the dividend.

---

* As explained in Chapter 12, mutual fund dividends paid from *short-term* capital gain are treated as ordinary dividends, not capital gain.

Tax Efficiency in Mutual Funds

Consider two different mutual funds. One pays dividends equal to 5% of share value and the other pays dividends equal to only 1% of share value. Suppose that after reinvesting the dividends, you get the same amount of growth from both funds. Which is better?

The fund that pays the smaller dividend is better. It's providing you the same amount of growth with a smaller annual tax hit. It's more *tax-efficient*.

We aren't talking here about differences between exempt bond funds and stock funds. The comparison here is between funds in the same category, especially different stock funds. There are wide variations in the tax-efficiency of stock funds based on the buying and selling patterns of the managers.

Mutual fund managers can improve the tax efficiency of their funds in various ways. When they reduce their holdings in a particular stock, they can take care to sell the highest basis shares first. They can try to avoid selling winners until the gains are long-term, or postpone gains until after the end of the year. In short, they can do many of the same things individual investors do to manage their capital gains.

Not all mutual funds pay attention to these issues, though. One reason is that many of their biggest investors are retirement plans and other nontaxable entities. These institutional investors don't care whether the mutual fund is tax-efficient, so a mutual fund manager intent on pleasing these investors won't be concerned about taxes. Another reason the manager may not focus on this issue is that even among taxable investors, most are mainly interested in the overall return of the mutual fund. Anything that can boost that return will be attractive to the manager even if it results in a higher tax bill for investors.

It's useful for you to be aware of the tax efficiency of mutual funds when choosing where to invest. Other things being equal, a more efficient fund will provide a better after-tax investment return. Here are some points to bear in mind:

Index funds. One way to classify mutual funds is to divide them between *actively managed* funds and *index* funds. In an actively managed fund, the manager attempts to choose investments that will achieve superior results. These choices may entail buying and selling activity that results in undesirable dividends. In an index fund, the manager seeks to have the fund perform the same as an index, such as the S&P 500 index. These funds sell stocks less often than actively managed funds, so they're likely to generate smaller dividends.

As a result, one way to improve the tax-efficiency of your mutual fund investments is to invest in index funds. You should be aware, though, that not all index funds are equally tax efficient. Consider what can happen in a *mid-cap fund*—a fund that invests in medium-sized companies based on their total capitalization (the value of all their stock). If one of the companies in the fund becomes highly successful, its stock price will rise and the company may "graduate" from mid-cap to large-cap. This stock will no longer be part of the index, so the mutual fund will have to sell it, creating a large gain, and a dividend for the fund's shareholders. The success of this company lifted the value of the fund, and that's good—but the sale of the shares caused the fund to pay a dividend, and that's bad.

Normally, you can expect excellent tax efficiency from broad-based index funds where the list of stocks that make up the index is relatively stable. Funds based on narrower indexes may be less tax-efficient.

Exchange-traded funds. A recent innovation is the offering of exchange-traded index funds. Like traditional index funds, these funds seek to match the performance of a stock index. Unlike traditional index funds, their shares trade in the stock market. It's possible that these funds will be more tax-efficient than traditional index funds in some conditions.

The reason is that if investors decide to pull money out of traditional index funds, those funds may be forced to sell shares. Those sales may produce gains, and there-fore produce unwanted dividends for the investors who remain in the fund. In an exchange-traded fund, investors who want to sell their shares don't pull their money out of the fund. Instead, they simply sell their shares in the stock market. The fund itself isn't forced to sell shares, so it won't have to create gains that result in dividends.

There's some question whether this possible advantage over traditional index funds is significant. Some people argue that the only time investors are likely to pull large amounts of money from index funds is when the stock market has performed poorly. If the stock market has declined, the index fund may be able to avoid unwanted capital gains by selling shares purchased when the stock market was at a higher level. For now, it's impossible to know whether exchange-traded funds will turn out to be significantly more tax-efficient than tradi-tional index funds.

Tax-managed funds. Another relatively recent innova-tion is the *tax-managed* fund. These are actively managed funds that have tax efficiency as one of their goals. The managers of these funds take tax considerations into account when deciding whether, or when, to sell shares of stock held by the fund. If you find a tax-managed fund that meets your investment objectives, there's a good chance it will be more tax-efficient than a comparable managed fund that isn't tax-managed.

Tax load. Some advisors suggest that you consider the *tax load* of a fund before investing. A fund that holds shares that have gone up in value a great deal has a large tax load. New investors may end up paying tax on those inherent gains when the mutual fund sells the shares. When you think about it though, the way a fund gets to have a high tax load is by investing in stocks that grow and holding those stocks for long periods of time. That's a recipe for tax-efficiency. As mutual funds like to remind their investors, past performance does not guarantee future results, and that holds for tax-efficiency as well as pre-tax returns. Yet I wonder whether a high tax load should be considered a negative in all cases, when you consider that the tax load may indicate tax-efficient operation of the fund in the past.

Averaging Methods for Sales of Shares

Tax planning for mutual fund investors includes the choice of methods to use in determining the basis of shares you sold. Chapter 5 discusses the methods that are available and considerations in choosing among them.

Chapter 32
Tax Planning for Traders

Traders have some tax planning concerns—and opportunities—that don't apply to investors. In particular, if you're a trader (as defined in Part V of this book) you should consider whether you would benefit from the mark-to-market election. Traders also sometimes wonder whether they would be better off forming a corporation or other entity.

The Mark-to-Market Election

Chapter 26 explains the mark-to-market election, which has three main consequences:

- Trading positions held at the end of the year are treated as sold for fair market value, with profit or loss from those positions taken into income.

- The wash sale rule doesn't apply to trading losses.

- Profits and losses from trading are treated as ordinary income, not capital gain.

Clearly this election involves a trade-off. If you make the election, you lose the ability to defer taxation by holding winning positions at the end of the year. You also lose whatever benefit you would get from treating trading profits as capital gain. Yet for many traders—probably the vast majority—these are not important issues. By definition, traders are in and out of positions very quickly. They're unlikely to have much unreported gain at the end of the year, and all or nearly all of their profits are likely to be short-term capital gain, taxed at the same rates as ordinary income.*

As a result, the negative aspects of the mark-to-market election are usually not very important. That's especially true when these disadvantages are weighed against the sometimes-crucial advantage of making this election: it eliminates the $3,000 capital loss limitation.

It's a sad fact of life for traders that even the best of them sometimes suffer losses. In particular, traders sometimes have a net loss for the year that is far in excess of $3,000. Without the mark-to-market election, they receive little current tax benefit from those losses, even if they reported large profits from trading in a previous year. Capital losses can be carried forward, but not back.

Consider the person I mentioned earlier in this book, who had $400,000 of trading profits in 1999 and $400,000 of losses when the market for technology stocks went sour the following spring. If she had made the mark-to-market election, she would have been able to use the $400,000 loss against all her income for 2000. If the loss exceeded her total income for that year, it would produce a *net operating loss* that she could carry back to the previous year, obtaining a refund of taxes previously paid. Without the election, though, the tax law allows her to deduct only $3,000 of the loss. Unless she returns to profitable trading, she'll use the loss at the rate of $3,000 per year for as long as she lives. Meanwhile, the tax on the 1999 profit is gone forever.

With one exception, I strongly urge stock traders to make the mark-to-market election at the earliest opportunity. Consider it an insurance policy against a bad tax result if your trading turns sour. It's bad enough to suffer losses in the market. Getting stuck with losses you can't deduct is even worse.

The exception is people who *already* have large capital losses from a previous year. Presumably, if you've continued to trade after incurring those losses, you're antici-

---

* Sixty percent of profit or loss from trading section 1256 contracts is long-term capital gain or loss, however. See Chapter 14.

pating profits in the future. Those profits will allow you to use the capital loss carryover created by your previous losses. If you make the mark-to-market election, your hoped-for profits will become ordinary income. You won't be able to soak up your previous capital losses.

> **Example:** Let's reverse the facts of the case we've been discussing. Suppose this trader had $400,000 of losses in one year and $400,000 of profits the next. Without the mark-to-market election, the loss carried from the first year eliminates all but $3,000 of the gains in the second year. If this trader makes the election in the second year, though, the profits turn into ordinary income. The capital loss from the first year still carries forward to the second, but only $3,000 can be used because the profits aren't capital gain.

Some people will find themselves in a position where the election is a tough call. Perhaps you got started trading near the end of the year and lost $20,000. At the start of the next year, you're hoping for profits but it's too early to know how the year will turn out. If you make a profit for the second year, you'll be better off without the election, because your profit will be capital gain, which absorbs the $20,000 loss from the previous year. Yet it's also possible you'll have losses much greater than $20,000 in the second year. In that case you'll come out much better if you made the election, because the loss from the second year won't be subject to the $3,000 capital loss limitation.

Timing. As discussed below, corporations and other entities can make the mark-to-market election within two months and fifteen days after the start of their first tax year. Other taxpayers—people like you and me—must make the election no later than the unextended due date of their tax return. Nearly all individuals file on the calendar year, so that means filing this election by April 15. As explained in Chapter 25, you have to file the election with your tax return or with an extension request filed by that date.

What if you begin trading in August? Unless you had the foresight to make the election in the previous April, the apparent position of the IRS is that you can't make the election until the following year. If you have losses in your first months of trading (as most traders do), there's no way to convert them from capital losses to ordinary losses. For this reason, if you're thinking of getting into trading in a big way, and it's late in the year, it might be a good idea to wait until January so any losses you incur at the outset can be covered by the mark-to-market election.

Corporations and Other Entities

Traders often wonder if they should form a corporation, partnership or limited liability company (LLC) for their trading business. Doing so may have a positive or negative effect on your tax situation. For most people I don't think the benefits outweigh the costs.

In the discussion that follows I'll focus on corporations. You can't form a partnership with just a single owner, and if you're going into a trading business with a partner you should work with a lawyer to structure your business and not rely on a few words from this book. As for limited liability companies, in most states it's possible to form an LLC with a single member, but the tax law completely disregards single-member LLCs. In other words, if you're the sole owner of an LLC, you're treated the same as if the LLC didn't exist and you directly held the assets of the LLC and carried on its activities.

That's not true of corporations. The tax law doesn't disregard a corporation that has a single owner. If you form a corporation for your trading business, your tax situation is likely to change. The question is whether that change is a good one.

C corporations and S corporations. For tax purposes, corporations come in two different flavors. Both are formed the same way under state law. The difference is simply a matter of filing an election with the IRS. If you file this election, your corporation is an *S corporation*; if not, you have a *C corporation*.

Large corporations with familiar names like Microsoft and McDonald's are always C corporations. Yet even a small corporation owned by a single person can be a C corporation. This type of corporation isn't well suited for a trading business, though. The main reason is that if your trading is very successful, you may end up paying double tax on some of your earnings: the corporation will pay tax at rates up to 35%, and you'll pay additional tax on what's left when you receive it as a dividend. There are strategies for avoiding double tax, but no way to completely remove the risk of ending up in that situation. I would be very reluctant to recommend a C corporation for a trader.

Some traders may want to consider forming an S corporation, though. This approach has advantages and disadvantages, and on the whole I suspect most people are better off without the expense and paperwork of maintaining a corporation. If you're interested in this approach, here are some of the main points to consider.

Flow-through taxation. For tax purposes, an S corporation is treated as a "flow-through" entity. That means any tax consequences of the corporation end up on your tax return. If the corporation has a short-term capital gain, *you* have a short-term capital gain. As a general rule, the corporation itself doesn't pay federal income tax. This is why the double taxation issue mentioned above for C corporations doesn't apply to S corporations.

Trader status. I've heard the suggestion that it's easier to qualify for trader status if you form a corporation. I don't believe that's correct. The IRS should apply the same standard for determining trader status without regard to whether you carry on the activity through a corporation.

You are not a trader. If you form a corporation to carry on a trading business, *you* are not a trader. The corporation is a trader. You are the owner of the corporation and also a person (most likely the only person) who works for the company. This fact has important implications as follows.

Because you work for the company you set up, you can be an employee. The company will pay you wages for your services, and those wages can be the basis for contributions to a retirement plan. This is one of the most important benefits a trader may obtain by setting up a corporation. Normally, a trader can't establish a retirement plan because trading income doesn't qualify for this treatment, even if the trader makes the mark-to-market election.

There's a flip side to this benefit, however. Traders don't have to pay self-employment tax on their trading profits. Yet any amounts your corporation pays as wages for your services will be subject to social security tax. Half of this tax is withheld from your pay and the corporation pays the other half, but you own the corporation so in reality you bear all the cost. The tax is substantial. Depending on the amount of earnings, you may pay $10,000 or more additional tax by reason of operating a corporation that pays you wages.

It gets worse. Generally speaking, if you own an S corporation, you can control the amount of wages you receive from your own company. You can choose to retain some of the profits in the corporation or receive them in the form of *distributions* instead of wages, avoiding social security tax on those amounts. Yet if you "pay yourself" too little, the IRS can challenge that result, saying a corporation with earnings that high should have paid a higher wage to its employee-owner. The IRS sometimes uses this argument to collect more social security tax from S corporations and their owners.

There's an advantage to paying social security tax: the more you pay, the higher the benefit you'll qualify for when you retire. Yet most people given the choice of paying $10,000 less in tax for the current year wouldn't hesitate to pay the lower tax, thank you very much. If you consider whether to form an S corporation for your trading business, you need to consider carefully whether the advantages outweigh the cost of this additional tax.

Mark-to-market. There's one other advantage in operating a trading business through a corporation. As noted earlier, an individual can make the mark-to-market election only in the first months of the year. If you begin trading after April 15, you have to wait until the next year to make the election. The main cause for concern here is that your trading may produce a loss in the first year. If you don't have the mark-to-market election in place, that loss will be subject to the $3,000 capital loss limitation.

If you form a corporation for your trading business, the corporation can make the election within two months and fifteen days after the start of its first tax year.* In the case of a corporation, the election is not filed with the IRS. You make the election by entering it on the books and records of the corporation. Be sure to document this action in a way that leaves no doubt that you acted within the specified time.

> **Example:** You begin your trading business in August. If you don't form a corporation or other entity, you won't be able to make the mark-to-market election until the following year. Losses you have before January 1 of the next year will be capital losses. If you form a corporation for your trading business, you can make the election effective immediately.

Bear in mind that if you incur losses *before* forming the corporation, those losses will still be capital losses. The mark-to-market election will apply only to assets and transactions of the corporation.

Only you can judge whether the benefits described above justify the cost and paperwork of forming and maintaining a corporation. In my experience, only a small percentage of stock traders want to work through a corporation.

---

* A corporation's first tax year begins on the first day it has shareholders, owns assets or conducts business. To avoid possible disputes, it's best to make the election within two months and fifteen days after the date the corporation is formed.

Appendices

Appendices

IRS Publications

IRS Forms and Instructions

Plain Language Books on Taxes

Professional Resources

Books on Personal Finance and Investing

About Fairmark Press

IRS Publications

The Internal Revenue Service has hundreds of information publications available free from their web site at **www.irs.gov** or by telephone at (800) 829-3676. On the web site, you can read or download the documents in PDF format (requires Acrobat Reader), or visit another area of the web site where you can browse the documents online. The ones most relevant to the topics in this book are:

Publication 17, Your Federal Income Tax. This is the IRS publication J.K. Lasser doesn't want you to know about. In 300 or so pages this free book gives a plain language explanation of all the basic tax rules that apply to general situations.

Publication 334, Tax Guide for Small Business. If you're a trader, your trading activity is treated as a business for tax purposes, and some of the information in this publication is likely to be helpful.

Publication 505, Tax Withholding and Estimated Tax. If you have investment income, you may have to pay estimated tax. This is where the IRS explains the rules.

Publication 554, Sales and Other Dispositions of Assets. In this publication you'll find details on determining when you have a gain or loss, how to measure it and where it should be reported.

Publication 550, Investment Income and Expenses. This publication covers many of the topics discussed in this book, including capital gains and losses, wash sales, short sales, constructive sales and straddles.

Publication 551, Basis of Assets. Look here for more details on determining the basis, used in measuring gain or loss when you sell an asset.

Publication 564, Mutual Fund Distributions. The title of this publication is a little misleading. In addition to mutual fund distributions, it covers the rules for selling shares of mutual funds.

Publication 929, Tax Rules for Children and Dependents. If you establish a custodial account for a child under 14 years of age, information in this publication may be helpful.

IRS Forms and Instructions

I often get questions from people who appear not to have read the instructions for the tax forms. I suspect in many cases people either aren't aware that the answers are in the instructions or don't have the instructions readily available, perhaps because they obtained the form separately or used tax return software to generate the form. Like the IRS information publications, forms and instructions are available on the IRS web site (**www.irs.gov**). Here are a few pointers about what you may find in the instructions.

Capital gains and losses. You'll find plenty of useful information, including how to report tricky transactions like wash sales, in the instructions for Schedule D, Form 1040. The most important thing people sometimes forget in dealing with capital gains is the special calculation you have to do to get the benefit of lower rates for long-term capital gains. You do this calculation either on Part IV of Schedule D or, if you qualify, on the worksheet provided in the instructions for Form 1040.

Estimating taxes. You use Form 1040-ES when you send in estimated tax payments. What you may not realize is that the instructions for this form provide useful information, including the inflation adjustments for tax brackets, standard deductions and personal exemptions.

Alternative minimum tax. At one time the IRS had a publication explaining the alternative minimum tax (AMT), but they discontinued this publication several years ago. There's a wealth of information about how this tax works in the instructions for Form 6251, which is used to report your AMT liability. If you paid AMT in a previous year, don't forget to check your ability to claim a credit on Form 8801.

Traders. If you qualify as a trader (or think you might), you may be interested to see the discussion of traders that was added to the Schedule D instructions beginning in 2000. I submitted informal comments to the IRS on that discussion and was please to see they acted on some of them, although the discussion is still lacking in some regards, particularly the failure to distinguish between the trading activity test and the substantial activity test for determining whether you're a trader.

Plain Language Books on Taxes

People sometimes ask me to recommend other plain language books about taxes. Here are some shameless plugs for my other books, followed by my favorites from other authors:

Consider Your Options: Get the Most from Your Equity Compensation by Kaye A. Thomas. This guide covers tax rules and planning opportunities for all forms of equity compensation, including stock grants, nonqualified stock options, incentive stock options and employee stock purchase plans (ESPPs). For more about this book and ordering information:

www.fairmark.com/books/consider.htm

Fairmark Guide to the Roth IRA: Retirement Planning in Plain Language by Kaye A. Thomas. Our web site has been a top-rated source of information about Roth IRAs right from the beginning. Now you can get all that information and more in a handy, attractively priced book. For more about this book and ordering information:

www.fairmark.com/books/roth.htm

The Best Way to Save for College: A Complete Guide to Section 529 Plans by Joseph F. Hurley, CPA. While the main focus of this book is on state-run college savings plans that provide special tax benefits, you'll also find thoughtful comparisons to other methods of saving for college. This book is updated regularly, and the author maintains a terrific web site:

www.savingforcollege.com

Tax Facts 2 on Investments (National Underwriter Company, new edition issued annually). Behind this unassuming title is a volume that provides detailed tax information on investments from stocks and bonds to equipment leasing and cattle. It's written for professionals, with many references to the Internal Revenue Code, revenue rulings and other authorities, yet it's a reasonably readable book in question and answer format.

J.K. Lasser's Your Income Tax (annual series). If you're wondering which of the tax preparation manuals is the best, this is the one. Clear, thorough, accurate.

Professional Resources

For those who may be interested, I list here the main professional resources I rely on for tax research.

Internal Revenue Code and Tax Regulations. Perhaps it's redundant to mention this, but the indispensable resource for professional research in taxation is a current copy of the Internal Revenue Code and the Tax Regulations. I use the version published by CCH, with the Code in two large volumes and the Regs in six.

U.S. Master Tax Guide Plus from CCH. This is an online service that very economically provides access to an extensive database of tax authorities. I found it invaluable, for example, in researching the older cases dealing with trader taxation.

OneDisc Federal Tax Research Library. This is another way to research an extensive tax database. Strangely enough, the "OneDisc" library consists of several discs, including discs devoted to chief counsel guidance and court cases.

Tax Management Portfolios from BNA. These publications provide in-depth analysis of particular topics. Often they go beyond merely stating the law to give insights from the author, who is often a leading practitioner. Available in hard copy and in CD-ROM.

Financial Products: Taxation, Regulation and Design by Andrea Kramer. This is the bible on this subject, with complete details from the leading authority on the subject. Covers all kinds of financial products, from the most familiar to the most arcane.

Books on Personal Finance and Investing

I've read dozens of books on personal finance and investing. For those who are interested, here are my favorites.

First, on the subject of accumulating wealth, try *The Richest Man in Babylon* by George S. Clason. This thought-provoking little book deserves its status as a perennial best-seller. Another excellent book in this category is Stanley & Danko's *Millionaire Next Door*.

On the subject of investing in general, anything by Andrew Tobias is good, especially *The Only Investment Guide You'll Ever Need.* Jane Bryant Quinn provides excellent coverage of all kinds of personal finance issues, including investing. So does Suze Orman—her status as a television performer is built on solid knowledge and good judgment.

For stocks in particular, Peter Lynch's books are interesting and witty, but to gain a good overall grasp of the subject, two books are indispensable: *A Random Walk Down Wall Street* by Burton G. Malkiel, and *Stocks for the Long Run* by Jeremy J. Siegel. On the subject of mutual funds, anything by John Bogle is worth reading.

Option traders. Before trading stock options you should read *Characteristics and Risks of Standardized Options.* This booklet is available free from the exchanges on which options trade. You should receive a copy when you open an options trading account with a broker. If you don't receive one, contact one of the options exchanges (such as the Chicago Board Options Exchange) and request a copy or read it on their web site.

If you're serious about buying and selling options—
and you shouldn't touch them unless you are serious—
you need to study a serious book on the subject. *Options
as a Strategic Investment* by Lawrence G. McMillan is one
of the best.

About Fairmark Press

I formed Fairmark Press Inc. to carry on my tax publishing business. Most publishers begin with books and use a web site to promote them, but I started the other way around. For a number of years I provided tax information to people who asked questions on computer message boards and similar forums. Some of the questions were repetitive, so I began posting material on the Web. That way I could simply tell people, "look here for the answer."

That project grew into the *Tax Guide for Investors*. People sometimes ask where they can buy this book, and I have to tell them it isn't a book, just a web site located at **www.fairmark.com**. Although we don't have a large staff to maintain this site, it has repeatedly been selected as one of the most useful sites on the Web by magazines such as *Newsweek*, *Forbes* and *Money*.

The heart of this web site is a series of tax guides. Many web sites provide articles on various tax topics, but we like to provide people with a way to learn all they need to know about a given topic. We don't cover everything in the world of taxation, or even every aspect of investment taxation, but we have extensive information on many topics of particular interest to investors, including capital gains, mutual funds, Roth IRAs, custodial accounts for minors and much more.

The web site also features a very active message board where visitors post questions and receive answers from various people with tax knowledge. Readers of this book are invited to visit the bulletin board to comment on this book or ask questions about the contents.

There's much more on our web site—tax news, easy access to tax forms and publications, reference materials—and it's growing all the time.

Books. We published our first book in January, 2000. *Consider Your Options* was an instant success and sold over 25,000 copies within 10 months after it was published. We've been gratified by the strong reviews, including favorable ratings from readers on Amazon.com.

Capital Gains, Minimal Taxes was our second book, and we now offer a third book, *Fairmark Guide to the Roth IRA*.

Index

Notes

Notes

Order Form

Order more of our books from our web site (**www.fairmark.com**), or by mailing or faxing a copy of this form.

Fax: (630) 434-0753   Mail: Fairmark Press Inc.
                                                P.O. Box 353
                                                Lisle, IL 60532

Quantity

_____   *Fairmark Guide to the Roth IRA* @ $13.95   _____

_____   *Consider Your Options* @ $23.95   _____

_____   *Capital Gains, Minimal Taxes* @ $19.95   _____

                  Total for books   _____

                  Shipping (flat rate per order)   _____ $4.00

                  Total   _____

Illinois residents add 6.75% sales tax.

Ship to:

Name: _____

Address: _____

Address: _____

City, State, zip: _____

Phone: _____

Email: _____

Payment

_____   Check   ____ VISA ____ MasterCard
                             _____ AMEX   ____   Discover

Card number: _____

Exp. date: _____

Credit Card Info (if different from shipping)

Billing name: _____

Address: _____

City, State, zip: _____

Notes

Order Form

Order more of our books from our web site (**www.fairmark.com**), or by mailing or faxing a copy of this form.

Fax: (630) 434-0753   Mail: Fairmark Press Inc.
                                            P.O. Box 353
                                            Lisle, IL 60532

Quantity

_____   *Fairmark Guide to the Roth IRA* @ $13.95   _____

_____   *Consider Your Options* @ $23.95   _____

_____   *Capital Gains, Minimal Taxes* @ $19.95   _____

                        Total for books   _____

                        Shipping (flat rate per order)   _____$4.00

                        Total   _____

Illinois residents add 6.75% sales tax.

Ship to:

Name: _____

Address: _____

Address: _____

City, State, zip: _____

Phone: _____

Email: _____

Payment

_____   Check   ____ VISA ____ MasterCard
                                ____ AMEX   ____   Discover

Card number: _____

Exp. date: _____

Credit Card Info (if different from shipping)

Billing name: _____

Address: _____

City, State, zip: _____